# THE QUEEN'S PRIZE

*Queen Victoria firing the inaugural shot on Wimbledon Common, 1860. A watercolour by G. H. Thomas, reproduced with the kind permission of Windsor Castle, Royal Library. © Her Majesty The Queen.*

# THE QUEEN'S PRIZE

## The Story of the National Rifle Association

Susie Cornfield

Pelham Books

First published in Great Britain by
Pelham Books Ltd, 27 Wrights Lane, London W8 5TZ,
1987

British Library Cataloguing in Publication Data

Cornfield, Susie
The queen's prize: the story of the
National Rifle Association.
1.  National Rifle Association—History
I.  Title
799.2′13′06041      GV1163.N2/


ISBN 0 7207 1751 5

Typeset by MCL Computerset, Ely, Cambridgeshire
Printed and bound by
Butler and Tanner, Frome, Somerset

*To Alex, who got me into this,
and to Pat, who helped get me out.*

*And with thanks to Lord Cottesloe
and John de Havilland.*

# Contents

# Foreword

The National Rifle Association, born less than half a century after Waterloo out of a fear of invasion by the French, was founded in 1859, and the first shot of the inaugural Imperial Meeting fired in July the following year by Her Majesty Queen Victoria. Since its foundation, the NRA has played an incalculable role in the development of the rifle, in the defence of Great Britain during two World Wars, and as an ambassador throughout the Commonwealth and, indeed, the world. And yet, the rifleman, trained to keep his eye on the target, almost to look into the future, has for too long lost sight of a history of which he should be justly proud.

My father, a former chairman of the NRA who won his first prize at Wimbledon in 1879, was co-author of a history which ended in 1909, and concluded with these words: 'It is hoped that men will not be wanting at intervals shorter than fifty years, who will find a pleasure in gathering up old memories and adding another volume to this history.'

Susie Cornfield has put us all in her debt by putting together this story which is neither a mere compilation of lists or figures, nor a story assembled with dry facts. It is a book of pageantry and passion, of fascination and humour, and it throbs with life. It gives a clear, bright picture of times long gone, with an undistorted view of where we are today.

I believe my father would have enjoyed and savoured this book as much as I have done, as much as anyone, be they marksman or no, will do.

# *Preface*

We were introduced by a mutual friend one blustery afternoon in early spring. It seemed a highly improbable match. He was much older, a little frayed round the edges, of the Old Empire. He was into rifles and shooting. And I, well, I wasn't. But a spark was lit. I wrote the script for the BBC TV documentary and video, in which he, the National Rifle Association, Bisley for short, was the star.

But the involvement didn't end there. In the course of research, the director, Alex Leger, pointed out that there was no definitive history, no book which told the story of the NRA from the beginning until the present day. 'What a marvellous picture book it would be. It wouldn't need many words,' he said. I agreed. Dick Douglas-Boyd at Pelham Books thought otherwise. He liked pictures but what he really wanted was words, 65,000 of them. Immediately, my home was under occupation. Bisley had moved in. Several months of blood, sweat, toil and 95,000 words later *The Queen's Prize* was born.

On the face of it, we remain an unlikely couple—but, as in so many cases, opposites can and do attract. Although Bisley has moved out of my home, he will always have a place in my life and, yes, the old devil, in my heart.

*Susie Cornfield*
*December 1986*

# CHAPTER ONE

# *The First Shot*

It was the year in which Chekhov, J.M. Barrie and Gustav Mahler were born. The year that Abraham Lincoln was elected President of the United States, the Russians founded Vladivostock, and Garibaldi proclaimed Victor Emmanuel King of Italy. Thackeray began editing the new *Cornhill Magazine*, and Wilkie Collins's *The Woman in White* and George Eliot's *The Mill on the Floss* were published. It was also the year that a rifle was fired in a London park one summer's day by none other than Her Majesty, Queen Victoria.

There were many witnesses to the shot fired on Wimbledon Common that sunny Monday afternoon, 2 July 1860, among them Prince Albert, the Prince Consort, Lord Palmerston, the Prime Minister, and Mr Sidney Herbert, Secretary of State for War.

But this was a shot fired not in anger nor to signal the monarch's entry into a mighty battle ... Queen Victoria fired the shot to mark the inaugural meeting of the National Rifle Association, whose annual summer meeting is now firmly established in the British sporting calendar. And not just the British calendar, the July Meeting (or Imperial Meeting, as it is known to most competitors), now held at Bisley in Surrey, has developed a reputation for the finest rifle shooting in the world, its competitions attracting hundreds of keen marksmen, particularly from countries in the British Commonwealth.

Nowadays, the Meeting is a purely sporting event, edged, as ever it was, with numerous social events, but its origins were military, the presence of the Queen and of her Secretary of State for War at that first Meeting in 1860, indicating the country's concern at the time for the defence of the realm.

A period of relative stability in Europe, established after the Napoleonic Wars by the Treaty of Vienna in 1815, was drawing to a close by the mid-19th century with the emergence of more aggressive politicians such as Bismarck in Prussia, Cavour in Piedmont, Gorchakov in Russia and Napoleon III of France. These men, who replaced the signatories to that treaty, were less concerned with the maintenance of the balance of power in Europe. Their priority was the aggrandisement of their own countries.

The Crimean War of 1854–6 marked a turning point in modern history. According to *New Cambridge* historians, as well as a shift in alliances in Europe (France and Britain found themselves in the unusual position of joining forces with the Turks to oppose Russia), dramatic improvements in the speed of communications by railway, steamship and telegraph encouraged the development of news agencies such as Reuters (founded in 1851) and meant that war correspondents could send their reports in minutes rather than days. Almost immediately, the public were made aware of the horrifying effects of the new weaponry being employed as well as the inadequacies of the Army commanders, who were completely out of touch with modern methods of warfare. In Britain, one result of the whole disastrous episode was the reorganisation of the administration of the Army, and the establishment and development of the Army Medical School and Army training camps, such as Aldershot which had been purchased in 1853.

Despite a fledgling Anglo-French alliance, nurtured by Palmerston and the French monarch, a fear grew in England of an invasion by France where the new Napoleon, elected President of the Second Republic in 1848, had overthrown the constitution and four years later had had himself proclaimed Emperor Napoleon III. Partly to distract his countrymen's attention from internal problems and partly to continue in the steps of his illustrious uncle, Napoleon III was anxious that France should expand its territories abroad and that it should become a diplomatic force to be reckoned with.

So it was that after French victories against the Austrians in 1859 at Solferino and Magenta, the British public began to feel increasingly apprehensive about the strength of the French military. On the other side of the Channel, the French Press remained convinced that Britain was determined to undermine Napoleon's sovereignty, while the British Press reflected the country's nervousness about an invasion from across the water. British travellers, returning from the Continent, confirmed that the only conjecture in people's minds was *when*, not if, the invasion was to take place. The demand grew rapidly within the country for the right to organise civilian defence groups.

Initially, the Government was less than enthusiastic to re-form a force which had been disbanded in 1814, with the Commander-in-Chief, the Duke of Cambridge, maintaining that such a proposal would destroy the spirit of the Regular Army. But as invasion fever grew, a meeting was held in London in April 1859 at which a strong protest was made about the inadequacy of the country's defence system. The meeting came to be called

The Long Acre Indignation Meeting and it inspired the Poet Laureate, Lord Tennyson, to pen these words which were published in *The Times* on 9 May 1859, under the title, *Form, Riflemen, Form*.

> There is a sound of Thunder afar,
> Storm in the South that darkens the day,
> Storm of battle and thunder of war,
> Well, if it do not roll our way.
> Storm! storm! Riflemen, form!
> Ready, be ready, to meet the storm!
> Riflemen, riflemen, riflemen form!
>
> Let your Reforms for a moment go,
> Look to your butts and take good aims.
> Better a rotten borough or so,
> Than a rotten fleet or a city in flames!
> Form! form! Riflemen form!
> Ready, be ready to meet the storm!
> Riflemen, riflemen, riflemen form!

Ultimately, the Government was forced to bow to the strength of public pressure and on 12 May 1859 the establishment of a Volunteer Force was sanctioned by the then Secretary of State for War, General Peel. This gave power to the Lords-lieutenants to appoint officers under which a Volunteer Rifle Corps, or in seaside towns, a Volunteer Artillery Corps, could be formed. The enthusiasm with which this was met can be estimated by the number who enlisted: in the first two years men were reckoned to be recruiting at the rate of 7,000 a month, so that by 1861 the Volunteer Corps stood at 170,000. And the rallying cry for the defence of the realm was continued in the *Volunteer Service Gazette, and Military Dispatch* which, in its first issue, 26 October 1859, expressed the nation's fears while encouraging a strong military stand:

'Let us look at our *ally* on the other side of the channel. France is not idle, although she possesses a standing army numbering half a million of men, and a navy which almost rivals that of England; on the contrary, she is straining every nerve to put her army on the most efficient war footing and increasing her fleet. Her arsenals and dockyards are fully and incessantly employed ... We hear, also, of orders given for the building of steam transports, each capable of conveying three thousand men, with cavalry and artillery. The whole coast of France is being rapidly covered with fortifications, as if a naval war were imminent ... There is but one country against whom this vast machinery of war could be necessary or useful, and that country is England ... There is but one way of averting, *as well as of meeting*, it, and that is by speedily organising well disciplined and serviceably equipped Volunteer Artillery and Rifle Corps throughout the length and breadth of the land, and placing our national defences in such a state that invasion would be madness ... '

It was hardly surprising that the vast majority of the new Volunteer force were totally unskilled in the use of rifles and, while the Hythe School of Musketry sought to rectify that deficiency, it was not many months after the formation of the corps, that two separate groups began to realise the importance and value of a national competition. Their aim was to stimulate an interest in the corps as a movement, allied to a hope that such an event would also encourage and secure a high standard of shooting—which, considering the unreliability of the current weaponry, was certainly something to aim for.

On 29 October 1859 the two groups, the Hythe Volunteer Force and the London Rifle Brigade, assembled for a meeting called by Earl Spencer at his London home, Spencer House, where they passed a resolution proposing the formation of a National Rifle Association for 'the encouragement of Volunteer Rifle Corps and the promotion of Rifle Shooting throughout Great Britain'. And at a further meeting, chaired by Lord Elcho, at the Thatched House Tavern in St James's Street, the proposal became a reality. Thus, the National Rifle Association was born on 16 November 1859.

Lord Spencer assured the meeting that the Association had the support of the Prince Consort and the goodwill of the Government, while Lord Elcho proposed Mr Sidney Herbert, the Secretary of State for War, as the NRA's first president. Lord Elcho also mooted that subscription to the Association be one guinea for a year, or ten guineas for life. One resolution was that the Association should hold competitions for all riflemen, whether members of a volunteer corps or not. Captain Wilbraham Taylor moved 'that the first Meeting of this Association be held in the neighbourhood of London on the first Monday in July 1860, or as near that date as can conveniently be appointed', while it was hoped that subsequent meetings would be held at different venues in England, and in Scotland every third year.

No one, continued the Captain, could be certain that they would be able to meet next year. It depended a good deal upon a certain august ally of ours whether they would have to meet to shoot for prizes, or to meet him and his followers. He was a man of peace, the Captain assured the meeting, and had therefore joined the corps, believing that if such a corps were formed throughout the country, there never would be a war.

It then came to the election of the Association's officers—three Trustees;

twelve Vice-Presidents; a Council of fifteen, with five extraordinary members; and a Working Committee.[1]

The first meetings of the NRA's Working Committee took place at Spencer House but it soon became necessary to secure more permanent offices, as well as appoint a salaried Secretary. Rooms were taken at 11 Pall Mall East, and Captain Edmond H. St. John-Mildmay, who had served in the Austrian Army and subsequently become equerry to the Duke of Cambridge, the Commander-in-Chief of the British Army, was appointed the Association's first Secretary, a role in which he continued until 1889, the last year the NRA held its Meeting at Wimbledon.

As befits a birth, the announcement of the formation of the National Rifle Association was made through the columns of *The Times* in a letter from Lord Elcho, who had been elected the Association's first Chairman. Another reason for the publication of the letter was the influx of correspondence to the Pall Mall office which indicated a general lack of understanding as to exactly what the NRA was setting out to do. The Association was formed, wrote Lord Elcho, to 'give permanence to the Volunteer Force, and to render it, as it ought to be, part and parcel of our institutions … What the bow was in former times, the rifle now should be. Competition is the life and soul of our national sports. How long would cricket flourish without "Lord's" or horse-racing without "The Derby"? We want then, to encourage Volunteers and rifle shooting in Great Britain, by establishing an annual "Rifle Derby".'

On 7 March 1860 a Volunteer Levee was organised by the Council of the NRA and the Committee of the Volunteer Service Club, and in the evening a dinner for the officers of the Volunteer Corps was held at St James's Hall, which was followed by a ball. It was, by all accounts, a glittering occasion, the rooms were festooned with flowers and chandeliers. 'Two Queens of Beauty,' enthused the *Volunteer Service Gazette*, with what could be described as a military attention for detail, 'the Duchess of Wellington and the Duchess of Somerset … occupied the centre of the gallery. The Duchess

---

[1] The Trustees proposed were Lord Eversley, Lord Ashburton and General Peel. The Vice-Presidents were the Duke of Buccleuch, the Earl of Derby, the Earl of Ellenborough, the Earl de Grey (from 1871, the Marquess of Ripon), Earl Spencer, the Earl of Malmesbury, the Earl of Wemyss, the Earl of Tankerville, the Speaker of the House of Commons, Lord Palmerston, the Lord Mayor, and Lord Vernon. The Council: Lord Lichfield, Lord Grosvenor, Lord Elcho, Lord Panmure, Lord West, Lord Radstock, Sir de Lacy Evans, Colonel Francis Seymour, Captain Adam Gladstone, Mr Deedes MP, Mr Laird, Mr Horatio Ross, Mr Fairbairn, Mr A. Boyle, and General Hay, commander of the Hythe School of Musketry. The Working Committee: Lord Spencer, Lord Elcho, Captain Montague Hicks, Captain A. Gladstone, Lord Cowper, Mr Warre and Captain Templer.

of Wellington wore a head-dress of dark-green leaves glittering with diamonds ... Her face wore an air of pensive sweetness ... The Duchess of
Somerset (was) attired in an Eastern turban of black velvet and gold, she
looked stately and superb as a Sultan.' Some five thousand people danced
the evening away, watched by Mr Thackeray, 'surveying the scene with
delighted eyes'; the celebrated former *Times* correspondent, William Russell, no doubt finding plenty for 'entertaining comment in his new military
journal'; and Mr Coroner Wakley who had 'found his way here as a distrac-
tion from *Lancet* leaders and Middlesex inquests'.

'Not less than three thousand volunteers were present in uniform,'
enthused the *Volunteer Service Gazette*, adding, with a patriotic sting, 'and
there is scarcely a uniform in the room, be it green or grey, fancy cut or
regulation pattern, rifle or artillery, that is not much more becoming and
gentlemanly than the evening dress of ordinary wear.'

Before every guest at the dinner had been placed a copy of the NRA's
rules and the Duke of Cambridge proposed a toast to the Association which
was duly acknowledged by Lord Elcho. Within the week, a circular was
sent out to all the commanders of the different Volunteer Corps, urging
them to encourage their members to join the NRA to ensure its survival and
to collect sufficient monies together to 'offer prizes worthy of being competed for by the Volunteer Force'.

The NRA, which had used as its model Switzerland's biennial rifle meeting, the Tir Fédéral, hoped to raise as much money as did its Swiss counterparts, that is to say a sum of £10,000. But they were to be disappointed, the
response to the appeal raised only £254. 'The Association has neither then
nor subsequently had the peculiar art of successful begging on a large scale,'
Humphry and Fremantle reflect sadly in their *History of the NRA, 1859–
1909.*

Nevertheless, the NRA did have the support of the Queen, who founded
an annual prize for a competition among the Volunteers of £250, a considerable sum of money for the time, sufficient to buy a small house on the
outskirts of London or, as not infrequently used by winners of The Queen's
Prize, to establish a tradesman in business. To this day, The Queen's Prize
remains the most prestigious in the Association's Meeting and the winner is
carried from the ranges shoulder high by fellow competitors in an oak chair
dating from 1883.

The Queen's husband, the Prince Consort, who had agreed to become
the Association's patron, gave an annual prize of £100 to be competed for
by all comers from all nations. While the Duke of Cambridge offered an
annual prize of £50 for breech-loading rifles, with the intention of pro-
moting the improvement of the unstable infant.

The NRA resolved to award two medals—one gold to be awarded to The Queen's Prizewinner, the other silver for the runner-up, both designed by G.F. Watts and executed by George Adams.[1]

The next resolution to be made concerned the subject of rifles. For the shorter distances of 300, 500 and 600 yards, and for the first stage of The Queen's Prize, the long Enfield was chosen, this also being the rifle with which most of the Volunteers were armed. But for the longer distances of 800, 900 and 1,000 yards, at which the second and final stage of The Queen's Prize was competed for, the long Enfield was considered to be too inaccurate. The Council of the NRA let it be known that they were in favour of using the acclaimed Whitworth, a rifle made by Mr (later Sir) Joseph Whitworth of Manchester. The decision brought a howl of disapproval from Mr J.D. Goodman, chairman of the Birmingham Small Arms Trade who objected to the Association's decision to use the Whitworth with its minimum bore of .451. The Birmingham manufacturers were working on a model which had a .453 minimum bore and felt that they would be unable to manufacture a new rifle to the smaller specifications and then produce the forty rifles that the Association deemed were necessary for the competitors to use.

In a letter to *The Times* on 20 April 1860, Lord Elcho replied that the NRA 'were anxious that the chief prize should be won by the Volunteer whose eye is clearest, whose hand is steadiest, and whose nerve is strongest and not by the man who, from his experience in rifles, has found out the best description of arm, the cost of which might possibly place it beyond the reach of the mass of competitors.' This was not the time to enter into a dispute with the very people the NRA were trying to involve in their work,

---

[1] George Frederick Watts, 'England's Michelangelo', was a celebrated Royal Academician whose paintings hang in a number of English country houses including Longleat. Watts, who was married but briefly to the actress Ellen Terry, was an enthusiastic shot and had joined the Artists' Volunteer Corps along with Lord Frederic Leighton and Rossetti. His country home at Compton, near Guildford, which he had built in 1890, included a rifle range where he taught the youngsters in the village how to shoot. Watts's original sketches, done on the back of an envelope, show how he worked to link defence past with present through the figures of a Plantagenet archer and a rifleman of the 1860s, while incorporating the NRA motto, *Sit perpetuum* ('Let it last forever'). Watts created the design for the Running Man which was introduced in 1863, the same year as was Sir Edwin Landseer's design for a Running Deer, the original drawing of which hangs in the Bisley Museum. The Queen's Medal was cut by George Gammon Adams, a talented and highly respected sculptor and medallist, who had worked at the Royal Mint in his early years. As well as cutting the medal for the Crystal Palace Exhibition of 1851 and the Queen's Jubilee medal in 1887, Adams sculptured a number of leading figures of the day such as Gladstone and Napier, while his model of the Duke of Wellington remains the definitive study.

and it was deemed politic to hold rifle trials to which manufacturers from all over the country were invited to submit their rifles. The competition duly took place at Hythe on 1 May.

It was not a great success—except for Mr Whitworth. The London gun-makers declined the invitation altogether and the United Gunmakers were only able to submit for trial a paltry ten rifles all of which were manufactured in the Whitworth mould. The United Gunmakers also insisted that the rifles should be tested using a machine-rest, which was all well and good considering the trials were beset by howling gales, but as all the United Gunmakers had omitted to bring their own machine-rests they were forced to use the one constructed for the Hythe School of Musketry ... which just so happened to have been built by Mr Whitworth. Mr Whitworth, using his own machine-rest, immediately proved the superiority of his rifle. At 800 yards with a target eighteen feet square, half of the forty shots from the United Gunmakers failed to hit the target. None of the Whitworth shots missed it. If anything, the test at the longest range was even worse for the United Gunmakers. And, in fact, after deploying two of their best rifles in the trials, the United Gunmakers admitted defeat. The Council of the NRA, as well as Mr Whitworth and his rifle, had won the day.

The next, and most urgent, matter was to find a suitable venue to hold the Meeting which was scheduled to be in just two months. A number of places were considered, among them Woolwich, Aldershot, Epsom and Chobham. It was the NRA's Secretary, Captain Mildmay, who suggested that Wimbledon Common was suitably spacious to accommodate the Association's needs as well as being conveniently placed near to London. What luck that the lord of the manor was a Vice-President of the NRA—Lord Spencer, who when facing local opposition to the proposal was able to meet it not only dressed in his uniform as a Volunteer officer but armed with its fighting spirit as well. The little local difficulty was soon routed.

The ground was inspected by Colonel Clark Kennedy, on behalf of the authorities of the Horse Guards, who submitted his report on 11 May to the Quartermaster-General. The Colonel's report was most favourable: 'Provided that the usual and proper precautions are observed, I do not consider that a safer or more eligible site for the Meeting of the Association could be found than Wimbledon Common.'

Wimbledon Common, thus decided upon, needed a little work to get it into shape. How much work was slightly under-estimated. Colonel Clark Kennedy had recommended the land as hard and dry, needing little labour to fit it for the purposes required, but neither he nor the NRA had reckoned on the vagaries of the English climate. A total of £872 was thought to be adequate to cover the costs of erecting butts and the necessary fences, but not long after the ink was dry on the estimate the heavens opened. A flood of English summer began, continuing until just a few days before the Meeting, turning the Common into a quagmire. Ditches had to be dug, extensive draining carried out, and roadways constructed from hundreds of yards of planking. As time ran out, so did manpower and the NRA was forced to call in military aid. Fatigue parties of the Guards and sailors from Woolwich Dockyard came to the rescue, working long hours and well into the night. The estimated cost of preparation doubled. But at least, with the promise from the War Office of the loan of tents, targets, mantelets (bullet-proof shelters open back and front), and the like, the Association was spared another financial headache.

Then, on the day of the National Rifle Association's first Meeting, the grey cloud lifted and the sun came out. *The Times*, in its report of the proceedings, captured the high spirits and the enthusiasm which greeted the festivity of the occasion combined with the punctual arrival of Her Majesty the Queen and the late arrival of summer. 'The 2nd of July may really be marked as the first genuine day of summer we have had; and that it should have favoured the first national fete of the kind was universally felt as a good omen—a circumstance of bright promise ... Wimbledon did its best to support the Council and do honour to the occasion. It raised an arch of welcome of the "forest green," hung out banners and flags in the street, shut up its shops, and betook itself to the adjoining common, or to the upper windows, and made it a holiday ... Every villa within a circuit of 20 miles must have contributed its chariot ... The whole scene was more like the Hill at Epsom, on the Derby-day ... '

The stalwart Mr Whitworth and his team of assistants inadvertently kept the crowds entertained for several hours as they stood on a crimson-carpeted platform, surrounded by beds of brilliantly coloured flowers, fixing the rifle on its mechanical rest, adjusting it in line with the target, and then shooting a great number of trial shots. 'Considerable was the surprise expressed,' *The Times* report continues, 'that the ball should take so much time in reaching its destination. This simple wonder ... is an indication that the fairer portion of the assembly were much more familiar with the older English practice of archery than with the vile guns that owe their existence to the discovery of Bartholomew Schwartz.' A reference, undoubtedly, to Berthold Schwarz, an early 14th-century German monk, possibly legend-ary, who is reputed to have discovered, or at least introduced, gunpowder to Europe.

At about 2.30 p.m. a band of uniformed Volunteers, most of whom were intending to compete, marched into the enclosure and formed a line on either side of the platform along which the Queen would walk towards Mr Whitworth's rifle. Following them, behind the flag of the Swiss Confederation, came a group of about 150 Swiss, the best shots in their respective cantons. 'They appeared to be of the urban rather than the rural population,' reported *The Times*. 'That this Swiss representative corps are not exclusively or even principally mountaineers of the Tyrol, is an advantage. They will show us that quickness of the eye and steadiness of hand are not possessed by the peasant only ... '

Naturally, *The Times*, with its highly-tuned social filter, had no problems in knowing the exact whereabouts of the Royal presence. Her Majesty, says the report, left Buckingham Palace at 2.45 p.m. and arrived at Wimbledon a little before four o'clock, having travelled across the Pimlico suspension bridge, through Battersea Park and Wandsworth. The Royal party, occupying seven carriages, was escorted by a detachment of the 10th Hussars and, when they arrived at the Common, they were greeted by the tumultuous cheers of crowds who had been gathering since early morning, among them the Volunteers in their long-skirted tunics, 'more picturesque than soldierly'.

The Royal Standard was hoisted above the Pavilion as the Queen, dressed in a black silk dress with a white mantle, a silver grey bonnet on her head and carrying a white parasol, stepped out of the carriage. She was accompanied by the Prince Consort and the Prince of Wales, in Eton jacket. With them were Princess Alice, the young Duke of Edinburgh in Highland garb and the Duke of Connaught, the future Commander-in-Chief, then aged ten; Princess Helena and the seven-year-old Duke of Albany. The Royal Family were met by the Prime Minister, Lord Palmerston, Lord Elcho, other officials of Government and the NRA, and the Association's President, Mr Sidney Herbert, Secretary of State for War and 'a ceremony of interest was enacted before the highest in the land'.

The Queen, who had been seated on a throne to listen to Mr Herbert's welcoming address, rose to give her reply in a few simple, yet succinct words: 'I receive with sincere satisfaction the sentiments of attachment to my throne, person, and family which have been expressed by the President and Council of your Association; and I assure you that I, together with my Royal Consort, have gladly given encouragement to a body whose object it is to render permanent an armed force, limited exclusively to defensive purposes, and founded upon voluntary exertions. I have witnessed with pleasure the manner in which the ancient fondness of the English people for manly and sylvan sports has been converted by your Association to more important ends, and has been made an auxiliary instrument for maintaining inviolable the safety of our common country.'

Prince Albert's response was equally to the point: ' … In establishing a prize, open to the competition of all nations, my object was to give our British marksmen an opportunity of comparing their own arms and their own skill with those of other countries; and I am convinced the result will show that, as the British manufacturer is already second to none in the fabrication of the arm itself, so the people of this country are not to be surpassed by any in the knowledge how to use it.'

To the cheers of the crowd, the Royal party moved to the rifle-tent where the industrious Mr Whitworth was presented to the Queen to explain the workings of the mechanism she was to use to fire the first shot. The lesson over, she was handed a scarlet silken cord attached to the trigger, and, with a gentle tug, Her Majesty Queen Victoria fired the opening shot of the National Rifle Association. A red and white flag was held up before the target, indicating the Queen had hit a bull's-eye at a distance of 400 yards. Another cheer echoed round the Common. The Queen declared the Meeting open and both she and the Prince Consort received a duplicate of the Association's gold medal from Lord Elcho. As the Royal party returned to the Pavilion a salute of twenty-one guns announced the opening of the competition to the thousands in the crowd who had not heard Her Majesty's inaugural words.

Lord Elcho explained the arrangements of the ground and the competitions to the Royal party who went on to examine a selection of guns and rifles exhibited in an adjoining marquee. Then, to more loud cheers, the Queen and her party toured the ranges where, at each firing point, competitors stood under a mantelet which protected the rifleman from the elements while affording the spectator a view of him and his target. The Royal party left Wimbledon Common at about five o'clock which was the signal for a goodly number to follow in its wake, certainly sufficient for *The Times* to note that 'an apparently interminable line of carriages' blocked the roads both to Wimbledon and to the City. 'Again the resemblance to the Derby-day was evident—in dust, puzzled driving, and confusion, it was complete. The excitement in Wimbledon when the detachment of Guards with their splendid band, gorgeous in new uniforms, marched through on their way back to the station, almost reached the point of wildness. The place will not recover its self-possession for many days.'

The first Meeting of the NRA lasted but one week, ending on Saturday, 7 July, the crowds being greater on the opening day and on the day of the finals, despite the fact that entrance was two shillings and sixpence per person (one shilling more than on other days), while carriages and those on horseback were charged five shillings (twice the price of entrance on other days). There were 1,314 entries for the sixty-seven prizes to be won, of which forty were open to all comers. There were seventeen Swiss entrants and one Russian, but, from the Volunteer force of 120,000 of which 1,200 were eligible, only 299 entered. The results of the competition were less than impressive, as can be gauged by the NRA's report of the first year's proceedings: 'This being the first Meeting of the Association, and the Volunteers having had very little time for preparation and practice, the Council refrain from expressing any opinion upon the shooting.'

The *Illustrated London News*, however, saw fit to be more enthusiastic about the winner of The Queen's Prize, nineteen-year-old Edward C.R. Ross, of the 7th North Riding, one of five sons of a former MP for Montrose, Captain Horatio Ross. Young Edward, who was about to go up to Trinity College, Cambridge, had developed an interest in rifle shooting when he was five years old, and was much encouraged by his father, himself a renowned deerstalker, so that by the age of ten, he had killed his first stag. When he stepped up to receive his prize from Lord Elcho, he had already received from him two minor prizes. 'When called to receive the Queen's prize of £250,' reports the *ILN*, 'the band struck up "See the conquering hero comes", and the applause that had greeted him before was redoubled. He bore his honours with great quietness of manner, receiving the prize just as coolly as he shot for it. He is tall, slight, and very youthful in appearance. He was congratulated on his skill and his success by the president, the different members of the council, and a knot of friends: among them was his father, the famous deerstalker. Mr Ross was called on to show his gold medal, and, finally, to put it on: he held it up to the spectators, but could not comply with the other request—the medal had no "fixings".'

The NRA held its first prizegiving at the Crystal Palace. As Mr Sidney Herbert was unable to attend, the ceremony was overseen by Earl de Grey and Ripon, the Under-Secretary for War, who was also one of the Association's twelve Vice-Presidents. And, before a crowd estimated to be 20,000, Lord Elcho announced that it was Her Majesty's intention to continue to give her prize annually at the Meetings of the Association.

When the ceremony was over, the crowd adjourned to the grounds outside the Palace where the Volunteers engaged in 'athletic sports and pastimes … (and) fountains played at five o'clock, and the scene in the gardens during the evening was magnificent'. In the evening the Council entertained the Swiss visitors and its staff to a private farewell dinner in one of the dining rooms at the Crystal Palace. All the speeches were delivered in French, Lord Elcho presiding and proposing the toast to the Queen: 'La Reine—la première carabinière d'Angleterre'. Monsieur de la Rive, the Swiss Minister, proposed a toast to 'England, and the development of her military spirit'. To achieve that, he added, there were only two requirements—men and arms.

At the end of the year, as the fear of war with France subsided, the National Rifle Association numbered but 1,387. Not as healthy a figure as they would have liked, particularly when comparing their membership with that of other societies such as the Royal Agricultural Society (4,600), the Botanical (2,294) and the Zoological (1,721); even though, the annual report reflected sadly, NRA membership included the right of free admission to the enclosure at the Annual Rifle Meeting.

Nevertheless, nothing daunted, the following month Lord Elcho wrote to the Lords-lieutenants of the counties, on behalf of the Council of the NRA, urging them to promote the formation of rifle associations in their areas, modelled on the National Association. In return, the NRA would loan the necessary equipment to set up the local group and would institute a bronze medal, and prize money 'if the state of our exchequer admitted of it,' to be competed for at an annual local meeting. ' ... We claim your favourable consideration,' wrote Lord Elcho, 'in the belief that what has been found to work so successfully in Switzerland, and to contribute so much to the strength and security of that country, will not be found ill-adapted to our own land.'

The year ended hopefully. Lord Elcho informed the Council that the Queen had given permission for Volunteers in the Indian Empire and the Colonies to compete for The Queen's Prize, and, despite the expense of mopping up Wimbledon Common during the summer, the NRA found itself in credit to the tune of £600.

*The Times*, in a leader published on the day of the Association's prizegiving, perhaps best encapsulates the NRA's aims and enthusiasm for its cause in that first year: 'We intend to have 100,000 men who can hit a dinner plate at 200 yards and a six-foot target at 1,000. We intend to make it an all-pervading feeling among our young men that he is not a man who cannot handle a rifle. We intend to make the position of Mr Ross, as the champion rifle shot of England, the envy of every youngster when his father teaches him to shoot. This is what the National Rifle Association has been started in order to effect. This is the interpretation of the Queen's act, when she sped the first bullet to the bull's-eye upon Wimbledon Common.'

# CHAPTER TWO

# *Wimbledon Fortnight*

Royal patronage, the enthusiasm of competitors, and the size of equally enthusiastic crowds must have cheered and encouraged the founding fathers of the National Rifle Association and the organisers of the first Meeting, but no one could have envisaged then that the Meeting would grow to the extent that it did. In 1860, there were 299 entries for The Queen's Prize and some sixty-seven prizes to be won; in 1878, entries reached a record 2,498; and in 1889, the final year that the Meeting was held on Wimbledon Common, there were 2,313 entries for The Queen's Prize, and the prizes numbered 3,201. What is more surprising, perhaps, is that it was not long before the Meeting developed into an important event in the social calendar. In the Victorian Age, Wimbledon Fortnight meant not the volley of tennis racquets but the volley of fire from rifles.

Within a few years, Wimbledon Fortnight came to mean a Common inhabited by several thousand Volunteers, living under canvas, in what was termed Tent Town or Canvas Town. It meant a street of shops, known as the Bazaar, everything from a barber to a florist, to a cycle shop. It meant camp fires and late-night sing-songs, conjurors and clairvoyants, clowns and fireworks, music from military bands, gymnastic displays, and divine service and concert parties in the Umbrella Tent by popular artists of the day such as the Swedish nightingale, Jenny Lind, who lived in the town. It meant a review of troops which could number as many as 22,000, and spectacular sham battles led by the Duke of Cambridge. It meant displays in the Exhibition Tent of the increasing number of magnificent silver trophies, and rides between the ranges on a specially installed tramway. Wimbledon Fortnight saw the start of numerous competitions such as the Vizianagram, the popular match between the House of Commons and the House of Lords, and the Elcho, the oldest international match, shot for by teams of eight from England, Scotland and Ireland.

Wimbledon Fortnight also meant garden parties and dinners organised by the NRA Chairman and his lady which were attended by Royalty, important visitors from overseas and, in their wake, of course, the very chic, the most fashionable of the London set. In addition, the event attracted thousands and thousands of ordinary men and women, who flocked to the Common to watch the competitions and to enjoy the peripheral entertainments. For many families, living not far away in London, the Meeting became an enjoyable and inexpensive way to spend a Sunday. And, increasingly, came enthusiastic riflemen from all over the world.

With fear of an invasion from France a real concern in the early months of 1860, it must have been particularly gratifying to the founders of the NRA that among the visitors to the Meeting in 1861 was Commandant Nessler, Head of the French School of Musketry of Vincennes, who, together with members of his staff, had been sent over especially by the French Emperor to report on the proceedings and on the organisation of the Association itself. Save for one representative rifleman, the Swiss were absent from the 1861 Meeting, busy at home with their own biennial Tir Fédéral. But there were visitors from elsewhere: as well as two members of the Royal Jersey Militia, the NRA noted with pleasure the attendance of an Australian Volunteer, Mr MacFarlane, who was one of the competitors in the first stage of The Queen's Prize. 'Mr MacFarlane is, it is hoped, only the forerunner of the many colonial competitors who may be expected to come to Wimbledon ... ', Lord Elcho stated in the proceedings for that year. With eight Colonial Rifle Associations (South Australia, New South Wales, Queensland, Victoria, Nova Scotia, New Brunswick, Prince Edward Island and Upper Canada), joining the sixteen County Associations in Scotland and England seeking affiliation to the NRA in 1861, Lord Elcho's hope was not long in being fulfilled many hundreds of times over.

Although, initially, the NRA had resolved that the Meeting should seek a new venue each year, the cost of the first one made the Council realise that such an idea would be prohibitively expensive. And, with local opposition quelled, the Council determined that the NRA should look upon Wimbledon Common as 'the permanent and only place where the annual prize meetings can be advantageously held'. The Council also recognised the value of having a site close to London, and therefore, to a vast amount of potential visitors who could swell their limited funds. At the nine-day Meeting of 1861, for example, 21,771 people were admitted, together with 1,062 carriages, and 799 horses which brought in a revenue of £1,786 19s 8d.

The Windmill on the Common, a building first recorded as being erected by Edward Hall in 1613, became the focal point of the NRA Camp. Appropriately, perhaps, because it had once served as a meeting place for duels, the most famous being one which took place in 1798 between the Prime Minister, William Pitt, and the member for Southwark, William Tierney, after the latter had taken offence at remarks made by the Premier in the House of Commons. The Cottage, a building near to the Windmill, became the residence of the Chairman and his wife during the Meeting. The roped-off lawns in front encompassed the tents containing the Association's offices as well as accommodation for its staff, and also served as the venue for the various 'At Homes' held by the Chairman to which members of London society were invited. Such events, in themselves, caused considerable crowds to gather to watch the comings and goings of the fashionable and the mighty whose carriages often jammed the roads into the town.

It was at the Mill House that Sir Robert Baden-Powell, founder of the Boy Scouts, wrote the movement's bible, *Scouting for Boys*, in 1907. Thirty-three years earlier, as Private Baden-Powell, he had travelled to Wimbledon with his school party when, for the first time, Charterhouse entered a team in the Public Schools' match for the Ashburton Shield. The school did not win the trophy, but one of their team was the only competitor in the match to score a bull. His name was Baden-Powell.

Around these buildings were the refreshment tents, the tents of the gunmakers, and the Prize Exhibition Tent. 'The ground here being sound, dry and intersected by gravel roads, and commanding a beautiful view of Richmond Park, offered advantages possessed by no other part of the common,' records the NRA's report for 1861, while noting that to one side of the Windmill, lay the encampment of the Metropolitan Police and a vast stretch of land that was offered to any Volunteer who wished to pitch his tent and camp on the Common for the duration of the Meeting. In 1861, only the Victoria Rifles and Lord Radstock took advantage of the offer, and the NRA reflected that in future perhaps it would provide the Volunteers with tents, believing that such an encampment would become a popular feature of the Wimbledon Meeting, and 'be of use in initiating the volunteers in the mysteries and contrivances of camp life'.

The Prize Exhibition Tent provided the NRA with another valuable source of income: silversmiths, watchmakers and gunmakers were invited to display articles 'suitable for prizes', and charged five shillings entrance fee for the privilege 'as a check against the sending of inferior articles'. Prizes, which numbered ninety-three in 1861, included a pair of field glasses worth twenty-one guineas, twenty-five engravings worth 250 guineas, and a patent safe, value twenty-four guineas, donated by Mr George Price of Burnley. 'This prize, which weighed 7 cwt, occasioned much amusement ... ', admitted Lord Elcho, in his report that year, while hastening to assure potential donors that the Council was quite prepared to accept anything 'provided they are of sufficient value'. But the amusement which greeted the safe must have been as nothing to that which greeted a prize donated in 1887, exhibited 'in suitably decorated rooms' erected by the donors, Messrs Atkinson and Co. of Westminster Bridge Road. It was a complete set of furniture, valued at forty guineas, 'for a bachelor bedroom'.

∽ ∼ ∾ ∾

Like Topsy in *Uncle Tom's Cabin*, the Volunteer Camp at Wimbledon just grow'd. What began in 1861 with one corps, one lord and their respective tents pitched on the Common, developed over the years into a camp which accommodated, at times, more than three thousand, and, alongside them, the facilities, and the little luxuries, thought necessary for a man away from his home, not to say his club, for as long as a fortnight.

In 1862, when 674 people, including 212 Volunteers, encamped on the Common, water was laid on, lavatories and washing sheds constructed, and twenty-five commissionaires were engaged together with twelve shoeblacks. At this time, tents were supplied by the Government. One tent provided accommodation for either two officers, or six non-commissioned officers and privates (which caused not a little discomfort and disquiet among the ranks). The officers' tents were each kitted out with a bedstead, mattress, pillow, washstand, basin, water can, bath, easy chair, pole strap, lantern, toilet glass and matting for the bedside.

Also that year, at the suggestion of Lord Ducie, tents were pitched for individual County Associations (the precursors of the clubhouses at Bisley Camp), where competitors could meet, 'deposit their cloaks, rifles, ammunition, etc.' and have their rifles cleaned. Each marquee was fitted with tables, benches and rifle racks, and manned by a commissionaire.

The following year, when a Pocket Companion for the Meeting was first produced and more than 1,100 people were staying in Camp, a large tent was pitched to serve as a club room. It was for members of the Association, but, on payment of one shilling, any Volunteer in the Camp could use its facilities which included the provision of daily newspapers, writing materials, a piano, and a billiards table. It was in this tent that Jenny Lind gave a concert. She was accompanied by Mr Blagrove, a renowned violinist, who wore the uniform of the Artists' Rifle Corps.

That year the NRA began a long and happy association with the Manchester caterers, Messrs Jennison, which, after a four-year break beginning in 1868, finally came to an end in 1877. The staff, who travelled down from Lancashire every year for the Meeting, included waiters who doubled as handymen to construct the huge Refreshment Pavilion, built substantially of wood and covered in with double canvas. Inside it had sufficient ovens and cooking apparatus, the *Illustrated London News* reported with a degree of awe, to supply hot dinners every day. 'The building altogether is upon a scale of sufficient magnitude to supply not only the army and the ground followers, but all the public who may feel disposed to patronise the proprietors.'

Just how much food the crowd could get through is indicated by another caterer's order for two days in 1869 when 25,000 customers were served by a staff of 450: 8,000 lb of bread; 16,000 rolls; 5 cwt of biscuits; 1,000 fruit pies; 4 cwt of butter; 5,000 eggs; 4 cwt of cheese; 2,500 lettuces; 1.5 tons of potatoes; 600 quarts of shelled peas; 600 quarts of ices; 780 gallons of tea; 130 gallons of coffee; 350 gallons of milk; 100 tongues; 100 hams; 5 cwt salmon; 156 lb of eels; 20 turbot; 480 lobster; 900 heads of poultry; 6 tons of meat; 5 tons of ice; 80 hogsheads of ale and stout; 760 gallons of claret cup; besides wines, spirits, liquors and aerated waters.

In 1863 it was decided to change the date of the annual Meeting, from the first Monday to the second Monday in July, to avoid the time when there was considerable pressure of work on banks and mercantile offices, following the end of the half-year accounts. A fact which again indicates the increasing popularity of the Meeting, as well as the profession of some of the men attracted to it.

The following year saw the arrival in Camp of a great attraction, the tramway, The Association Wimbledon Line, which ran along the back of the firing points, and was drawn by a horse ridden by a soldier from the Military Train. Passengers sat in long side cars, back to back to enable the conductor to pass along and collect the fares. 'The Tramway,' said Lord Elcho in his annual report, 'was a great success, notwithstanding one or two trifling accidents that unfortunately occurred to the passengers, the result of too great a speed, as is frequently the case in railway travelling.' In spite of the dangerous speed of horsedriven carriages, the tramway was extended and converted to steam in 1877. And, despite the issue of an abundance of hot air, the engine was named, without a murmur of dissent on his part, after the then Chairman, the Earl of Wharncliffe. It was opened, prior to the Meeting, by the Prince of Wales, later Edward VII. It was electrified and again extended in 1884.

It was in 1864, when Mr Jennison first constructed his wooden Refreshment Pavilion, that the large tent which had been used as refreshment area became free for other events. In the beginning, the tent was called the Parasol or Umbrella Tent; the fact that the latter name was the one which stuck gives some indication as to the weather which predominated at the Meetings. The Umbrella Tent served as a railway station, concert room, and, on the middle Sunday in the Meeting, as the place where Divine

Service was held. In 1864, the Archbishop of York, who was Chaplain to the Inns of Court Volunteers, travelled down from York to hold the service. Among the most popular entertainers in the Umbrella Tent were the Moray Minstrels. So popular, in fact, that the NRA Council quickly established an admission charge after their first recital—ever conscious of ways to bolster the Association's meagre funds. And, at one shilling a ticket, which raised £50 at the next concert, it proved to be a decision made just in time.

The Camp abounded with flowers and ferns, which blossomed in specially constructed boxes or in trenches dug out at the side of a tent. Volunteers often decorated the outsides of their tents with amusing, welcoming notices to identify the occupants from their neighbours. The Earl de Grey chose as his welcoming mat, a fierce, toothy crocodile, undoubtedly, to the considerable relief of his friends, one that was dead and stuffed. To make himself feel more at home, Sergeant-Major Kethro took to his tent in 1869, a brightly-coloured green parrot which, reported the *South London Press*, was much admired for its voice. 'Not only does it give utterance to some very droll sentences as clearly as any human being, and sing several pieces of music accurately from beginning to end, but also gives all the bugle calls for commencing and ceasing fire ... ' The reporter makes no mention, however, of the feelings of the parrot's and Sergeant-Major Kethro's close neighbours. A trip round the Volunteer Camp was as much fun for some visitors as watching the competitions.

Sunday was the great visiting day, 'undisturbed by the popping of rifles,' reported the *Illustrated London News* in 1880. A day for quiet sociability when families came to visit Papa, but 'the imperfect privacy of a tent, with some portion of its canvas drawn aside to let in the fresh air, but opening the whole interior to the view of passers-by' did have its drawbacks. Families were 'too often disturbed by the mercenary importunities of fruit-vendors and other peripatetic small tradesfolk, who keep up an incessant clamour to proclaim their wares for sale throughout the camp.'

The 'harmless art of photography' also came in for some gentle, if more wry, criticism. 'If it be subject to no restrictions of place, (it) may be inconvenient, possibly, to a young couple roving towards the sequestered nook, where they do *not* know, or suspect, that "there is an eye to mark their coming." The gallant swain has presently to cover his disappointment by ordering those ruthless professors of the art to execute a shilling portrait of his beloved companion, which is sure to be utterly unlike her ... '

It soon became the custom for competitors staying on the Common to meet in the evening round a camp-fire, and, in 1862, the NRA Council thought to use this habit to set up a Rifle Parliament, where everyone could exchange their ideas and opinions on shooting, on rifles, and on Camp life in general. Notices were put about inviting competitors to a Midnight Meeting, which was actually held at the more convenient hour of 10 p.m. Once again, a heavy storm threatened to put a dampener on NRA proceedings, if not wash it out altogether, but almost as soon as it started, the storm blew itself out and a magnificent double rainbow emerged, casting its light over the entire Common.

It was a good omen. And if the spirits were lifted only marginally by it, they must have been raised considerably more by the Victoria Rifles' promise to supply all-comers with an unlimited amount of punch.

Round a huge pile, some forty feet high, of blazing furze, distributing smoke and spitting sparks to the poor souls who were unfortunate enough to be downwind of it, the motley parliament of some 1,400 assembled. Duchesses and other noble ladies mingled with shoeblacks and shop-keepers, Guards officers, barristers, sailors, policemen, and Volunteers of all classes. Jenny Lind was there as was, of course, the popular Chairman's equally popular wife, Lady Elcho, who was cheered loudly when someone referred to her as an 'enthusiastic volunteer'. Such a mixed social gathering caused the correspondent of the *Illustrated London News* to reflect how times had changed: 'Years ago no one could have dreamed that such a meeting could take place, and even now we believe that in no country in the world save our own could such a scene pass over without a single untoward incident or unpleasant reminiscence ... '

Lord Elcho presided over this first Rifle Parliament at which the discussion encompassed topics such as accommodation, targets, rifle-testing, prizes and, what became a long-running issue, the position riflemen should adopt to shoot. Should it be the Hythe position or should an individual have the right to choose? The Camp administrators were thanked, Lord Elcho remarking that he had received only one complaint from a man who had been disturbed to find three earwigs in his hat.

The crowd received the news with a sympathetic roar of laughter: earwigs were the bane of life on the Common. So much so that, three years later, when the Midnight Meetings had to be abandoned, partly because of the fire hazards in an increasingly populated Camp, and partly because the space was needed to accommodate extra bodies, two letter boxes were put at the entrance of the Council tent, one decorated with the figure of an owl (for wise suggestions), the other, to receive complaints, having at its head an earwig. (These figures can be seen to this day in the NRA offices at Bisley.) Both creatures, who so closely shared, or worried, the life of the Volunteer on the Common, later gave their names to Camp newspapers and then to competitions. Indeed, for some time, the Victoria Rifles

*Wimbledon Common in the 1860s — 'the white tents . . . like a nest of poached eggs shining in a dish of verdant spinach'.*

*Whitworth's Ammunition Tent on Wimbledon Common in the 1860s. Mr (later Sir) Joseph Whitworth assembled the rifle fired by Queen Victoria at the inaugural Meeting of the NRA, and Whitworth's rifles were used by entrants to The Queen's Prize in the early 1860s.*

LEFT Lord Elcho, first Chairman of the NRA, from a copy of a painting by John Sargent.

RIGHT A Captain and his comrades enjoying the outdoor life on Wimbledon Common, 1864.

BELOW The Cottage on Wimbledon Common in the 1860s: the scene of garden parties and numerous other events held by NRA Chairmen which became highlights of Wimbledon Fortnight and, indeed, of the Victorian social calendar. In the foreground is the Honourable Artillery Band and just visible in the background is the Windmill.

BELOW RIGHT The Scottish team who won the Elcho Trophy in 1864. Seated front, left, is the young Lord Elcho.

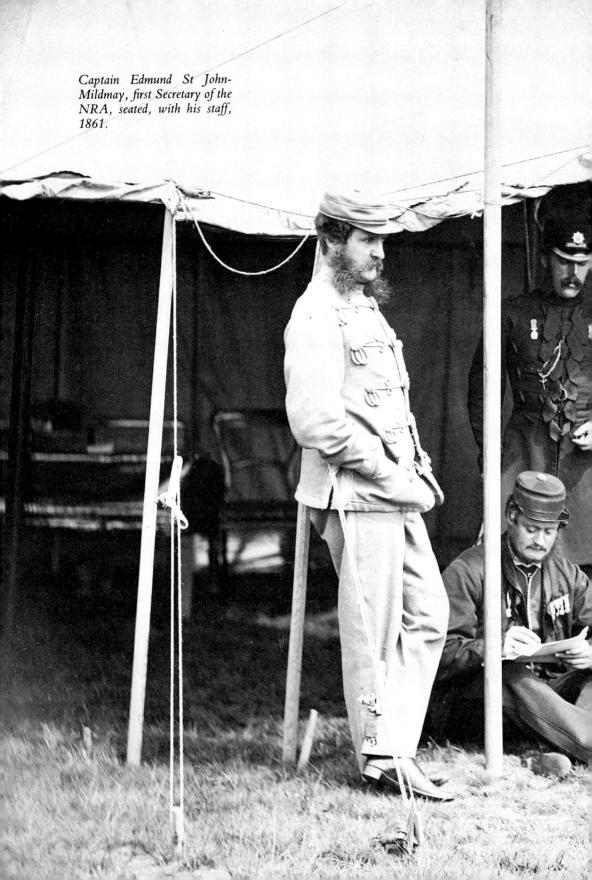

Captain Edmund St John-Mildmay, first Secretary of the NRA, seated, with his staff, 1861.

*Major (later Sir) Henry Halford and his wife (1864). At their home at Wistow, which he left to his protégé Thomas Fremantle, Lord Cottesloe, Halford worked with William Metford on the development of the rifle. A member of the English team in the first Elcho Shield Match, Halford was also a popular captain of several British teams which competed against the US and Canada. He died in 1896.*

*Private Angus Cameron, winner of The Queen's Prize in 1866 and 1869, who celebrated his victories with a cup of tea.*

*A caricature of Earl Spencer, who chaired the meeting at his London home, Spencer House, which led to the formation of the NRA. He became its second Chairman (1867–8).*

mounted on top of their huge distinguishing totem pole in their camp, a large golden earwig.

A Master of Revels ensured that the first Rifle Parliament never got too serious, and an interval was given over to music and comic recitations. Later in the evening, the proceedings were again interrupted by a figure claiming to be Robinson Crusoe and carrying what seemed to be an endless supply of cups and mugs for people to dunk into the steaming cauldrons, placed near the fire, which were overflowing with hot punch.

cᴐ cᴐ ᴐ ᴐ

By 1864, the Camp had expanded to cover a space one mile in circumference. Mr Bennett, who was a regular contributor in the Exhibition Tent, fitted up a clock, with a bell weighing 300 lb which could be heard all over the Camp, not to say the Common. 'Those who rise with the lark speak in rapturous terms of the spectacle of sunrise—a sight not too familiar to Londoners; and are equally eloquent on the delights of the early morning "tub and rub" outside their tents, after the fashion of the Japanese,' enthused a correspondent in the *Illustrated London News* in 1876. 'Breakfasts are enjoyed in the open air; and the free and easy matutinal life is very different from the brilliant but staider evening gatherings, when sweet girlish faces and gossamer garments lend variety to the green and drab, grey and scarlet uniforms of the Volunteers, and Wimbledon Camp is *en fête*.'

In 1867, ivory passes were instituted for life members, and, the following year, to accommodate the increasing number of lady visitors to the Camp, what was termed the Junior Wimbledon Club was opened. Subscribers paid one guinea annually or, 'if properly introduced', a subscription for a day, to avail themselves of a spacious marquee, 'tastefully fitted out and supplied with much of the current literature of the day'. Ladies were not permitted into the Camp, however, until morning ablutions were over—though quite whose modesty was being spared is not made clear.

The Bazaar of shops continued to expand. Every year there were rows of stores containing everything a rifleman could possibly consider to be necessary, alongside everything else that he might think to be unnecessary. There were cigar divans, cycle manufacturers, lamp and hammock makers, tea and provision merchants, manufacturers of gymnastic equipment. And, with a visit from that very special guest impending, a chap could always avail himself of the services of a barber and a florist, and, if the need should arise, a photographer. The post office did thriving business. In 1874 30,564 letters were despatched and 17,678 delivered. In 1878, following an enthusiastic report from a member of a rifle team who had competed in a match in the United States, the telephone was introduced to speed up the delivery of results from the butts. 'Though, as might reasonably have been anticipated, there were some failures in the instruments and the manipulation of them, yet the telephonic communication was decidedly more convenient, and gave rise to fewer misunderstandings than the electric bells hitherto in use.'

Notwithstanding the volatile nature of the early rifle, combined with the initial inexperience of the handlers, medical reports are remarkably free of serious accidents or illness. The main problems which afflicted the Camp each year were either constipation or diarrhoea, which gave rise to a strong recommendation that unauthorised purveyors of fruit and beverages should be excluded from the encampment.

In 1880, when the Meeting was clouded over by an issue involving rigging the markings, the weather was equally unclear. 'At times the fog (was) so dense as to obscure the targets, and on one occasion to necessitate a suspension of the firing,' records the NRA report that year. One Tuesday in 1868, the *Illustrated London News* reported that 'the heat was so intense that many of the competitors retired from the contests. Stewards' thermometers registered the greatest heat in the shade at 101.'

Sometimes there was the wind and, of course, always, always the rain. On 13 July 1867 the Prince of Wales arrived on the Common to lead a welcoming party for more than 2,000 Belgian visitors, including the Gardes Civiques. Crowds lined the route to watch the spectacle. They, along with everyone else that day, were drenched to the skin in a torrential downpour which carried on throughout the entire ceremony and beyond. In 1873, after a day of continual rain which reduced the entire Camp to the conditions of a swamp, a gale arose of such ferocity that it blew down the Umbrella Tent. Luckily, the few people underneath it, though shaken and certainly stirred, were not seriously injured.

Two years later, day after day of rain put most of the Camp under water. Several hundred yards of planks had to be laid down simply to connect one part of the Camp with another. On the fifth day of the Meeting, the situation had got so bad that the Committee went so far as to suspend the regulation which stipulated that Volunteers had to shoot in uniform. Even the most particular, most conscientious members were seen on the ranges *sans* shoes or stockings.

The weather, however, never seemed to dampen people's enthusiasm. 'Not only do the Volunteers owe a debt of gratitude to the National Rifle Association, Society finds in the Wimbledon Meeting relaxation from the continual round of the Row and the Drive, the Opera and Dances,' wrote the reporter for the *Illustrated London News* in 1878, with a delicate world-weariness that makes one positively swoon in sympathy. How the poor soul reacted to the continual sound of gun-fire is not, alas, recorded.

There were the garden parties, the Chairman's 'At Homes', firework and gymnastic displays, reviews and, in the early days, Sham Battles, which involved as many as 15,000 men, and covered the Common with alarum and excursions. 'This was one of the finest sights of the day,' a reporter enthused at the first Meeting in 1860. 'The evening was getting just a trifle dusky, the brightness of the day had ceased, and in this slightly-diminished daylight the lines of fire at each discharge were seen distinct and bright through the white smoke which partially concealed the men. With the rapidity of lightning the small tongues of flame played from the right of companies along the extended line; and then came one, and another, and another simultaneous well-delivered volley, which seemed as though the crest of the hill were vomiting fire and smoke ... ' And when the grand event of the day was concluded, 'the sun, as his last rays glistened upon the bayonets of the men marching to bivouac over the brow of the hill, seemed to smile approvingly upon the efforts of that earnest and patriotic band.'

In 1867, after the prizegiving, the review on the Common involved some 22,000 men, including some of the London Volunteer Corps, the House-hold Brigade of Cavalry, four battalions of Foot Guards, several batteries of the Royal Artillery and Horse Artillery and the Belgian Volunteers. The spectacle was watched by His Imperial Majesty the Sultan of Turkey, who arrived punctually at six o'clock on a white Arabian horse, with a magnifi-cent saddle-cloth. On either side of him were the Prince of Wales and the Duke of Cambridge, the Duke of Aosta, second son of the King of Italy, and Prince Teck, and in their wake, a party of nearly ninety staff and field officers, aides-de-camp, Albanians, Turkish, Arab and Circassian chiefs 'whose costumes were gorgeous and picturesque'.

Royalty showed its support of the Association not only by donating prizes each year, but in regular attendance at the annual Meeting. In 1887, the year of the Queen's Jubilee, Wimbledon Common throbbed with its blue-blooded visitors and, in a marquee attached to the Cottage, Lord and Lady Wantage gave a banquet for more than a hundred guests including the Prince and Princess of Wales, the King of Greece and his son and heir, the Duke of Sparta. The entire Camp was illuminated for the occasion and after dinner, the guests were entertained by a band of musically-talented Volunteers who performed under the verandah of the Staff Pavilion. The Prince of Wales was a frequent visitor to Wimbledon Fortnight, and enjoyed taking the odd shot himself, particularly at novel competitions such as the Running Deer, first introduced by the gunmaker, Lancaster, in 1862.

The distribution of prizes was frequently carried out by a noble lady, members of the Government often in attendance. In 1860, 1862 and 1863, the ceremony was held at the Crystal Palace, before cost became prohibitive, and was followed by a display of athletics. In 1862, two years before he did battle with Bismarck over the problem of Schleswig-Holstein, the prizegiving was attended by Lord Palmerston. At the grand old age of seventy-eight, it was noted that he appeared to be in excellent health and that as he mounted the platform, he was greeted with loud and long-continued cheers.

Numerous prizes were introduced in those early Wimbledon years, and several traditions begun, among them the custom of carrying aloft from the ranges the winner of The Queen's Prize in a chair which was presented to the Association in 1883 by Charles Wainwright, once a member of the London Rifle Brigade. But when after thirty years on the Common, the NRA had to leave, traditions were not left behind. 'If anything were necessary to prove the deep hold which the love of rifle-shooting has taken of the English people,' said *The Times* in 1865, 'it would be the fact that not even the excitement, tumult, and conflict of passions attendant on a general election can put a stop to the great annual trial of skill at Wimbledon.'

☙ ☙ ☙ ☙

It is hardly surprising that, considering the size and popularity of such an event, an unruly element was attracted to the Meeting on the Common, a fact which disturbed the NRA Council and, not unnaturally, annoyed local residents who objected to the crowds which descended on the town, particularly on Sundays and after evening gun-fire. In 1882, in an attempt to rectify the situation, and pacify the locals, the Council imposed a ban on the sale of alcohol to visitors on Sundays, and closed the Refreshment Pavilion on weekday evenings to all but Volunteers in the Camp and to soldiers. They also prohibited entertainments after 8 p.m., except by their permission, adding sternly, 'This permission will never extend to fireworks, balls and dancing parties.'

Initially, the ban meant a loss of visitors, as well as a considerable loss of revenue because the Association had to pay compensation to the refreshment contractors. But, it seems, the problem did not go away. At least, in the eyes of certain local residents. In 1886 a short-lived periodical, *The Wimbledon, Tooting and Merton Temperance Gazette*, ran a series of readers' letters under the heading 'Intemperance In Wimbledon Camp', which began with a correspondent who used the *nom de plume*, Achilles.

'Cannot something be done to stem the tide of drunkenness and immorality at the Wimbledon Camp meeting?' he bemoaned. 'I am quite sure, from long experience, that alcoholic drinks do not assist any man hitting the target ... No "crack shot", or good marksman will argue that drinking alcoholic liquor will improve his sight or enable him to make a true allowance for wind and distance when he faces the targets ... If any one will tell me that he shoots better because he has been primed with alcoholic liquor, I can point to a score, who are prepared to prove that liquor has no more to do with good shooting, than comets have to do with cabbage stalks ... '

By the following issue, Achilles had generated supportive responses from Vigilance and A. Ratepayer, the latter stating that, 'Of an evening, which is the only time many of the residents in the locality have time to go on the Common during the Camp, it is not a fit place for any respectable person to walk about ... '

The matter was brought to a close in the following issue by a reader with slightly different views, and tastes, who had noticed Vigilance's desire to ban the sale of alcohol at the Camp. 'You might just as well try to cure rheumatism or gout by act of Parliament. You can't do it ... If the Teeto-tallers do not like the drinking at the camp, I say, let them stop away. Hoping you will publish this, and so oblige a large number of the inhabi-tants of Wimbledon, I beg to subscribe myself, Drink.'

*The Wimbledon, Tooting and Merton Temperance Gazette* folded not long after, though the Temperance movement itself flourished for many years, fighting what G.M.Trevelyan called 'one of the major evils of city life'. Achilles, Vigilance and A.Ratepayer must have been inspired by The Queen's Prizewinner of 1866, Angus Cameron, a small, boyish nineteen-year-old private with the 6th Inverness Corps, who was a self-confessed abstainer. Three years later, at the grand old age of twenty-two and now promoted to the rank of corporal, Cameron again won The Queen's Prize. He was hoisted on to the shoulders of two strong men and carried off to the Council Tent, cheered by the crowd while the band of the Victorias played 'See The Conquering Hero Comes'. His gun was checked, found to be perfectly regular, and he was eventually borne aloft into the regimental tent of the London Scottish where the reception he received was, as for every victor, overwhelming—except, that is, for Cameron. As the *Illustrated London News* reported: 'Everybody insisted on drinking his health; but Mr Cameron himself, as a strict total abstainer, refused even the cooling ref-reshment of a draught of claret; and, having modestly thanked his friends and fellow-countrymen, retired to the establishment of Messrs. Spiers and Pond, to take a cup of tea.'

೧ ೧ ೧ ೧

'Who does not know Wimbledon? Wind-driven Wimbledon! … Who does not know the white tents resting on the fragrant heather like a nest of poached eggs shining in a dish of verdant spinach?'

So wrote one of the noblest visitors to the Meeting. A man whose sentimental feelings were sometimes writ as large as the drink-sodden nose he stuck into affairs. It was a nose often plastered, as it were, over the pages of his own magazine. He was, of course, Mr Punch. Mr Punch enjoyed himself enormously at the Meetings, if only because it gave him free rein to become his querulous self, a state in which both he, and his readers, were happiest.

In 1875 Mr Punch set off for Wimbledon in an amiable frame of mind which disintegrated, delightfully, as the journey progressed. The problems began at Clapham Junction, he recalled, when he was 'invited to change carriages, and found that the Railway Companies, with that forethought for which they are renowned, had prepared a little preliminary puzzle for the Volunteers, evidently with a view to testing their knowledge of military tactics. The tunnel underneath the Station was in the hands of the plasterers; and as all the ordinary directions on the walls had been carefully painted out, it was a matter of chance if you turned up on a platform "right" for Brighton, or got into a train warranted to carry you all the way to Exeter in something less than no time.'

After an hour spent searching for a train to take him to Wimbledon, Mr Punch gave up. Instead, he boarded one which took him to a station nearby. Thus, he arrived in Putney, reflecting on his arduous journey, his temper not in the best of health, his wit improving all the time. 'The comparative dexterity with which this feat was accomplished, was strongly suggestive of a third-rate conjuring trick performed by a fourth-rate conjuror.' Putney, Mr Punch recalled bitterly, was but a short step from Wimbledon, 'that step was the step that divided the Sublime from the Ridiculous.'

Eventually, Mr Punch, having tersely refused an invitation to have his portrait taken, arrived at the Camp. Over the years, it became a sight which did not fill his eyes with pleasure. Not surprisingly, he made remarkably speedy progress through the ranks from Private to Field-Marshal Punch, which led him to write down his own rules and regulations to spruce the place up a bit. One disquieting matter to catch his beady eye, was the variable dress adopted by the Volunteers—the subject of forest-loads of correspondence in the newspapers and in the NRA's own reports.

Thus, 'Field-Marshal Punch, Chief Inspector-General of the Auxiliary Forces, etc., etc., acting for himself … begs to inform the troops under his immediate command, that he has noticed, with much pain, in years gone by, the want of discipline often observable in the Volunteer Encampment, held annually at Wimbledon ... With a view to ensuring uniformity, the Field Marshal begs that the following regulations may be strictly observed by all taking part in this year's gathering. He may add that experience has taught him that none of the rules published below can be considered unnecessary.'

Camp Orders—No one is to sleep in more than two tents at once. Snoring not allowed until 11 p.m., and then only in unison with the drone of the bagpipe which will give the key-note. The Camp Guard will be selected at 9 p.m. from those who can distinctly pronounce the countersign 'Statistical Calculations' ... The picket will reverse arms, sections outwards, dress by the right, and advance by subdivisions at the halt.

Dress—Officers ordered to attend in Full Dress parade, will not appear in white neck-ties, lavender kid gloves, and swallow-tailed coats ... Non-Commissioned Officers taking part in Battalion Drill should never unfurl their umbrellas without the command of a Brigadier-General ... A Major (in the absence of his Commanding Officer) should never hold a Church Parade in a straw-hat, a sword, and a pair of goloshes. Kid-Gloves should never be of more than three distinct patterns and colours when worn by Privates belonging to the same Company.

Small Bore Regulations—The following excuses for failure in shooting will be disregarded:—That the competitor forgot to clean his rifle, or to alter his sight, or to put in a bullet, that he put two bullets in, that he had too long a walk, that he was shaken in a 'bus, that he has no appetite, that he dined out and had too much—well—salmon, and had in consequence too high elevation, that just as he fired the target suddenly took two paces 'right close' ... That he forgot to make proper allowance for the rotation of the Earth, the attraction of the Moon, and the idiosyncrasy of the asymptote trajectory of the trygonometrical barometer ...

Bands—No Band in future will be permitted to take up its station within a radius of six yards from another Band. As a rule, Bands practising within ten yards of one another, should select tunes of more or less the same character. For instance, if Band A plays a quadrille, Band B should rehearse the 'Lancers'; if B and C commence a polka, Band D may perform a lively waltz; and so on.

In the Lords and Commons Competition, any position will be allowed, but no motions or speeches. The Members will be selected by

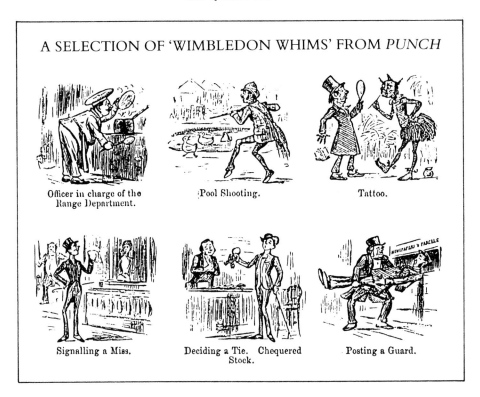

## A SELECTION OF 'WIMBLEDON WHIMS' FROM *PUNCH*

Officer in charge of the Range Department.

Pool Shooting.

Tattoo.

Signalling a Miss.

Deciding a Tie. Chequered Stock.

Posting a Guard.

divisions, and in any disputes about the sights, the 'ayes' have it. All complaints … are to be referred to the Secretary's knickerbockers … One of the Council by rotation will take steps to provide a 'running man' to be shot at.

At times, Mr Punch relished a little gentle didacticism. 'Here it is necessary to say, for the benefit of the Public (who are wholly and entirely ignorant of all military matters), that the Marksman is the person who fires off the rifle. The rifle is a weapon consisting of a certain amount of wood and steel. This weapon is loaded (that is filled) with an explosive composition called gunpowder, and a missile made of lead yclept (called) a bullet. The gunpowder is put into a tube (called a barrel) first, then a bullet. When ignited, the powder propels the bullet through the air … '

In the guise of a contributor who had not won a prize, Mr Punch allowed himself less spleen and a lot more sentiment as he pondered some 'Whys' of Wimbledon:

Why is the Camp situated between two Railway Stations, and near neither?

Why must you to get to your destination, either puff up a high hill or pick your way over a rutty common?

Why must you live in utter discomfort in a bell-tent with a lot of other fellows for a couple of showery weeks?

Why is the Staff permitted to revel in boarding, carpets, elaborate furniture, and flower gardens?

Why is the Members' Camp permitted to assume the appearance of a collection of Stock Exchange boudoirs?

Why is the shooting so badly managed?

Why is the marker invariably asleep when a fellow clearly makes a bull?

Why does one's rifle, so good at practice, always go wrong when it comes to competition?

Why do all the earwigs take my tent for a trysting place?

But, when the sticks are down, Mr Punch's enormously sentimental heart, almost bursting from his breast, can't help but lead him to conclude: 'Why, after making up one's mind never to come to Wimbledon again, does one always find oneself under canvas within half a mile of the windmill?'

Mr Punch was not best pleased when George Ranger, as he dubbed the Duke of Cambridge, gave the National Rifle Association notice to quit. True, he did toy with the idea of continuing Wimbledon Fortnight—without the shooting—but, instead, he sharpened his spleen and settled down to write a new set of rules, under the heading 'Vale, Wimbledon', in order that 'the property of the Illustrious Personage may be injured as little as possible'. Volunteers were not permitted to walk on the grass. No one was allowed to use pegs to erect their tents, for fear of damaging the turf. Smoking was not permitted within six miles of the Duke's residence and no person 'on any consideration whatever, will be allowed to open a soda-water bottle that has its neck pointing towards His Royal Highness's property, for fear of accidents.'

Mr Punch, however, being a particularly perceptive clairvoyant, could guess why the Duke was perturbed at the consequences of the National Rifle Association staying at Wimbledon. His vision appeared in 1887 under the heading, 'A Long Shot At The Future':

41

SCENE—The Interior of a Villa Residence in a secluded part of the Isle of Wight. Domestic circle discovered assembled at lunch.

PATERFAMILIAS. I have brought down *The Times* to read—(the paper is suddenly torn from his hand and carried through the window with a crash). Hallo! What's this!

SUPERSTITIOUS SPINSTER. Brother, I have always told you that this place is haunted! The incident has unnerved me. Nephew, I think I *will* take another glass of sherry.

YOUNGSTER. All right, Auntie!

(Raises decanter to pour out wine, when both bottle and glass are knocked to pieces.)

MATERFAMILIAS. How careless of you, Charley! Have I not told you a hundred times that—(The chandelier comes down with a run.)

SCHOOLGIRL. Oh, Mamma, what can be the matter? The poor canary is lying on its side, with a hole through the wire of its cage!

PATERFAMILIAS. Dear me! Well, this is very strange! (Suddenly looking at heading of paper.) Why, to be sure! How thoughtless I am! I did not notice the date. Why, of course this is the first day of the Volunteers at Wimbledon. We had better take our plates as usual downstairs, my dears, and eat our luncheon in the cellars! (The family act upon the suggestion.)

~ ~ ~ ~

The relationship between the NRA and the town was, at best, cordial; at worst, a long way from that. Admittedly, the shopkeepers, publicans and traders revelled in the extra business. 'Indirectly,' the *Surrey Comet* reflected in 1878, 'the arrival of the camp season stimulates the business of Wimbledon, but there is the doubt that the lion's share of the extra pickings finds its way into the pockets of the cab proprietors and publicans. The Wimbledon boys, however, with an enterprise worthy of a better cause, dog the footsteps of volunteers going up and down Wimbledon, and insanely offer to "Carry your gun for you, sir?" ... Apparently, no one as yet has accepted their kind offer, but it is impossible to go up and down the hill without hearing the cry repeated to an indefinite extent.'

In 1879, however, a storm blew up. A storm far greater than the one which had threatened the original Meeting, and one which damaged severely the relationship with the local inhabitants. The trouble concerned the NRA's decision to impose an entrance fee, after evening gunfire had ceased, of sixpence. The reasons were twofold: to restrict the unsavoury element which was still attracted to the Common and upset local residents,

## COMING OF AGE.—N. R. A., WiMBLEDON, 1880.

"The National Rifle Association has now attained its majority, and in a befitting way celebrates the twenty-first year of its existence by showing more vigorous signs of life than ever."—*Daily News.*

COMING OF AGE IN THE MODERN TIMES, AND MANY HAPPY, HAPPY RETURNS OF THE DAY.

TWENTY-One this year!
  *Punch* uplifts his beaker,
And, in accents clear,
  Cordial as the speaker,
Loud enough to reach
  Over all the Island,

Swift from beach to beach,
  Shouts with Punchian smile, and
Drinks "The N. R. A.,
Twenty-One to-day!"

Seasons Twenty-One
  (On Time's roll a trifle)

and to boost the NRA's coffers which were suffering as a result of having to issue some 8,000 or more free passes each year to local ratepayers as a result of the Wimbledon and Putney Commons Act of 1871.

The decision caused a furore, or 'a feeling of extreme dissatisfaction in the place', reported the *Surrey Comet*. 'The arbitrary and unfeeling manner in which the Council have acted cannot but be condemned. True, the camp after gun fire, is hardly so orderly as it might be, in consequence of the roughs and tramps who pour in directly the gates are opened, but we would urge in the strongest possible manner that the Wimbledon working man can hardly be included in that category ... '

Nevertheless, the Wimbledon working man and a few of his peers decided that they could not wait for the NRA to reconsider the matter and showed 'their righteous indignation' by pulling down part of the fencing which surrounded the NRA Camp. One of their leaders, Mark Crook, was fined £2 2s 6d, and the local newspaper began to carry letters of disgust at what people saw to be a gross miscarriage of justice. Their argument was that the NRA had itself broken the law, as laid down in the Wimbledon and Putney Commons Act, by prohibiting the residents free access across the common land. 'I intend before this meeting is over to demand a right of way across from Stagg-Lane to Wimbledon after "gun-fire", and I contend that no one can legally stop me,' wrote a furious Frederick Ely of Alexandra Road, Wimbledon.

A few days later, the *Surrey Comet* reported the outcome under the heading, 'Serious Rioting on Wimbledon Common'. Printed notices had gone up in the town inviting people to a meeting at 8 p.m. on Thursday, 24 July, to be held near the White Houses entrance, in order to demand admission to the Camp. Some 800 people took up the invitation and, as news of impending trouble had reached the authorities, they were met with a body of police, mounted and on foot, stationed at various strategic points. As the gates were shut, a well-dressed man knocked to be admitted, tendering his sixpence at the same time. He was not allowed in, and thereupon jumped over the fence, offering his entrance fee again. But to no avail; he was arrested and marched off to the police station in the custody of three policemen.

At this point, Mr Edward Newitt, of Wimbledon Hill, drove up to the gate. 'This was a signal for a complete uproar,' records the *Comet*. 'The fencing began to move visibly, and soon yards of it came down with a crash, the crowds cheering lustily. At length, a cry was raised. A delinquent had been captured, and five policemen appeared, bearing in their arms a poor little boy of six years old. The hooting and hissings at such a proceeding can be better imagined than described ... '

If the *Comet* was shocked by such a development, the crowd was truly incensed. More fencing was torn down and, while the police staggered to uphold the rest of it, half a dozen men were taken into custody. At this point, Mr Newitt tried to approach Captain Mildmay, the NRA Secretary, and other NRA officers, to demand permission to use the roadway to Roehampton. The permission was refused. Mr Newitt then offered bail for the men who had been arrested. This offer caused some little confusion in the NRA ranks, as it transpired there was no bail book at the Camp police station, the nearest one being at Wandsworth Police Station. Was Mr Newitt prepared to make the journey? Yes, said Mr Newitt, quite definitely he was. But not before he had climbed on a wagonette to join Mr C.C.Casey in rallying their troops. The police were only doing their duty, maintained Mr Newitt, but before he left the meeting he wanted to inform everybody that a subscription list was to be opened for the defence of the arrested men.

After about an hour's deliberation, Mr Newitt departed and travelled to Wandsworth with a handful of policemen. By now it was getting dark and it looked as though the crowd was about to disperse and make its way home. 'But,' reported the *Comet*, 'little did the police know the trouble they would have. Ominous sounds of falling fencing arose from the lower end of the Common. The furze appeared alight in three or four places near the Rounds, and the exasperated mob deliberately pulled down the boards and threw them in the flames. The exasperation was intense, and the police could not cope with the offenders. The result was that the regulars were called out, and endeavoured to extinguish the flames. The disturbances did not end until very late in the evening, when the actors and spectators in a scene, which had never before been witnessed on the common, took their departure … '

Charles Henden, a brickmaker, Garrett Jacob Nunn, a carman, Robert Simpson, a compositor, Henry Paxton, a patent leather-dresser, Alfred Lake, a weaver, and Charles Beadle, a labourer—all men who lived in the locality, were charged with breaking the fence, the property of the NRA, on Wimbledon Common. 'I see no reason why every inhabitant should not enjoy the glories of our Common. The humble Cottager and the luxurious City merchant, there is room for all,' Edward Newitt proclaimed in the pages of the *Comet*, while a Wimbledon ratepayer applied for a summons to be taken out against Captain Mildmay for refusing to admit Wimbledon residents into the Camp, under Section 52 of the Wimbledon and Putney Commons Act which directed that the Common should be thrown open to the public after gun-fire.

'Owing to the spontaneous and handsome manner in which the

inhabitants subscribed to the Wimbledon Commons Defence Fund,' the disgruntled residents were able to employ the services of a respected barrister Mr Montagu Williams. Such was the strength of the argument, if not Mr Williams's eloquence, that Counsel for the NRA was forced to express his regret at the inconvenience caused to the defendants who were subsequently all discharged. The *Comet* reported the outcome of the case with satisfaction, but expressed anxiety that the question of the admission charge after gunfire had not been settled. They need not have worried. The NRA could easily mend one set of broken fences but the Council realised that it had a considerable amount of rebuilding to do with the local community. The admission charge was not re-introduced.

∽ ∽ ∾ ∾

Gradually, just as the Meeting grew in size so did the town. The population, about 4,500 in 1861, had more than trebled to become just under 16,000 by 1881. As more and more land around the Common was used for residential purposes, so the danger from stray bullets increased. Something had to give way, and it had to be the NRA.

As early as 1862, the Council was paying out compensation to tenants who were in some way inconvenienced by living or working so close to the rifle ranges. Ironically, the land most affected, the Coombe Estate, was owned by the NRA's own President, the Duke of Cambridge. In 1865, rumblings began in that quarter when, it was reported, stray bullets were coming over part of the estate which meant that it became unsaleable for building purposes. The Council wrote a polite letter to the Duke's agent in which, they said, 'they disclaim any right to use the Rifle Ranges at Wimbledon in any way prejudicial to the property of His Royal Highness, and to assure you that they would not allow any forbearance on the part of H.R.H. to be made use of hereafter for the purpose of establishing such a right.' But the problem did not go away.

In 1869 the Council received a letter from the solicitors to the Duke of Cambridge stating that unless they had an absolute assurance that steps would be taken to prevent the possibility of rifle bullets travelling across the Duke's estate during the Meeting, they would be obliged to apply for an injunction to stop the firing. A sum of money was settled on a particularly aggrieved tenant of the Duke's, and, once again, for a while at least, the matter was resolved.

The Wimbledon and Putney Commons Act of 1871 regularised the NRA's presence on the Common, without guaranteeing it a long-term tenancy, while the public's interest was protected by setting up a watchdog body, the Conservators. The Act directed the Conservators to allow the Association certain freedoms such as enclosing a defined area for a defined time both before and after the Meeting, as well as the right to prohibit the entry of unauthorised people except on Sundays. Under the Act, the NRA had to pay the Conservators a rent of £100 a year, while the Conservators were given the authority to give the Association six months' notice to quit.

The Conservators were vigilant in their protection of their Common. They objected to the NRA pruning trees and bushes overhanging the ranges, and digging up the turf to make flower beds. As a result, anyone wanting a bit of floral decoration had to bring in their own earth, and take it away afterwards. When the NRA wanted to plant some trees to hide an ammunition shed, the local MP, Mr Henry Peek, went so far as to withdraw a prize he had donated to the Meeting for the previous eight years. The NRA carried on the Henry Peek prize, calling it instead the Olympic, though Latin scholars and wits of the day insisted that it be called the Olim Peek. The matter of the screen of trees was settled and Mr Peek reinstated his prize, content with the new name. Of Olympic, that is.

The normal rights affecting common land, and the rights of owners of land behind the butts, were not affected by the Act, but they were at times strengthened by it as has already been illustrated, when in 1879, the NRA tried to impose an entrance fee after gunfire. The writing on the wall was writ larger and although still unseen by many, it was at least observed, if not fully appreciated, by a correspondent writing in one of the Meeting's newsletters, *The Camp Magpie*, in 1879:

' ... Now that I have got into the hands of the conservators I cannot be expected to live for ever, but as long as a creak is left in my dormant sails, or two stones are left in my substructure, I shall re-echo the motto of the National Rifle Association, *Sit Perpetuum*. I have sat still so long that I might be suspected of wishing to perpetrate a joke, were such a thing admissible, in the columns of so serious an organ as our new friend the *Camp Magpie* ... I laugh when I hear the mean threats and see the puny efforts of a paltry clique to abolish the annual national gathering which we name simply the meeting of the NRA. What can these bumbles do in the face of such an evidence of patriotism as the Volunteer force and its doings afford? Shut up the camp? I should like to see it tried. Where else can a mass of fifty thousand of such people be collected and remain as well conducted and orderly through all a summer Sunday as I see around me here on a fine Middle Sunday? ... '

In 1882 some residents in Wimbledon, Wandsworth and Putney got together to complain to the Council about rowdy behaviour in the neighbourhood which, they said, was caused by visitors who spilled out of the

Camp in the evenings, particularly on Sundays. After lengthy discussions, it was agreed that the Pavilion would close at 9 p.m., that on Sundays no alcohol would be sold except to soldiers and Volunteers in Camp, and that the NRA would ensure that the Camp was cleared by 10 p.m. Again, such a restriction forced the NRA to pay compensation to the caterers. In the end, however, it was not the Conservators who brought about the removal of the NRA from the Common, but the Duke of Cambridge.

It was in 1887, when the NRA Council began to discuss the need for a considerable outlay on repairs and extensions, that the Duke made his intentions quite clear and gave the Council notice to quit the Common. As usual, as President of the NRA, the Duke took the chair at the winter AGM held at the Royal United Services Institution in London. The news had leaked out already, beyond the knowledge of Council members, and the atmosphere at the meeting was electric with expectation. But the Duke proceeded with matters in military order. He began by summarising the report of the Council and confirming the unusually healthy financial position in which the Association found itself. Then he dropped his bombshell. Since the publication of the report with its ambitious plans for improvements, said the Duke, he had felt it only right to give notice to the Council to quit. He had no desire to hurry the Association, he said, but the course taken was absolutely unavoidable, for though every care had been taken, his tenants were becoming seriously alarmed at the danger of stray bullets. There was nothing more to say on the subject, he added, only that he was anxious that there should be no mystery.

The Duke continued with reports on other business which were taken up and discussed by members of the Association, and it was not until the end of the meeting that the matter was touched on by the retiring Chairman, Sir Henry Wilmot, who announced, to the considerable relief of all present, that the Council had already formed a working party to consider all the problems which a move would entail. Understandably, very little could be done at such short notice and, at the spring general meeting, it was announced that the Duke, again taking his place in the chair, had agreed that the 1888 Meeting could be held on the Common.

With many members of the Association fearful for the future not just of the Meeting but of the NRA itself, the 1888 Meeting was not a happy occasion. The singularly unsettled weather that July only underlined the gloomy mood which prevailed. 'The men under canvas spent a very uncomfortable time on the night of July 10, there being a strong wind and a deluge of rain, followed by very low temperature. The thermometer went down to within nine degrees of the freezing point, and though the weather was fair on the 11th, it was cold and dull. A great part of the Common was converted into a sort of bog, so that the competitions were carried on under considerable difficulties,' reported the *Illustrated London News*.

The move from Wimbledon pre-occupied the minds and the general meetings of the Association that year. Initially, the Council determined that the least disruptive and possibly cheapest solution lay in offering to buy from the Duke of Cambridge 120 acres running up to Coombe Wood. At the winter meeting, the new Chairman, Lord Wantage, had to report that the Duke, through his solicitors, had rejected the proposal, 'as such a sale would be a most serious injury to his estate and might interfere very materially with its development hereafter ... ' There was also, the Duke's solicitors pointed out, 'an immediate prospect of the general introduction of a small-bore military rifle for practice, with which it is understood Wimbledon Common will be absolutely unsafe ... '

That winter meeting bubbled with regrets and anxieties. Lord Elcho, now the Earl of Wemyss, 'deeply regretted' the Duke's decision. If they had to leave the Common, he said, they would virtually cease to exist as a *National* Association. Mr H. Trelawny Boodle, a Wimbledon resident, thought that the Association should carry on in its struggle to retain the present shooting ground. He maintained a belief that a larger number of residents deemed it an honour to have the great NRA Meeting on their Common, and certainly preferred having riflemen there for a fortnight as opposed to being hemmed in the whole year through by a stack of smoking chimneys. Sir Henry Halford said he had not given up hope, and wondered if the Duke could be persuaded to sell all his land behind the butts. Lord Wantage, with an eye on the never very abundant coffers of the Association, was quick to knock that ambitiously expensive idea on the head.

At this point the Duke who had been absent from the gathering, entered the arena, took his place in the chair and proceeded with the ordinary business of the meeting, seemingly quite oblivious to the issue of main concern. However, he was not allowed to get very far before a Mr Gratwicke rose to his feet. The Duke's speech was very interesting, said Mr Gratwicke, as his speeches always were, he hastened to add courteously, but a far more pressing matter had been under discussion before the Duke entered the room, that of the future of the Association's annual Meeting. The Duke interposed. The matter, the Duke felt, would be better discussed when he was not present. Mr Gratwicke bowed and concurred. For the Duke, and now also the NRA, the matter of remaining on Wimbledon Common had come to an end. And it says much for the strength of the relationship between the two that when it came to the close of the meeting and the election of officers, the motion to re-elect the Duke was 'carried with acclamation'. The Duke was touched. He would not have taken it amiss, he said, if they had elected another President, 'they might easily find a better one.' He felt their kindness the more because he had been obliged to take a line not acceptable to them. But as the NRA must have realised, and a fact which the Duke himself gave voice to, it was to the advantage of the Association to have as its President the Commander-in-Chief of the Army.

Yet the problem remained. Some other location had to be found, and quickly. But where?

At the spring general meeting, held in May 1888, the NRA appeared to be closer to a solution. Lord Wantage reported that a number of sites had been suggested and rejected. Among those some thought more worthy of consideration, despite various drawbacks, were Nazing Common, near Broxbourne, whose cold, wet soil was thought to be unhealthy as well as unattractive for the encampment of troops; Epping Forest (cold, clay soil, and possibly too small); various sites in the vicinity of Brighton (too far south); Staines (low-lying, and surrounded by rivers); a site on the Berkshire Downs between Didcot and Compton (thought to be too far from London, despite the advantages of a healthy chalk soil, large extent of ranges, and good railway links). Another location considered by the Council was Pirbright, but 'although healthy, (it) has a soil which, after a little use, becomes no better than a sand-hill, and it is, moreover, subject in summer to a "mirage", which renders rifle shooting at times impossible.'

There was one site, however, which Lord Wantage and the Council had grown increasingly enthusiastic about—Richmond Park. It was an idea keenly supported by the Queen herself—on one condition—that the proposal met the approval of the Ranger of Richmond Park who was none other than the Duke of Cambridge. 'No site offers such advantages as Richmond Park,' enthused Lord Wemyss. The Royal park had all the advantages of Wimbledon Common, in that it was close to London; in addition, it had a lot more available space. Investigations and negotiations began in earnest, the ground was surveyed and plans were drawn up though, not unnaturally, the proposal met with a good deal of local opposition. But then on 23 August, Lord Wantage had more bad news for the Association: 'The Duke has, I regret to say, considered it his duty to withhold his sanction, basing his objections on the ground of the interference it would entail with the privileges of free access to the park now enjoyed by the public, and on the unsuitability of a site in the neighbourhood of dwelling houses to rifle practice with the new rifle about to be issued.'

Valuable time had been lost in visiting possible sites and then in trying to secure Richmond Park as a venue for the next Meeting. No location appeared to be as perfect as Richmond but on 9 August, Lord Wantage offered the Council a solution—a gift of some 500 acres on the Berkshire Downs. At a meeting on 22 August, the Council met to consider two sites: the land offered by Lord Wantage and another near Cannock Chase, which appeared to have almost unlimited space for the ranges as well as for accommodation.

A decision was postponed, however, in order that a conference, arranged between a Special Committee and Mr Stanhope, the Secretary of State for War, could determine what assistance the Government would be prepared to offer the Association. Prior to the meeting, various sites had been inspected: Staines, Guildford, Lewes, Brighton and Pirbright. Guildford was rejected as being far too small a site, but the location which most appealed now was a stretch of Government land adjoining Brookwood station on the London and South Western Railway, with a parcel of common land of which Lord Onslow was lord of the manor. And he was more than enthusiastic to give whatever support the NRA needed. Not only was the Brookwood site not far from London but, with the Army camp at Aldershot not far away, it had the added advantage, it was thought, of drawing the Volunteer and Regular Forces closer together. But would the Government agree to give the Association the land, as well as the money to assist in developing it?

On 21 November, the NRA received the answer they had wanted for so long. They could expect no money from the Government but they could expect support, and providing the site was examined and found to be suitable, the scheme also had the approval of the Army's Commander-in-Chief, the Duke of Cambridge. At a meeting of the Council on 5 December, Lord Wemyss urged the members to decide in favour of the site. It had been inspected thoroughly and approved by all concerned. 'Once established,' said the old campaigner, 'it is hoped permanently, on the Brookwood site, the National Rifle Association will have no cause to regret their removal from Wimbledon.'

However the Chairman of the Council, Lord Wantage, still favoured his land on the Berkshire Downs, while Council members with northern connections were more inclined to support the site near Cannock Chase.

On 27 February, the Council met to make the final decision which had to be announced at the winter meeting of the Association the following day. Each member of the Council had been given a printed statement presenting the arguments in favour and those against the respective sites, and many had an opinion to express. There was an air of excitement in the room, and the debate was long and lively but, when the vote was finally taken, there was no doubt as to the outcome. The majority voted decisively in favour of the Brookwood site.

On Thursday, 28 February 1889, Lord Wantage announced that the Council had adopted the Brookwood site as the place where the NRA would hold its annual Rifle Meetings, and that, in future, the site would be called Bisley Common.

Now, at last, all the plans which had been outlined and drawn up could be put into operation. Negotiations began with the War Office, to whom most of the site belonged, to determine that the Association could make use of the land and purchase any further space required. (In the end, more than £12,000 had to be paid for the additional land.) The War Office took on the responsibility of negotiating with Lord Onslow to close any public rights of way and, in return, it was agreed that the War Office should be able to make use of the entire site at times other than the annual Meetings.

The Commander at Aldershot, Lieutenant-General Sir Evelyn Wood, was given permission by the War Office to assist the Association in preparing the site, and a company of Royal Engineers and working parties quartered at Aldershot were employed in raising the butts and laying the tramway line from Brookwood station into the Camp. Meanwhile, the London and South Western Railway set about enlarging their station at Brookwood, and also made a donation of £1,000 towards the Association's funds.

But even before the spring meeting in May 1889, it was clear the new site would not be ready that year and the Duke of Cambridge gave his permission for the Meeting to take place once more on Wimbledon Common.

'Fate invariably decrees that the men under canvas shall know what rain means,' reported The Times, when, after ten hours of bright sunshine on the previous Saturday, the first shot of the final Meeting on the Common was fired under a gloomy sky with rain falling, which it continued to do the whole of that first morning. The closing hours were somewhat more cheerful. Lord and Lady Wantage, and a host of distinguished guests, attended a full-dress dinner held, bravely, in the open air, in the camp of the London Scottish. As the meal came to an end, a swirl of tartan sprang into the middle of the assembly, and, amidst whoops and cheers, performed a sword dance by the blazing light of a myriad of illuminated torches. There followed a song, 'Farewell to Wimbledon', and as a troop of Scots escorted Lord and Lady Wantage back to the Cottage, the crowd sang 'Auld Lang Syne'.

It was at the end of the Meeting that Captain Edmund St John-Mildmay resigned his post as Secretary to the Association, a position he had held since its formation thirty years before. He was respected as a quiet, diplomatic man who commanded great respect from his staff and from competitors alike. His departure, many people felt, indicated that an old era was indeed well and truly over. There was an added poignancy in that year's prizegiving when, among the men who stepped on to the platform to receive their prize from the Countess of Wharncliffe, was the first ever winner of The Queen's Prize, Edward Ross.

At the service held in the Umbrella Tent on 20 July, before a crowd of several thousands, the Bishop of London preached a sermon, reading from the New Testament. 'Nevertheless,' he read, 'I tell you the truth, it is expedient for you that I go away. For if I go not away the Comforter will not come unto you, but if I depart I will send Him unto you.' The Magpie column in the *Wimbledon Times* had its own words of farewell: 'Good old Wimbledon Meeting! Thy glory has departed. Thousands of persons from London and the surrounding districts visited the town and Camp on Sunday, and availed themselves of the last opportunity they will have of enjoying one of the most delightful outings of the year.'

As the 1889 Meeting, the final Meeting on Wimbledon Common, drew to an end, *The Times* came to its own conclusion: 'By successful organization, by offering high prizes, and by using every endeavour to follow out its original design the National Rifle Association has entitled itself to lay claim to the honour of having raised the standard of rifle-shooting in Great Britain, in the colonies, and abroad, and of having rendered honour at Wimbledon the summit of every rifleman's ambition.'

# CHAPTER THREE

# *The Foreign Connection*

'These Wimbledon meetings have promoted peace by training the finest marksmen in the world, but more than this, these gatherings of representatives from town, counties, colonies, and nations have done an immense deal to cultivate cosmopolitan sympathy and to foster fraternal regards between people who would otherwise have been for ever separated by ignorance and prejudice.'

The words were penned by a correspondent of the *Weekly Mail of Toronto* in the 1870s, but the sentiments live on. There may be cliques in rifle-shooting circles, as there are when any body of human beings congregate, but it is a sport which transcends class and culture, creed and colour. 'There is a duke and next to him a dustman,' members of the NRA delight in pointing out. Lying on the ground, often in extreme discomfort brought about by the fickle nature of an English summer, appears to be a great social leveller. Rifle shooting is a sport which seems to know no boundaries, and since the early days on Wimbledon Common, the annual Meeting has attracted enthusiastic competitors from all over the world, most particularly from the Commonwealth. In fact, with its biennial Tir Fédéral, Switzerland, where 'rifles are as common as walking sticks, every citizen being an enthusiastic rifleman, was naturally looked to for precedent and example,' admitted the Association in its early reports. This fact was underlined by the attendance of some 150 Swiss who helped to form a guard of honour, alongside the British Volunteers, for Queen Victoria at the inaugural Meeting on Wimbledon Common in July 1860.

That year, seventeen Swiss entered the competitions, together with one Russian. Despite their undoubted prowess, the Swiss scores were not unduly high, which must in no small measure be the fault of the French who stopped them at the border and confiscated their powder stock as well as a number of their rifles. Nevertheless, nothing daunted, they entered some of the competitions for which they were eligible. The *Jersey Independent and Daily Telegraph*, for one, was particularly struck by the Swiss manner of shooting, resting the barrel on the left fist, just in front of the trigger. They did not use cartridges, the correspondent remarked, and their rifle preparation included the use of linen discs which they lubricated by rolling round their mouths and then rammed into the gun. They stood legs apart, breathed in very deeply, and used their noses as a rest. 'Puffed out like the bull-frog emulous of passing for a bull, the inflated Switzer can no more bend to one side or the other than a hard-rammed sausage.' Quite understandably, this extreme position meant that bullet and breath left the Swiss with almost equal ferocity.

The following year, the Meeting attracted only one Swiss entrant, the others being too busy 'bull-frogging' their way through their own competition at home; also two members of the Jersey militia; and 'perhaps the most gratifying and novel feature in the Prize Meeting, as far as regards the attendance,' a sole Colonial, an Australian by the name of MacFarlane, who was one of the competitors in the first stage of The Queen's Prize, and who, after competing with his Terry's breech-loader, also carried off an extra prize, an engraving valued at ten guineas. 'Mr MacFarlane is, it is hoped,' said Lord Elcho in his annual report, 'only the forerunner of the many colonial competitors who may be expected to come to Wimbledon now that Her Majesty's prize has by her special desire been opened to Colonial Volunteers.' It was a hope that was to be fulfilled many, many times over with the arrival of hundreds and hundreds of rifle enthusiasts. In that year, sixteen County Associations, and eight Colonial Associations affiliated to the National Rifle Association.[1]

Such good reports ricocheted around the Continent after the first Meeting that the Emperor of France, commander of what was reputed to be the strongest army in the world, felt it necessary to send to the second Meeting the head of the French School of Musketry in Vincennes, Commandant Nessler, with strict instructions to report on the organisation of the proceedings and of the Association itself. And the following year, as well as a complimentary letter to *The Times* from Captain Jules Gérard, an

---

[1] In 1861, there were sixteen County Associations (Angus and Mearns, Berkshire, Cheshire, Dumfriesshire, Essex, Galloway, Gloucestershire, Hertfordshire, Inverness-shire, Kent, Lancashire, Northamptonshire, Nottinghamshire, Shropshire, Staffordshire, Yorkshire); and eight Colonial Associations (South Australia, New South Wales, Queensland, Victoria, Nova Scotia, New Brunswick, Prince Edward Island, and Upper Canada) affiliated with the National Rifle Association. By 1889, the number had risen to seventy-six County Associations in England and Scotland, four in Ireland, and sixty-one throughout the rest of the world (four in Australia; twenty-five in Canada; two each in China, in New Zealand and the Channel Islands; twelve in India; one in Japan and one in Mauritius; three in the West Indies; and nine in South Africa).

officer in the French Army, who was also a celebrated lion-shooter, the National Rifle Association could also point with pride to the praise meted out to it in the French paper, *Le Moniteur de l'Armée*. Although the latter's enthusiasm for the skills of shooting in England were mingled with a goodly dose of post-revolutionary egalitarianism, albeit one tinged by a new Napoleonic Empire:

' ... The competitors had not a roof to shelter them, to rest themselves after the fatigue of the contest ... Everything strictly necessary for the contest was alone provided in order that the chances should be equal and the result better ... The Government is perfectly indifferent as to the weather. That fact proves that it knows it may rely on British stoicism, which is not to be alarmed by torrents of rain or by storms, and which will not give up sport for any caprices of weather ... Everybody admits that there can be no great deviation of the ball when fired by an English hand and from an English firearm ... The English aristocracy has adopted national shooting; it covers it with its powerful protection. Several members of the House of Lords thought it not derogatory to learn the exercise from a non-commissioned officer ... It is asserted that the Wimbledon shooting produced an effect which was not expected. That mixing of the commercial classes and operatives with the nobility for a common object destroys prejudices, and gives place to warm sympathy and general confraternity ... Thus the institution of the Wimbledon rifle shooting will make England stronger both against her enemies at home and abroad. One cannot immediately understand the influence the rifle may exercise on the pacification and the fusion of parties, but even if the anticipated result be only half obtained the English will not have to regret either their time or their money ... '

Just over a decade later, in 1875, the techniques which were being tested successfully on Wimbledon Common resulted in a request from the French Minister of War, that he be sent a detailed description of the NRA's new mechanism for raising and lowering targets.

In the early days, the strongest foreign links were with the Continent, in particular with Belgium, a country of especial strategic interest to Britain as it controlled a passage across the Channel. The Belgians also put a high value on strong internal defence, in their case to protect a monarchy which had enjoyed its independence from Holland for only thirty years. On more than one occasion, the Belgians had found cause to be grateful to the British Prime Minister, Lord Palmerston, for the protection he afforded them against the acquisitive French. In Belgium, the National Rifle Association was supported out of government funds, the NRA noted ruefully, but it never soured the relationship between the two.

In 1865, a party of English Volunteers were given a warm welcome when they visited Brussels to take part in the Tir National and when 150 Belgians, 'with few exceptions ... all robust, fine-looking men,' the *Illustrated London News* reported, made a return visit the following year, the cheering reception they received was such 'as Englishmen and volunteers alone can give'. A dinner held in the Refreshment Tent was packed with VIPs, and a rousing speech made by Lord Elcho was punctuated periodically by the Belgians springing to their feet and cheering the patriotic sentiments the noble lord was expressing. And, as the guests left the dinner at 10.30 that evening, they walked out into a Camp which had been brilliantly illuminated in their honour. That year, the NRA presented their allies with a trophy to be shot for at their Tir National. The cup was presented by Major Irvine of the 1st Surrey who delivered his speech in French at the carriage door of the Ambassador, Monsieur Van de Weyer, who, as he was 'suffering from a late accident, was obliged to remain in his carriage.'

In 1867, more than 2,000 Belgians, including members of the Gardes Civiques, journeyed to Britain to compete in the Meeting, travelling from Gravesend, up the Thames to the heart of London, in six steamboats. The next day they brought City traffic to a halt, as they marched, six abreast, with two bands playing all the while, from Somerset House, through the Strand, along Fleet Street, Ludgate Hill and Cheapside to the Guildhall where they were met by the Lord Mayor of London, the Aldermen and Councillors, the Dukes of Grafton and Manchester, Colonel Irskine, Inspector-General of Volunteers, Monsieur Van de Meyerer, and Monsieur Bartholeyns, the Belgian chargé d'affaires.

The formalities over, one of the bands struck up a polka, and hundreds of the Belgian men began to dance together—much to the amusement of the crowd. The Belgians were fêted all over town. They dined at Windsor Castle, danced the night away at a grand ball at the Alhambra in Leicester Square, were entertained at the Crystal Palace and, when they arrived at Wimbledon Common on the appointed Saturday lunchtime, were met by a guard of honour, a rousing band, a gun salute, and an official welcoming party led by the Prince of Wales, in his uniform as Captain-General of the Honourable Artillery Company. The Belgian commander, Colonel Gregoire, received from the Prince a Silver Challenge Trophy presented to him on behalf of the NRA and, in return, he presented the Prince with the Belgian Challenge Cup from the Chasseurs Eclaireurs of Brussels and the Belgians who visited Wimbledon in 1866, and a silver trophy from the

Gardes Civiques of the City of Antwerp. 'Let us hope,' said the Colonel, 'that it may be the destiny of England and Belgium long to journey side by side in the path of peace and progress.'

❧ ❧ ❧ ❧

However, it was not until eleven years after the first Meeting on Wimbledon Common that one of the strongest and happiest bonds was founded, a bond which has been unbroken, since that time, except during the war years. The year was 1871. In Europe, the political map was changing. After years of fighting and political manoeuvring, Bismarck had succeeded in unifying Germany under a Prussian king, and replacing France as the strongest country in Europe. Italy, another land of separate states and disparate factions, was also on the verge of unification. In that year, Britain welcomed to its shores not only several hundred Belgian Volunteers but another, smaller band of twenty Volunteers from one of its distant colonies.

Those visitors had travelled from Canada to compete in the twelfth annual Meeting. The welcome they received was considerably warmer than the weather during that fortnight which, for the most part, remained dull and overcast. Sir Peter Tait presented their commander, Captain McClenaghan of the 22nd Regiment, with a Challenge Trophy to take home. Sir Peter had clubbed together with a few English friends to collect £100 to be given as prize-money 'as a greeting to their Canadian brothers'. Rifle shooters are renowned for needing little excuse to celebrate, and the first Canadian visitors didn't have to search far for one. As they were in Camp before the Meeting opened, they found themselves away from home on 1 July, Dominion Day. The night before, the Camp commandant gave permission to extend the time for lights out and, as the clock struck midnight, a crowd of British Volunteers who had joined in the festivities, gave three lusty cheers for 'Our Young Dominion'. Having allowed a decent period to elapse between one set of celebrations and the next, at noon the following day, the Canadian team paraded in front of their tent and with three rounds of ammunition fired a *feu de joie*, and gave, as they called it, their 'war whoop' for the Queen, while the numerous flags in the Camp were dipped in honour of the Dominion.

There were other ways the Canadians joined in the fun, as the correspondent for the *Weekly Mail of Toronto* noted a few years later. There were foot races, jousts, tent-pegging and tent-pitching competitions, wrestling, sword and lance combats, 'taking one back to the days when knights of chivalry entered the lists with fair maids' favours in their bonnets.' The

Canadians always put in a good appearance, the writer noted with particular satisfaction, with the sorry exception, that is, in 1877, of Lieutenant Hunter, but then his entire belongings had been consumed in a fire. It was not only the figure of poor Lieutenant Hunter who caught the beady eye of the correspondent. One year, there was a prize he didn't like the look of either. It was a lamp, but no ordinary lamp, much to his disgust. The lamp 'is not an object of the most refined taste—a monkey (out of whose head is a large paraffin lamp) dressed like a lady, having her boots brushed by a monkey shoeblack, and exposing a striped stocking.'

In 1872, on only their second visit to Wimbledon, the Canadian team won the Kolapore, or as it was called then, the Raja of Kolapore's Imperial Challenge Cup, a competition begun the year before to be competed for by teams from India and the Colonies and a united team from the Mother Country. Their score was 532 compared with the home team's score of 524. (Canada won the competition again at Wimbledon in 1875, 1881, 1884 and 1889.) The *Weekly Mail* correspondent made a point of reminding his readers that Canada and, indeed, all the colonies, owed a debt of gratitude to the President of the Canadian NRA, Colonel Gzowski: 'When the idea of having the Colonies represented at Wimbledon was first suggested it was thought that Colonial competitors were qualified to shoot for the International Challenge Trophy, but an examination of the conditions under which that competition was constituted proved that it was limited to United Kingdom teams. Colonel Gzowski represented to the National Rifle Association through Lord Elcho that the Kolapore Challenge Trophy was at their disposal, and the conditions under which it was to be shot for were thereupon framed in accordance with his prompt suggestions.'

On that second visit, the Volunteers came from Nova Scotia, New Brunswick, Ontario, and from the Province of Quebec who won a Challenge Trophy donated by the Merchants of London. Corporal Larkin of the Nova Scotia Corps, who was in the team which won the Kolapore, had an extra reason to celebrate that year, as he also carried off the princely sum of £3 in prize-money for being one of the ninety best shots in the third category of The Queen's Prize.

The year 1875 brought an air of excitement to the Meeting. The Americans were coming.

Or were they? A lot of correspondence had crossed the Atlantic between the NRA office in Pall Mall and the headquarters of the NRA in New York, as the Americans had expressed a wish to shoot simultaneously with the three Eights competing for the Elcho Shield, not for the shield but for a cup which was donated in honour of the Americans' visit by Lloyd's. But, the Council of the NRA in Great Britain objected. A team could not be allowed to shoot in a match when they were not competing for the prize. Letters continued. First to Ireland, where the Americans were shooting in a return match with the Irish at Dollymount, near Dublin. Then to the Langham Hotel in London. The matter was resolved, at the eleventh hour, by the Americans agreeing to compete only against one another for a cup donated by the NRA of Great Britain. Yes, the Americans *were* coming. And the match was set to be held at 2.30 p.m. on Saturday, 17 July 1875.

Except that it wasn't. But this time it was not the NRA Council which prevented the match taking place. It was the weather. Rain, rain, and more rain. Three and a half inches fell during that Wimbledon Fortnight. And just under half of that on the day before the American match was due to take place. The whole Common was awash and one of the best American shots, Colonel Bodine, caught a bad cold. So bad, in fact, that he had to withdraw from the competition which was postponed until the following Wednesday afternoon. Nothing, however, seemed to affect the remarkable shooting of another American, Major Fulton. Using a Remington, he scored a total of 133 out of a possible 150—nineteen of his thirty shots were bull's-eyes.

The American team was entertained to dinner in the Cottage by the Chairman, Lord Wharncliffe. There were a number of prominent persons present, reported the *New York Tribune*, adding with finite relief, 'No speeches were made.'

On the morning after their own match, the Americans kept the targets for the Irish in the Elcho, and, more important, superintended their shooting. It was a closely contested battle, but for only the second time, the Irish team snatched a victory with a score of 1,506, over Scotland's 1,503 and England's 1,502. The jubilation which the Americans shared with the Irish that day on the Common was also shared in New York, where crowds of people had monitored the competition as it progressed. All over the city, in hotels, bars, armouries and any place which had newspaper boards carrying reports, the main topic of conversation was the Elcho Match at Wimbledon. The argument always concluding with the belief that as the Americans had beaten the Irish at Dollymount, and the Irish had won the Elcho, ergo the Americans could or would have won the Elcho Shield—if they had been allowed to enter.

The next day, the successful Irish team competed among themselves for the Lloyd's Cup (which had hastily been transferred into a competition to be competed for by each individual member of the Elcho Shield winning eight, and was won that year by Lieutenant Fenton, with 67 marks out of a possible 75). The debate continued to occupy the news in New York. Someone consulted an expert at Remington's on Broadway. Not surprisingly, they concurred with the general opinion. Yes, given the chance, the

Americans would have won. But it was to be a few years before a match between the two nations could be carried out, and the rifle skills of each could be thus compared. In the meantime, hypotheses reigned supreme, while the British could afford themselves a small smile of satisfaction when they learnt that the Council of the US Rifle Association were altering the targets at their range, Creedmoor, so as to conform to the latest Wimbledon pattern.

In 1876, the NRA welcomed Volunteers from the furthest afield to date, when five men from the Colony of Victoria, Australia arrived to compete in the Meeting. They were a smart-looking band, according to *The Times* reporter, as well as being pretty good shots.

The Meeting was remarkable that year for being held during a heatwave. Indeed, the temperature was mainly in the high eighties in the shade, and on the final day it had settled at 88°F. *The Times* reported that while the temperature had reached 143°F in the sun one day, no one was suffering ill effects through the heat, adding stoically, 'men who have a good deal to do are apt to forget the sun.' Nevertheless, the fine weather did not assist the Australians. Their limited number prevented them from taking part in the Kolapore, and so the Victorian Match was arranged in which they competed against squads of five from England, Scotland and Canada for five silver tankards presented by the NRA. The match was won by England with a score of 830 marks (out of a possible 1,050). Scotland was the runner-up with 827. The Australian team scored 755; the Canadians 701.

That year, Colonel Gzowski wrote to inform the NRA of the Canadian Rifle Association's intention of donating a Challenge Trophy to the NRA as a mark of the bond between the two associations, and the following year he himself presented the cup to the Duke of Cambridge at a ceremony in the Exhibition Tent. The correspondent for the *Toronto Weekly Mail* noted that among those present was Countess Wharncliffe, who wore a simple cream-coloured dress, adorned by a metal belt falling loosely to the right *à la militaire*. 'The trophy,' he described, 'is an oval silver shield about three feet high attached to a stand made of Canadian maple, walnut and oak. Imagine an oval target, in the bull's eye is a female figure representing Canada. In a broad convex border corresponding to an outer is an allegorical design of numberless figures in terrible contention ... in the seven great battles which make the empire and its colonies illustrious. On a silver border are the arms in enamel of the seven Provinces of the Dominion, and on yet another border, which is of ebony, are the monograms in wreaths of silver, oak and maple, typical of the union of the mother country and her eldest daughter.'

The *Weekly Mail* correspondent, well aware of how much money was raised through subscription in Canada, doubted that the sum collected covered the cost of the magnificent vessel. He was quite sure that Colonel Gzowski had dug into his own pockets, and deeply at that. It would be a typical gesture, claimed the writer, of a man whom the British Press were wont to dub the father of the Canadian Volunteers.

By now, the Canadian camp over which the Colonel presided was a pretty impressive sight. Designed on a letter H, there were about ten tents on either side with a suite of marquees for entertaining at one end, and dressing rooms in the centre. The centre bar consisted of lushly furnished and decorated dining and drawing rooms, carpeted and adorned with exotic plants and flowers. Outside there were shrubs and rows and rows of flowers. And, what's more, it was a popular place for all the Volunteers on Camp for the ready welcome they always received. Ten years later, the correspondent of the *Toronto Weekly Mail*, who was always quick to point out the Canadians' popularity, wrote, 'In the qualities that attract the attention of those who admire manliness and independence with gentle behaviour the whole of the team excelled, and I venture to say that every one of them, coming in contact as they did with crowds of mechanics, labourers, and yeomen, not to mention the many of the upper class who influence others, gave a most favourable opinion of Canada, than any number of lecturing agents ... In their character of talkers, without design concerning the life and resources of the great Dominion, these Canadians, in the full vigour of their manhood, coming annually to the largest and most comprehensive gathering in Europe, are doing an immense deal of good, and no other proof of the statement is required than that *everybody* visits the Canadian quarters.'

In 1877 the match finally took place against the Americans at Creedmoor in what they called the American Centennial Trophy and the Championship of the World. Sir Henry Halford, who was chosen as captain, set about selecting a team of ten, during a three-day event at Cambridge in the week immediately following the Meeting. One thing in particular that had impressed Halford when the Americans had been at Wimbledon two years before had been the success they had achieved by shooting from the back position. So impressed was he, in fact, that he had asked Major Fulton, the outstanding American rifleman, to give him lessons. Since then, Halford had never shot from any position other than the back position and had tried to encourage other English marksmen to do the same. He had also, he admitted candidly to the *New York Tribune* reporter, gone out of his way to try to select a team of back shooters—but without success. The team which was finally selected included Lieutenant Fenton, who was in the Irish team which had won the Elcho two years before, and Lieutenant-Colonel Cecil

Peel who wrote an extremely comprehensive report on the event which was to prove invaluable in organising future teams.

As soon as the match was fixed, a subscription fund was started to raise the necessary cost of the venture, and among the first contributors were the Prince of Wales and the Duke of Cambridge. The entire sum was amassed speedily and, on 16 August, the team set sail from Liverpool on board the SS *City of Richmond* which arrived in New York nine days later.

The two-day shooting match, on 13 and 14 September 1877, was attended by about 4,000 people, a remarkably poor turn-out, one newspaper sniffed apologetically, but the event itself warranted front page news. And not only news. Columns were eaten up not only with reports, but with large diagrams showing the position of the bullets on the targets. It was to be a competition, said the *New York Tribune*, that would 'cement the bond of friendship which at present exists between the two great nations represented in the match.'

Situated just outside New York, Creedmoor at that time was contained in about ninety acres, a perfectly level range with every target visible from the farthest point. It had several mechanisms for detecting variations in the wind, including a wind gauge, as well as scoring boards placed high above the heads of the crowds, and, what particularly impressed Peel and the rest of the British team, telephones on the ranges. What did not impress the Americans was the ragged appearance of the British team who wore all manner of apparel, including knickerbockers and white scarves round their hats, unlike the home team who were dressed, to a man, in a standard loose brown uniform. A number of Americans also remarked on the higgledy-piggledy manner in which the British turned up at the ranges, unlike their opponents who marched there all together as a team, chests out and heads held high.

'The surroundings of the range are green—the butts sheltered—the climatic and atmospheric influences less variable, and there is generally, as compared with Wimbledon, scarcely any mirage, whilst from the northern aspect of the butts the sun is never in the shooter's eyes. In short, Creedmoor is a perfect shooting gallery,' wrote one of the British team. Alas, while the British were thrilled with the results of some 'brilliant shooting', the perfect conditions did not help them to pull off a victory.

As it turned out, the Americans had had every reason to look and behave like winners. At the end of the two-day competition, they had beaten the British team by 92 marks. Bruce, the top American marksman, who made the highest score ever recorded on any range with 219 out of 225 marks, was fêted in the papers but remained modest about his achievement. 'Sharp's rifle did the work,' he told a reporter, 'with me back of it.' Lieutenant Peel, on his return from America, summed up the reason for the British defeat. 'First, Organisation. Second, Position. Third, Rifles.'

The importance of team organisation should not be under-estimated, Peel urged in a detailed report to the NRA Council, in which he didn't demur from pulling his punches as to the reasons for the British team's failure, as well as setting out his ideas for future success. 'To enter a Team composed as ours have always been against the Americans, is like expecting an undisciplined rabble to hold its own against a body of regular troops of similar numerical strength,' he wrote. 'If team shooting is to be carried on, study system and discipline, which are synonymous with organization.'

He also pointed out the weaknesses of shooting in the prone position (that is, lying face down) compared to the back position: 'A man who generally makes brilliant scores on his face, should he be suffering from indisposition or nervousness, or be out of sorts from any cause, goes to pieces altogether ... the three men of our team (all celebrated shots) who fired in the prone position made the three worst scores recorded in either team, whilst one of the highest scores on the American side was a man (in the back position) who was so ill that it was a question from round to round whether he would not have to give up shooting.'

As to the question of rifles, Peel tested the American Metford and Rigby against the British weapons and came to very definite conclusions on which he urged the Council to act. He suggested that all rifles should be brought together in the matter of sighting, that the weight of military breech-loaders be increased, and that 'a military breech-loader be the military rifle of the future, allowing any contrivance that science or ingenuity can invent to get the best shooting out of it for military purposes without destroying its efficiency as a military weapon. Set your faces against the further use of muzzle-loaders, even if proved to be better for match purposes than our present breech-loaders. The former are relics of a bygone age, and the chief obstacle to all improvement in a practical direction.'

Peel also had very firm ideas as to the composition of a strong team: 'I am decidedly of the opinion that the Captain of a Team should not himself shoot. He would find ample occupation in looking after his men ... the man selected as Captain should possess great tact and firmness, should be devoid of anything like fussiness, and should have had so much experience that the Team generally would be ready to give cheerful obedience to all his directions ...

'I should prefer that the choice of the men should be left solely to the Captain ... I do not think that the best individual shot is necessarily the most valuable man for a Team; far from it ... Many shooting men think it impossible that they themselves can make a mistake, and imagine that a miss or bad shot MUST result from some cause over which they have no control. Such men are unfitted for a Team, however brilliant their individual shooting may be ...

'The stamp of man I should select would be one having a clear light eye, a steady hand, a good digestion, and not knowing the meaning of the word nervousness ... '

At least the Association and its administration could take comfort in some, if not many, of Peel's words: 'In all relating to the order of shooting, squadding, and matters of executive detail, the Americans are behind us.' To their credit, not only did the Chairman and Council take Peel's strong medicine, they also recognised the report's general interest and its importance to all riflemen, and so sought his permission to publish what had originally been intended to be a private and confidential document. Peel agreed and the report was published in the *Volunteer Service Gazette*.

One proposition that Peel made was implemented by the NRA the following year when telephones were introduced at the long-range firing points and, although a proposal to restrict match-rifle competitions to breech-loaders was rejected at a meeting of the NRA the following year, the defeat at the hands of the Americans and Peel's report marked the end of the muzzle-loader. A few American breech-loaders made a distinct impression with the considerable success they achieved in the 1878 Meeting, most notably the Ballard belonging to Mr Farrow of New York, who made the top score in the single rifle section of the Martin Smith and the highest possible score, 35 out of 35, in the Ladies' Any Rifle competition. In 1879, Mr Farrow returned to Wimbledon and won the second stage of the Albert, and the princely sum of £100 which went with it, while coming second in the St Leger competition. A fellow New Yorker, Frank Hyde, who used a Sharp, came third in the Albert and was well near the top in a handful of other competitions.

That year was a good year for competitors from across the Atlantic, for while Canada lost the Kolapore, they could console themselves with the fact that one of their number, Lieutenant-Colonel, later Sir John, Gibson carried off the Prince of Wales's prize, with 94 out of 105 marks, which was presented to him by the Duchess of Connaught.

In 1880, the year the Welsh were admitted to take part in the International, the Americans came to Wimbledon after shooting against the Irish at Dollymount. A singularly observant, or simply over-imaginative, reporter had noted that on the targets at the 800-yard range in Ireland, one American had shot an almost perfect three-leaved shamrock while another had shot the design of the Stars and Stripes.

If there was something in the Irish air affecting the vision of the writer, there was a good deal more of it at Wimbledon that year which clouded the sights of the riflemen. It was fog. Dense fog which forced officials to abandon shooting one day—at the cost of £30 an hour. The Canadians were in despair, while one of the best American shots leaned on his rifle and told a reporter that the next year he would stay at home and shoot in the daylight, adding laconically, 'We didn't come here to shoot at a thousand yard range in the moonlight.'

Despite the variable weather, which one wag dubbed patriotic, and the 'disagreeable discovery of alleged fraudulent marking' which upset the entire Camp that year, the Anglo-American Match took place on the final Saturday of the Meeting, 24 July. There had been a suggestion that the Americans should compete against teams of four from England, Ireland and Scotland, but the NRA again insisted that there should only be one team representing the United Kingdom and the Americans withdrew their consent for a team match, though they still allowed members to compete as individuals. The result of the match, with teams got together by Halford and Hyde, was a victory for the home side—1,647 marks to 1,568.

Nevertheless, the Americans did well in other competitions. And Mr Farrow and Mr Scott figured prominently among the prizewinners. Mr Farrow, with his Ballard, carried off the Wimbledon Cup; Mr Scott, using a Remington, won both the first and second stages of the Albert; while Frank Hyde, armed with his Sharp, picked up the Association Cup. And, ironically, with the Americans once again in town, Ireland won the Elcho Shield, albeit by only one point above England's score, while one of their team, Lieutenant P. Godsal, scored the highest individual total—with an American Sharp.

In the summer of 1881, Europe sweltered. Madrid was reported to be like a 'fiery furnace', while in London, the streets were choked with dust as the water carts in the city dried up, literally. But the social season continued unabated, with Lord and Lady Brownlow holding lunches and garden parties at the Cottage. Among their guests that year were the King of the Sandwich Islands and the Canadian Prime Minister, Sir John Macdonald, who inspected the Canadian camp and assured his host, the Duke of Cambridge, that if England were unfortunate enough to find herself at war, Canada's forces would do their fair share of fighting in the field for the common cause and the common flag. The Canadian Volunteers, he said, were not a holiday force. And, as if to underline the point, the Canadians again carried off the Kolapore, in which Jersey and Guernsey competed for the first time that year, while, after a tie in which both competitors shot with a Sharp, the second stage of the Albert was won for the third year in succession by the American, Frank Hyde.

In 1882, after a certain amount of debate as to who should go first and where, a match was decided upon between the American National Guard and a British team, to take place at Creedmoor in the autumn, with the Americans undertaking to travel to Wimbledon the following year.

The British team, led by Sir Henry Halford, set sail in September on board the steamship *Alaska* and were met in New York, one early morning, by a delegation from the American Rifle Association on board a steamboat flying the British colours from her bow, the US flag from her stern, and streams of coloured bunting everywhere else. Also in the welcoming party was a correspondent from the *New York Tribune*, who was able to report that Sir Henry Halford was the first member of the British team to be spotted amidships, with 'his inseparable companion—a stumpy pipe—clenched in his teeth'. The British party transferred to the smaller boat, their luggage of tin cans, baskets, hat boxes, bags and trunks being tumbled over the side while the small wooden boxes, marked cartridges, were transferred by a red-faced captain 'with great care'. After warm greetings and shortish speeches, the party sat down to a lunch of sandwiches, salad and wine.

A train bore the visitors away from the docks and from the 'nauseating smells of Long Island City', taking them to Garden City, where the English team had stayed five years before. The party took over two cottages, and used an extra room as their headquarters. The Britishers, noted the correspondent, were singularly different from the Americans—they were so tall. The smallest was 5 ft 5 ins, the tallest just half an inch off being a foot taller than that. Some of them had been shooting for ten or fifteen years, much longer than any of the Americans, but they never boasted of their prowess. They remained quietly confident.

A lot of newsprint was spent on describing the forthcoming match, and in outlining the characters of the British team. There was first the captain, Sir Henry Halford, 'a man of imperturbable good humour', well known to the Americans who had visited England already for the hospitality he had shown them at his estate in Leicestershire where he had his own private rifle range. Then there was the thirty-two-year-old Major A. Humphry who had won The Queen's Prize in 1871. Educated at Rugby and Cambridge, Humphry was a barrister who had written a useful handbook, *First Hints in Rifle Shooting*. He was accompanied by his wife, who was at Creedmoor not merely as a spectator of her husband's exploits, 'for her deft fingers are the ones employed in the work of loading his shells—work requiring the greatest nicety, and which few riflemen are willing to trust out of their own hands.'

Among the British party from whom a team was selected were Rab

McVittie, a brawny Scots cabinet-maker, said to be the best shot in Great Britain; W.H.Walrond, the thirty-three-year-old Tory MP for East Devon; the adjutant, Henry Smith, a senior official in the Post Office, who was founder and honorary secretary of the North London Club; George Boulter, chief clerk in the Cheshire Post Office; P.Oliver, thirty-eight, a member of both the North and South London Clubs, who had scored the highest marks ever with a Metford rifle; the youngest member, twenty-five-year-old Henry Mellish; and William Caldwell who had served with the American reserves when he had lived in New York, and been wounded on active service three times. Caldwell's presence in the British team, with his former American status, was thought to counterbalance the inclusion in the American side of an Englishman, John Smith.

One matter, which the *New York Tribune* felt was an important factor in determining the choice of a rifleman was the colour of his eyes: 'It is a fact that in warm weather gray or blue eyes make better shots than dark eyes and this is the reason that light eyed men have been invariably chosen in the American teams.'

After their long journey, and the lengthy welcoming entertainments, the British party slept soundly and deeply that first night in New York, untroubled, they noted happily, by the dreaded mosquito. The next day was spent sightseeing, or, for some members of the team, on business trips. There were official entertainments, and trips out of town such as a steam-boat trip up the Hudson to visit West Point, with a band on board to provide musical interludes; and the news that a special medal was being struck by Tiffany's, the exclusive New York jeweller, which would be presented to the captain and all the members of the winning team. Then began the serious work—practice. The first morning on the range, the sky was slightly overcast and the 'light was of a grayish tinge which delights the rifleman'. But the clouds soon thickened and, as the two sides went in to lunch in the clubhouse at Creedmoor, the weather broke and down came the rain, so heavily, in fact, that a leaky roof often interrupted the welcoming ceremony which, as a consequence was 'almost solemnly performed'.

The Americans must have sensed a forthcoming defeat, though they didn't admit it. Time had wrought many changes since the Americans' decisive victory over the British five years before. Now the British were armed with far better weapons. Nevertheless, the crowds rallied to the ranges. The ferries from New York were packed as early as nine o'clock in the morning. 'At the foot of East Thirty-fourth street a large band of police officers stood ready to embark; their glittering uniforms embellished, as their portly frames filled the crowded cars.'

Newsboys travelled up and down the coaches, each offering the only official guide to the shooting, and, for light relief, there were always the comics. Some people arrived in their own luxurious carriages and parked next to farm boys in old spring wagons. And then, when everyone had settled themselves in for the day, there were plenty of refreshments to be had. Clam chowder. Water melons. Cigars, a dime each. All the tastes which a holiday crowd could possibly want were catered for on the stalls set up amidst the Camp's own tents which glistened like giant snowballs in the September sun. There were a few 'spacious and obnoxious persons' who blocked the view of the shooting and a few 'indiscriminate advertising agents made themselves obnoxious by their noisy buffoonery'. There was also a Broadway clothing house which was 'advertised by a crier with a voice like a steam siren'.

And there were other diversions. Small boys ran around, as small boys are wont to do, 'as lively as the Long Island grasshoppers that entangled themselves in the meshes of the ladies' hair.' And, of course, there were the ladies. Some quite familiar with the rifleman's language, others content simply to flirt under their parasols. An occasional vulture soared overhead in a wind which was also in the mood for some fun, and not just in interfering with the riflemen. It whipped straw hats off heads, playing havoc with the dignity of some as well as the boaters of others. And then, just as shooting was about to begin, a gust of wind whipped a parasol from a lady's hand and sent it hurtling across the range. After it, in hot pursuit went a gallant soldier who was heartily applauded by a laughing and cheering crowd.

The Americans had marched to the ranges under the command of Colonel Bodine, 'tall, dignified, straight as an arrow, he looked the very ideal of an officer,' while the British were escorted there by the 13th Pennsylvania Regiment. Once again, though, they were noted for 'straggling' and their disparate apparel, occasionally flashed with red and with the white cloth havelocks over their caps, presented a distinct contrast with the uniform blue dress of the Americans. Nevertheless, the headline in the *New York Tribune* after the two-day event, which had received columns of reports on the front page as well as diagrams of the targets, read 'Victory of British in The Great Rifle Match'. Victory, it was indeed, and a decisive one at that.

At every distance, the British had gained marks but their greatest lead came, as they had anticipated, at the long ranges where the Metford rifle came into its own. The combination of the smooth-grooved gun, with a British powder which, for those days, was relatively clean, gave the British team distinct advantages. The British won the Great Rifle Match by 1,975 to 1,805. The American Press blamed the windy conditions to a certain extent, and an excess of caution bordering on nervousness in the home team. Colonel Bodine, however, believed the defeat was due to the superiority of the British weapons: 'The arms used by the British team were undoubtedly superior to ours in many particulars. They are the products of the keenest rivalry between several prominent British makers, backed by capital and scientific talent, stimulated by the expectation that such arm as may prove best will be the one adopted to replace the present service arms—the Snider and the Henry-Martini—neither of which are popular with the soldiers or the officers.'

Judge Gildersleeve, a former captain of the American team, saw another reason for the British success. 'I have made some observations today that may be of interest,' he said in a speech at a dinner held after the match, 'The Wimbledon team should all be married men and their wives should go with them. If you watched the score you saw that Mr Humphry made the best score at 1,000 yards.' There was laughter and a good deal of cheering as the crowd focussed its attention on the smiling, blushing Mrs Humphry, and, after a pause, the Judge continued, 'If any of our young ambitious riflemen want to go to Wimbledon, let them look for wives immediately.'

An American team travelled to Wimbledon in 1883 in the bi-diurnal competition—if, in the meantime, any one of them had taken Judge Gildersleeve's advice, it is, alas, not recorded in NRA reports. The Americans were not inclined to camp on the Common, preferring to stay in Putney. Celebrations and entertainments were not too impaired by that fact, however, and among the welcoming parties was a banquet at the Criterion in London, attended by the Duke of Teck and the Earl of Wemyss. There was also a dinner at the Army and Navy Club in Piccadilly to which the American and Canadian teams were invited. And, by chance on 11 July, when the Americans went to practise at the Government ranges at Hounslow, a lecture on the subject of America was delivered in London by Oscar Wilde.

The conditions for the match were almost identical to those at Creedmoor the year before, but one matter that had arisen which caused a degree of difficulty was the admission of wind-gauge back-sights. The Americans had sights adjustable by screws which were not permissible under NRA rules, and while both sides appeared to think the matter had been settled to its own satisfaction, nothing was done until the Americans arrived at Wimbledon. By this time, the Council determined that the Americans could shoot alongside competitors with their screw adjustment back-sights, but not actually compete unless they removed them. Two did, and with success: Dr Scott won one of the new prizes donated by the American NRA, the Bodine (named after the captain of the American team, which was donated together with the Molineux, named after the American president of the NRA), while Mr Hinman carried off the St Leger.

However once again, there was an air of caution among the NRA in America about its team's chances. Only one member came out with fighting talk: 'If we are defeated, it will be because of a Jonah.' When news of the American defeat by 45 points came through on the wire, the NRA secretary in America admitted to being 'whipped and beaten fairly'. The Americans had nothing to complain of since the English had shot so well, he said, and the Americans did not have the long-range riflemen necessary to make the odds even. But there was still the thought abroad of a Jonah in the team who had brought down the spirits, as well as the scores, of the side.

Despite its defeat, the captain of the American team said his men had enough backbone left in them to join in the cheering of the home team and later, in the brilliant sunshine, he led them, in full dress uniform, to the prize-giving ceremony which was conducted that year by the Duchess of Teck. The NRA Chairman, Lord Brownlow, invited them on to the main platform which was reserved for state visitors and the Duchess shook hands with each and every one, including the Englishman who was shooting on the American side, John Smith.

In 1884, the Irish repeated their success of the previous year by carrying off the Elcho, and the Canadians once more captured the Kolapore.

With the promise, unfulfilled as it transpired, that the Australians were to send a team in 1885, the Duke of Cambridge made a rallying speech at the NRA's winter meeting on 24 February at the Royal United Service Institution: 'The coming of the colonists to Wimbledon as competitors with our Volunteers has always been most satisfactory, as showing the good feeling our kin across the sea take in the mother country but the warmth of our feelings is enhanced when we hear of our colonists coming forward in moments when they think there is a danger to the mother country, and when there appears to them a necessity for assistance, with the offer that they should stand shoulder to shoulder with the old country, should share her anxieties, and help to fight her battles side by side with the British soldier.' By today's standards the speech rattles with jarring patronising tones, but to those listening to the words a hundred years ago it was patriotism pure and simple and, as a consequence, inspired many cheers.

As far as *The Times* was concerned, 1886 on Wimbledon Common was 'symbolical beyond all precedents of the greatness of the Empire' and of 'that filial affection' which subsisted between the colonies and the mother country. That year, said the *Illustrated London News*, the Volunteer gathering's 'prize list is more munificent, its competitions more extensive, and its competitors more numerous and more fully representative of the entire British Empire than on any previous occasion.' It was the year that the Meeting welcomed teams from Canada, Australia, India, Jersey and Guernsey. And to honour the occasion of the visit, the City of London donated a silver cup to be competed for solely by Volunteers from India and the Colonies (and won by a Canadian, Sergeant Armstrong of the Governor-General's Foot Guards).

The Australian team, under the command of Colonel Sleep, had three members from Tasmania, five each from Victoria and New South Wales, and two from Queensland. With the Indian team, commanded by Lieutenant-Colonel Rivett-Carnac, the Australians were encamped next to the Canadians, commanded by the president of the Dominion of Canada Rifle Associations, Colonel Gzowski, for whom it was the sixteenth visit to Wimbledon. They, at least, must have been used to the way the Camp began its life on the first Sunday before the Meeting with the London Scottish marching to Roehampton for Divine Service, 'the sound of their pipes as they returned to their quarters attracting considerable numbers of spectators.' That year, in the regular Middle Sunday Service, the Reverend Canon Hole of Newark chose the words 'a devout soldier' for his text, and delivered an eloquent sermon which cited as examples of devout Christians, General Gordon and the Emperor Charlemagne.

On the opening Monday, 12 July, there was a surprise visit from a party of French riflemen, including Monsieur Merillon, a member of the French Chamber and President of the Union of the Rifle Associations of France, who watched some of the matches and then returned to the Camp the following day, to be formally introduced by the French Military Attaché to Sir Henry Wilmot, the Chairman of the Council, and to present the NRA with a valuable Sèvres vase. The presentation was made, they said, with the sanction of the French Government, and they also invited English riflemen to compete at the Concours National which was to be held at Vincennes the following month. Several members of the French party then shot at Pool and at the Revolver range, and two of them won awards which, because of the rules of qualification, were presented to them as courtesy prizes.

The French connection was particularly strong that year; two prizes were instituted, donated by two rivals in Rheims—Monsieur Eugene Clicquot who donated six dozen bottles of champagne, while seven dozen bottles and £25 were donated by Messrs Perinet and Fils. Such beneficence must have added to the disappointment of an Australian, Lieutenant Cork, who as an extra prize carried off a crate of lime juice.

The importance of the attendance of about eighty men from the Colonies was signified by the fact that the Princess of Wales agreed to give the prizes that year. She arrived on Wimbledon Common on the final Saturday of the Meeting, with the Prince of Wales, and her daughters, the Princesses Maud, Victoria and Louise, to be greeted by cheering crowds and the band of the London Rifle Brigade playing the national anthem. The Prince toured the colonial encampment and then returned to the Cottage outside of which a platform had been specially constructed, covered by an awning under which were rows of tables carrying all the glittering trophies. Among the guests were the Duke of Rutland, the Duchess of Westminster, Lord and Lady Wantage and the French Ambassador. The Kolapore was that year won by the home team (666 marks); runners–up were Canada (646), followed by Guernsey (636), Australia (632), Jersey (626), and then India (595). The cheers, noted *The Times*, were particularly reserved for the colonial riflemen as well as for Ireland who won the Elcho and for Ser-geant-Major Gaudin of the Royal Jersey Artillery who won the Prince of Wales, while, the newspaper noted, the Princess spent longer than average talking to Lieutenant-Colonel Rivett-Carnac, who commanded the Indian team.

The aphorism that the world is very small, is well illustrated at the Meeting on Wimbledon Common, wrote the correspondent of the *Weekly Mail of Toronto*. One of the Canadian team had been introduced by a friend to a man with the same name. Not only did it transpire that their quarters were adjacent and 'within the range of the ordinary tones of conversation,' but, on comparing genealogical notes the men discovered they were first cousins simply living at opposite ends of their vast country.

The world was indeed becoming a smaller place, while the annual Meeting grew larger, welcoming more and more foreign visitors. In 1887, came the first visit of a team from the Cape of Good Hope who took third place in the Kolapore, just two marks behind the runners–up, Canada. There were also teams from India and the Channel Islands, and, in that year, the year of the Queen's Jubilee, Lord and Lady Wantage held a ban-quet in a great tent next to the Cottage on the Common, to which came foreign dignatories and royalty.

The tent was decorated with festoons of coloured Indian muslin and a temporary drawing room was divided from the dining area by huge velvet curtains embroidered with gold. The sides of the tent were hung with tapestries and the floors were spread with rugs and carpets from the east. On one table, amidst bowls full of blooming roses, stood some of the Wimbledon prize cups which glittered in the light shed by the fairy lamps.

Among the guests at the banquet were the King of Greece, the Duke of Sparta, Princes Albert Victor and George, and the Prince of Wales, who pinned the gold badge on the arm of the Queen's Prizewinner, Lieutenant Warren, and the badge of his own prize on the arm of a member of the Canadian team, Private Gillies. There were 115 guests, including Council members and staff of the Association, and many past winners of The Queen's Prize and of the Prince of Wales's Prize.

That year, more Americans came to Wimbledon—twenty-two members of the Boston Honourable Artillery Company, who were visiting the HAC London. Their founder, Robert Keayne, had joined the London company in 1623 and, after migrating to Boston, had formed the American company in 1638.

In 1889, the last year on the Common, sixteen members of the Massachusetts Volunteer Militia visited the Camp. Their Springfield rifles, much admired by the Duke of Cambridge, prevented them from competing but they did not prevent the Americans from being made honorary members of the London Scottish. Both they and the American ambassador, Mr Lincoln, were shown round the Camp and the Massachusetts riflemen were invited to join in the celebrations for The Queen's Prizewinner, Sergeant Reid of the 1st Lanark Engineers. Cheering crowds gathered to watch the Americans give a display of their style of skirmish drill, despite heavy storms of rain and hail.

As ever, not even an English summer appeared to deter visitors to Wimbledon Common—be they from home or abroad, riflemen and shooting enthusiasts were welcomed always. The move to Bisley changed nothing.

# CHAPTER FOUR

# *Bisley—the New Wimbledon*

## PURELY A MATTER OF BISLEYNESS

Private R. Van Winkle opened his eyes, and, taking up his rusty rifle, marched towards his new ranges. 'Dear me!' said he, gazing with amazement at his surroundings, 'this is not at all like what I saw when I went to sleep.'

'No, RIP, it is not,' replied Mr Punch, who happened to be in the neighbourhood. He had been watching his sweetest Princess making a bull's eye at the opening ceremony.

'Why, it is twice as large as Wimbledon,' continued the astounded warrior … 'But where are the fancy tents, and the luncheon parties, and all the etceteras that used to be so pleasant at Wimbledon?'

'Disappeared,' returned Mr Punch, firmly. 'Bisley is to be more like Shoeburyness (where the Artillery set an excellent example to the Infantry) than the Surrey saturnalia.'

'And is it to be *all* work and no play?'

'That will be the general idea. Of course, in the evening, when nothing better can be done, there will be harmonic meetings round the camp-fires. But while light lasts, the crack of the rifle and the ping of the bullet will be heard in all directions, *vice* the pop of the champagne corks superseded. And, if you don't like the prospect, my dear RIP, you had better go to sleep again.'

But Private VAN WINKLE remained awake—to his best interests!

*Punch*, 19 July 1890

It was a day to be marked with white stone in the annals of the National Rifle Association, trumpeted *The Times*, when the National Rifle Association's new Camp at Bisley in Surrey was opened by the Prince and Princess of Wales on Saturday, 12 July 1890, and, following the example of Queen Victoria thirty years before, the opening was heralded by the Princess pulling a silken cord attached to the trigger of a magazine rifle and scoring an unquestionable bull's-eye.

75

For many, that Saturday had begun early with a journey from Waterloo Station. Unsuspecting travellers must have thought that London was under military occupation, with the presence of armies of Volunteers from all over the country, in and out of uniform, carrying piles of luggage of 'more or less a military aspect,' creating havoc and turmoil on the station concourse. The chaos increased as the day wore on, for as well as the ordinary traffic, there were two special trains to be prepared for the Royal party who were due to depart from the station shortly after three o'clock.

However, that departure was delayed somewhat so that the Princess could inspect an impromptu guard of honour formed by her own Yorkshire regiment which was on its way back to Portsmouth after a brief spell of duty at Wellington Barracks. 'The glitter of bayonets in Royal salute, the strains of the national anthem from the Grenadier Guards' band, which had come to play the Yorkshire regiment off, and the inspection of ranks, made an imposing little pageant for which the rail officers were hardly prepared,' noted the *Daily Graphic*. The Royal party left Waterloo amid cheering crowds of Volunteers, arriving at Brookwood some forty minutes later. The carriage containing the Prince and Princess, together with their daughters the Princesses Victoria and Maud, and the Duke of Cambridge, was then brought into the Camp by an engine, named the Alexandra, which was decorated with trophies of flowers and flags.

The Prince alighted from the carriage on to the platform to be met by the Association's Chairman, Lord Wantage, in the full dress uniform of Brigadier-General of the Berkshire Volunteers. A host of dignatories were gathered on the Pavilion platform, among them the Duke and Duchess of Westminster, the Turkish Ambassador, Prince Louis Esterhazy, Monsieur Pontavich, the French Military Attaché, Sir Henry Wilmot, Sir Joseph Savory, the Lord Mayor of London, Sir Henry Fletcher, Edward Stanhope, the Secretary of State for War, and Sir William Harcourt, the Attorney-General. The Common was awash with uniforms and medals—the Duke of Westminster and the Earl of Wemyss being conspicuous as the only members of the Council who appeared in plain clothes.

The Princess, in a dark purple dress embroidered with violets, the same flower which adorned her bonnet, accompanied the Prince and the young Princesses, dressed in fawn and beige, into the awaiting carriage to be driven to the rifle ranges, escorted by a detachment of Hussars through the lines of cheering and waving Volunteers and Regulars, while a band played the national anthem. Here they were joined by the Prince's brother, the Duke of Connaught, who had driven over from Bagshot, and then walked through the crowd, almost unrecognised, to the enclosure where several tents had been erected as a precaution against the storm which threatened, but never broke over, the proceedings. The weather had not deterred the fair, and the brave, from dressing in the daintiest and most delicate of summer dresses which lit up the grey afternoon and the more sombre colours of the uniformed men in the crowd which pressed against the ropes sealing off the enclosure and marking the safety limit on the ranges.

On a platform, under an umbrella-like awning, rested the rifle which the Princess was to fire. Sir Henry Halford, in his full dress uniform as Colonel of the Leicestershire Volunteers, stood guard over the rifle he had spent hours in sighting on the target. At his side, Captain Nathan, an officer from the Woolwich Laboratory, stood as stiff as a sentry, as though guarding Sir Henry.

The Duke of Cambridge, President of the Association, read a speech of welcome to the Prince, reminding him of his presence at the inaugural meeting on Wimbledon Common thirty years before. The Prince, in his reply, spoke of the importance of keeping up to a high standard the art and practice of rifle shooting as a military exercise: 'It is evident that the efficiency of our Army depends upon the skill which soldiers are able to acquire in the use of their weapons, and every possible facility should be given them to acquire this skill. To the Volunteers, in whose interest this Association has been more especially founded, I would say, that to attain a high standard of merit, and to make the rifle today what the bow was in the days of the Plantagenets, is a peculiarly appropriate object of ambition to those who stand forth in the defence of their country.' He wished the Association 'a long career of increased prosperity and extended usefulness', and, hoping that it 'may continue to meet with the countenance and support to which its national and patriotic character entitles it,' he declared the ranges open.

Then, after a speech of welcome from Lord Wantage, the Princess was conducted to the spot where the rifle rested. After a brief explanation from Sir Henry as to its workings, the Princess was handed a silken cord attached to the trigger. A bugler sounded the signal to commence firing and the ninety targets at the great butt rose simultaneously. The Princess pulled the cord, and the bullet shot from the gun towards the number twelve target. Even before the marker indicated the bull's-eye, the crowd had begun to roar its approval. It was a roar which increased when the indication was signalled, and more than one person noted the relief followed by the ripple of smiles which spread across Sir Henry's face.

The Royal party remained on the platform until Mr Hoey, the Clerk of the Works, brought over the carton which had been pierced by the bullet and delivered it into the hands of the delighted Princess, who then received from Lord Wantage the Association's Gold Medal as a memento of the occasion. At her particular request, the boys of the Gordon Home at Sandhurst, who had been working in the butts, were brought over for inspection. 'Well set-up lads, who promise to make good soldiers,' they gave three cheers for the Prince and Princess and 'one cheer more' for the Duke of Cambridge.

Acknowledging the cheers of the crowd, the Royal party climbed into a carriage and pair to drive up to the Clock Tower and look out over the entire Camp spread beneath them. Then it was time for tea in the Pavilion, before boarding the train back to London shortly after six o'clock. For other visitors, too, there was a train to catch home, but for many it was a night to be spent under canvas and an overcast sky. The National Rifle Association's new home at Bisley had officially opened, but there were still two days to go before the Meeting itself began, and for the competitors, that meant hours spent in acclimatising to the new location and, of course, preparing themselves and their weapons for the big event.

∽ ∽ ∽ ∽

The New Wimbledon, as some called it, met with instant and warm approval, despite the fact that it was twenty-seven miles from London. The *Illustrated London News* found the layout of the Camp 'compact and convenient', while *The Times* thought that as a camping ground, 'it is a capital place'. From the rifleman's point of view, *The Times* maintained, Bisley was far superior to Wimbledon. 'The aspect of the ranges is perfection, and the wind does not sweep across them with the fury which was characteristic of the Wimbledon plateau. Moreover, there is a certain amount of shelter both on the right hand and the left.' But *The Times* added a note of caution: 'The only fear appears to be that from the porous soil under the rays of a hot sun may rise that which riflemen call mirage ... which is worse for the rifleman than a thunder shower, and almost as bad as a Scotch mist.'

The *Illustrated London News*, having inspected the wild and desolate moorland the year before, took its readers on a guided amble round the little wooden and canvas town which had grown up on the Common:

'Most visitors will run up into the Camp by the tramway which has been laid down, from a point beyond Brookwood ... to a station in the heart of the Camp, the passengers alighting close to the club tents, the great refreshment pavilion, the exhibition tent, the bazaar, and the offices in which all the business of the Association, the Camp post and telegraph office, the Press reporters, and the Camp printers is done. These all lie to the right of the tramway; to the left are the tent lines of the National Rifle Association, in which the Volunteers, principally from the provinces, whose corps have not a regimental enclosure, are encamped. There are also, to the left, the regimental enclosures ...

'Beyond the tramway station, to the left, the range officers have their quarters; a little farther on, the Camp for members of the Association has been pitched. To the right of the tramway station ... are the Umbrella Tent, where men will congregate in the luncheon hour; the huts erected for the more luxurious shooting-men who shun the discomforts of a tent; the quarters for the police, those for the civilian staff, and the camps of some necessary services. As far as is possible, the hedgerows, bushes, and trees of the land in its former state have been preserved, while the rough ground has been made smooth.'

Bisley, said an enraptured Canadian correspondent, is a most delightful sample of the scenery characteristic of rural England, 'and all riflemen who have visited it unite in the opinion that it is, in all respects, an ideal place for such a gathering.'

The move had cost the Association a little short of £26,000—more than half that sum to buy the land, the rest being spent on erecting the new butts and targets, the offices and tramway—but the Council believed that the change of location to Bisley and, in particular, the first Meeting at the new site had proved to be a thorough success. Everyone appeared to be determined to make it so—even when, on the first Tuesday, a tropical storm broke over the Camp which that year accommodated nearly 3,000 men. Nearly two inches of rain fell that day, well over an inch of it in just an hour, forcing the shooting to stop temporarily and flooding many of the tents, 'causing the greatest discomfort'.

But spirits were not dampened. There were 2,320 entrants for The Queen's Prize, seven more than in the final year at Wimbledon, and the winner carried on the shoulders of his fellow competitors to the Council offices was Sergeant Bates of the 1st Warwickshire, a forty-eight-year-old grandfather, who had given up his job as a clockmaker to work on rifle and gun adjustment and had first shot at Wimbledon in 1869 when his name appeared in the Queen's Hundred. Because of the official opening, the Meeting closed with extra novelty competitions taking the place of the prizegiving or what the *Daily News* described as 'that monotonous ceremony'. But nothing altered the tradition meted out to The Queen's Prizewinner. After receiving the gold medal from the Duke of Cambridge, Lady Wantage pinned the gold badge to his arm and, amidst hearty cheering, Bates was lifted on to the Prizewinner's chair and carried round the Camp in triumph.

*The Times*, warm in its enthusiasm for the New Wimbledon, wrote at the close of the first Meeting at Bisley: 'The general verdict is that the place is excellent; that the arrangements are quite as good as anything which anybody has a right to expect in the first year; and that, if the Association can obtain, either from the voluntary subscriptions of the public or from Parliament, the funds which it certainly deserves to obtain, there ought to be no room for doubt with regard to success in the future.' On 25 November that year, the Association noted with pride that it had received from the Queen a Royal Charter of Incorporation.

The second year at Bisley was remarkable for one event, although it was seen by the *Illustrated London News* to be a 'minor incident of novelty'. Nevertheless, 1891 was the year that saw the arrival on the ranges of a lady rifleman. Miss Winifred Louise Leale, the nineteen-year-old daughter of Surgeon-Major Leale of the 2nd Guernsey, had been taught by her father and had gone on to become a more than proficient shooting member of the Guernsey NRA. When the Duke of Cambridge visited the Camp in the second week, he made a particular point of asking for Miss Leale to be presented to him so that he could congratulate her on her shooting record. It was a more remarkable feat, he said, because of her handling of the Martini-Henry rifle whose recoil was known to cause some raw Army recruits to pale with fear and consternation. Miss Leale, however, was made of sterner stuff and went on to become a regular visitor to the ranges at Bisley.

Happily, the serious nature of Bisley, as foreseen by Mr Punch in 1890, could not be maintained for long and in 1892, 'with a view to cheerful evenings in Camp,' the Council decided to organise concerts with the help of various willing and enthusiastic regiments. It was also the year that the English Eight decided to build a permanent clubhouse on the Common, at a cost of £176, as did an individual member, the renowned American revolver shot, Walter Winans. A wealthy man, Mr Winans, his abode on the Common being valued at £235. The following year, the wettest on record with the exception of the 1875 Meeting, buildings were erected for the English Twenty Club and for the Inns of Court Rifle Volunteers. The range of Camp entertainments also began to increase—actors and wags in various regimental dramatic clubs providing special amusement on summer evenings.

In 1895, when the Surrey Brigade, the Victoria and St George's Rifles erected permanent clubhouses at Bisley and, at times, the weather chose to be unkind to marksmen by whipping up winds of thirty m.p.h. which covered the targets in clouds of dust, The Queen's Prize was won for the first time by a Volunteer from the Colonies.

When Lady Wantage pinned the gold badge on to the Prizewinner, she

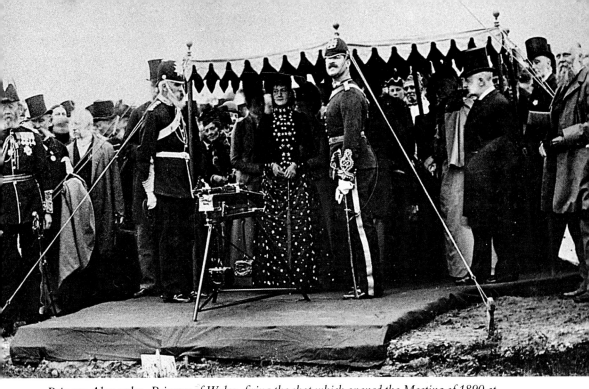

*Princess Alexandra, Princess of Wales, firing the shot which opened the Meeting of 1890 at the NRA's new home on Bisley Common.*

*Thomas Francis Fremantle, 3rd Baron Cottesloe and Chairman of the NRA, 1931–9, (left, and standing), next to Sir Henry Halford and Mr Henry Whitehead (seated, centre), at Bisley in 1890. Lord Cottesloe last shot at Bisley in 1946.*

*ABOVE/BELOW Postcards based on paintings by Ernest Ibbotson.*

TOP LEFT *On Bisley Common in 1890, as at Wimbledon, competitors enjoyed entertaining their families — but women were not allowed to stay in Camp until after the Second World War.*

LEFT *Inside a tent, believed to be the Members' Tent, at Bisley, 1890.*

*1895 was the first time a foreigner won The Queen's Prize, but Private T. Hayhurst, a toolmaker from Canada, actually hailed from England, from Kendal in the Lake District. In the foreground, the president of the Canadian NRA, Colonel (later Sir) C. S. Gzowski.*

*Private William Priaulx who in 1899 became the first competitor from Guernsey to win The Queen's Prize.*

*Miss Winifred Leale, an acclaimed shot in the Channel Islands, taught by her father Surgeon-Major Leale of the 2nd Guernsey, pictured here in 1896, who five years before at the age of 19 became the first lady to shoot in a competition on Bisley Common.*

The victorious American team competed against six other nations in the Palma Trophy Match in 1903 and later celebrated the occasion at the Trocadero Restaurant with a banquet given by the Duke of Cambridge.

ABOVE *The Bazaar, 1899.*

*The Prince of Wales (later George V), and the Princess visiting Bisley, 1904, the year the Prince became President of the NRA on the death of the Duke of Cambridge.*

**L'ESPRIT DE MON PÈRE M'EST TOUJOURS PROCHE**

*Mrs Kitty Way, wife of a Rand manager and an accomplished shot, who competed at Bisley in 1905, under a banner proclaiming that the spirit of her father was always close to her.*

*King Edward VIII at Bisley in 1905 — he had witnessed the inaugural shots fired by his mother, Queen Victoria, on Wimbledon Common in 1860, and later at Bisley in 1890 by his wife, then Princess Alexandra. Lord Cheylesmore is on his right.*

expressed her delight that the great prize should be captured by the most loyal of all—Canada, and the assembled crowd cheered, clapped, and war-whooped for fully five minutes. In fact, Private T.H. Hayhurst, a toolmaker by trade who worked in a hardware store in Hamilton, just south of Toronto, was not Canadian but English, having been born twenty-seven years before in Kendal in the Lake District. He had one elder sister, who was a nurse in a London hospital, but he himself had decided his future lay abroad and had emigrated three years before. After spending a year in the United States, he had decided to settle in Canada, so that one Canadian official pronounced on his return home, 'As he pays his taxes here, he's as Canadian as I am.'

Hayhurst's victory had been a close-run battle against the favourite to win, Private Boyd of the 3rd Lanarkshire. An enormous crowd had gathered to watch, the Canadians standing as close to their man as was permitted, using telescopes to watch the targets. Everyone in the crowd remained tense and silent. Only the two competitors appeared to be calm and collected. Until that is, the final shot was fired. It was Hayhurst's, it was an inner, and it was the signal that he had won The Queen's Prize. 'Thousands of hats, sticks, rifles, coats and flags were thrown up by the excited crowds, and the din of voices sounded at a distance like the roar of an angry sea,' reported Canada's *Daily Mail and Graphic*. And the Canadians wore out their voices as well as the soles of their boots, as they marched round and round the Camp singing their National Anthem, 'The Maple Leaf'.

When the news was telegraphed to Canada, no one could believe it. As the truth began to sink in, so the enthusiasm built up to give Hayhurst a hero's welcome. On 13 August, in Montreal he was cheered and mobbed by the crowds who thronged the streets as he was driven in a coach and four from his hotel to the Drill Hall which was decked out with photographs of his victory at Bisley and packed with chirruping ladies anxious to get a view of their latest heart-throb. In Toronto, it was the same. A lunch for 150 of the city's dignatories, followed by a public reception to which young ladies had poured in helter-skelter.

Then there was the journey home to Hamilton. As the boat was escorted into the harbour by a flotilla of tugs and small craft, the bay was filled with the sound of whistles, horns, booms of cannon fire, cheers and ringing church bells. There were bonfires on the hillside and in the harbour itself and everywhere there were myriads of Roman candles, fizzling and sending their sparkling fiery light over the boats, across the water, and on the land.

With his fellows, Sergeant Morris and Sergeant Skeddon who had won the *Daily Graphic* Match, Hayhurst was carried shoulder-high into the town in a mile-long parade led by hundreds of cyclists who had painted the wheels of their bikes in bright colours and had decorated them with Chinese lanterns. Bands of pipes and drums played throughout. The bells of the cathedral pealed. The City Hall was covered in a long streamer, emblazoned with the words, 'Welcome Home', and pictures of the three local riflemen. Every store and house was covered in bunting and flags and there were still more fireworks which sparkled in the fresh breeze. The park was ablaze with lights and more ladies packed the hall where the official reception was held.

It was almost too much for the stocky, broad-shouldered Hayhurst, whom compatriots described as 'steady, reliable, a good comrade and a gentleman'. He had by now been cheered and mobbed for days, but worse, he had been forced to reply to the eulogies of countless officials whom he had never met before and was highly unlikely to meet again. 'I can assure you,' he said at this largest and final thanksgiving, 'I feel very much the kind reception which you have accorded me, and if you will excuse me, I will not say more, for, to tell you the truth, I don't feel equal to the occasion.' For a while, the speeches stopped. The cheering for Hayhurst, however, went on a lot longer.

In 1896, the War Office began to re-arm the Volunteer Force with the Lee-Metford rifle, a smaller-bored rifle than the Martini-Henry. This called into question the conditions for the competitions and, in particular, those for the Match or, as it was then called, the Any rifle. This rifle, with its special sighting equipment and other mechanisms to assist the shooter, was considered to be a rich man's plaything as well as an aid to the scientific improvement of the weapon. But the change in the service rifle meant that the Any had to change, so at a meeting of the English Eight Club the maximum calibre of the Any, which in the next year became the Match, rifle was fixed at .315 (where it had been .450); this was considered to be the largest military calibre practicable as that of the Service rifle was .303.

A shadow was cast over the Meeting that year by the news of the death of the much loved Countess of Wemyss. In the early days on Wimbledon Common when she was still Lady Elcho, she had been dubbed that 'most enthusiastic volunteer' for her continual support of her husband and of the Association. The following year, 1897, saw the death of another much respected figure, Sir Henry Halford, and a Challenge Cup was instituted to his memory; also that year came the death of Major Perley, of the Canadian Engineers, who had been staying at Bisley to superintend the building of the Canadian clubhouse. He was interred with full military honours at the churchyard at Bisley, after the mid-Sunday service in the Camp.

It was the year of the Queen's Diamond Jubilee and the Meeting was generally blessed with fine and dry weather. In fact, the meteorological report noted that 'the duration of sunshine was phenomenal,' although one violent thunderstorm interrupted proceedings on the day the Chinese ambassador visited the Camp to enjoy a typical English garden party which he did ... to the accompaniment of a downpour during which half an inch of rain fell in half an hour. And one range official found himself in 'deadly peril': as he was talking on the telephone to an official in the butts, the line was hit by lightning. At times, it looked as though the storm was also attempting to eradicate all the reporters who were 'hard at work' in the Press room.

A steady breeze which occasionally whipped up into a wind of some thirty m.p.h. also caused grumblings among the riflemen. 'Not that grumbling is an unusual trait in the character of a rifle shot,' sniffed the *Daily News*, 'as no matter how favourable the elements be, there is bound to be some man who will lay the blame of a poor performance, not on himself but on one of the many varieties of atmospherical conditions which are apparently only known to shooting men.'

That year there was an unprecedented number of entries for the Kolapore. Besides the regulars from Canada, Jersey and Guernsey, there were teams from India, Victoria, Cape Colony, New Zealand, Queensland, and Natal. The cup was carried off by Victoria who scored three points more than the runners–up, New Zealand. One foreign rifleman who stood out from the rest was Subadar Mahomed Beg of the 1st Madras Lancers, whose gloriously sumptuous uniform was frequently spotted on the ranges where he proved himself an almost equally outstanding shot. The Duke of York, whose wife presented the prizes that year, expressed his delight at the number of friends from abroad who had come to Bisley to compete and who had carried off so many prizes.

It was particularly apt that in the Diamond Jubilee Year, the most frequent visitors, the Canadians, should open their new clubhouse which they did with a magnificent reception attended by the Lord Strathcona and Mount Royal, Sir Donald Smith, the High Commissioner for Canada in London, and the Association Chairman, Sir Henry Fletcher, who had turned the first sod of earth at a small ceremony in the spring. The building was completed within a hair's breadth of the opening reception and the walls were lined with specially imported Canadian shooting memorabilia such as a shield made of flints dating back thousands of years, and the heads of bison and moose. To call it a hut, wrote one visitor, is a misnomer for it is 'a very handsome and picturesque shooting lodge.' Colonel Gibson and Major Mason, assisted by their wives, entertained the guests who included a number of fellow Canadians such as the Bishop of Saskatchewan and the

Bishop of Toronto, while the band of the 2nd Battalion of the Liverpool Regiment, stationed outside on the lawns, played a selection of music.

Sir Donald Smith presented to Major Mason for competition at the Meeting the cup annually bestowed by the Dominion Rifle Association, for the highest grand aggregate score, and one from himself for the highest score by a Volunteer. Then Colonel Gibson presented to Sir Henry an illuminated address of thanks for his services in connection with the erection of the Canadian pavilion. 'Speeches expressive of the most fraternal feelings between Canada and the Mother Country were delivered,' the *Daily Telegraph* correspondent wrote, 'and a most agreeable afternoon was spent by the guests.'

As well as being the year that the Running Deer target, designed by Sir Edwin Landseer in 1863 and made of iron, was remodelled in a penetrable material and, as a consequence, lost his antlers, the Jubilee Year was also the year in which the Council lost if not such vital equipment as antlers then certainly some authority. A strong lobby of members managed to carry through a decision, against the wishes of the Council, that, instead of a Winter meeting in London, the Association should hold a general meeting at Bisley during the shooting fortnight in order to involve more members in Association business.

The first general meeting of members, held the following year in the Umbrella Tent, was deemed to be a success—even by the Council who, having had to bend to the pressure for change, placed on record their welcome for the opportunity the meeting afforded for a 'frank interchange of thought'. Perhaps it was an excess of hot air in the atmosphere which, added to the sunny, dry weather that year, caused the water supply to fail right in the middle of the Meeting which would have had to close if it had not been for the London and South-Western Railway, who ran the regular train service into the Camp, rushing hundreds of gallons of liquid relief in its tenders. The disaster which was so narrowly avoided encouraged the Association to build its own 60,000 gallon water tank.

Relief of a different kind came when the Council, in its search for new refreshment contractors, hired the services of the brewers, Ind Coope, who provided a hot midday meal for sevenpence and a cold one for fivepence, a Challenge Cup for a prize of their own name, and consequent satisfaction to many.

That year, Guernsey won the Kolapore Challenge Cup, beating by three points the previous year's winners, Victoria, but the following year, 1899, they claimed a greater victory when a twenty-nine-year-old bachelor, Private William Priaulx, of the 1st Guernseys, a 'sober, steady carpenter, albeit of no mean descent', carried off The Queen's Prize.

The ship from Weymouth on which Priaulx and his fellow riflemen, including team captain, Colonel Leale, and Miss Leale, voyaged home, sailed into St Peter Port which had been decked out for the victor's return. Thousands of cheering, flag-waving locals and holidaymakers packed out the quayside, while from the ships in the harbour, festooned with bunting, came an uproarious greeting, and a band played 'See The Conquering Hero Comes'. Priaulx, infinitely more relaxed than his excited and beaming father who was with him, was carried shoulder high to a small carriage driven by four greys which bore him to the Court House Terrace. Flags and bunting lined the route, and the street leading to the Court House was transformed into an archway of green foliage. And not for the first time, a Queen's Prizewinner was mobbed by a bevy of young ladies who vied with one another to catch their hero's eye.

At the Court House, Priaulx was greeted formally by the Bailiff, Mr T. Godfrey Carey, and the Lieutenant Governor General, Mr M.H. Saward, who sang the victor's praises not only for carrying off The Queen's Prize but also for being the highest individual scorer in the Kolapore. But praise was not deemed to be sufficient for Priaulx. The city officials had been scurrying around to discover more about their carpenter and fruit grower, and in doing so, had found that the family had crossed the Channel with William the Conqueror. One Priaulx had saved Richard the Lionheart from capture by the Turks, while another had married the daughter of the Bailiff on the island back in 1443. What could be better than a humble prizewinner with a noble pedigree!

Meanwhile, at home, the Council were still absorbing the report they had received from Major Thomas Fremantle, who had captained the English team which had fared so badly in the International Rifle Match in Holland in June, coming next to bottom in overall scores out of the eight competing teams. Unfavourable local conditions combined with 'fancy' rifles and a concentration on the standing position to shoot were deemed to be among the causes for the poor performances, but there was one consolation—Sergeant-Instructor Wallingford of the Hythe Staff carried off the Gold Medal for the highest individual score made in the prone position.

ﻌ ﻌ ﻌ ﻌ

The new century opened with a new role for the Association, given to it by the War Office: that of being the central organisation for local Rifle Clubs. At the general meeting that summer, Sir Henry Fletcher, the Association's Chairman, reported that the NRA already had ninety-two clubs with a membership of 6,000 affiliated to it, and some fifty or more were in the process of joining.

'It should be ingrained into the public mind,' the Duke of Cambridge had told the Winter meeting, when all assembled knew that many Volunteers were in South Africa fighting in the Boer War under Lord Roberts, and that the military were using the ranges at Bisley for target practice, 'that rifle shooting must become a necessary pastime for all classes, not with a view to making war, but in order for the country to be fully prepared when war should happen to break out.'

The rallying cry grew louder after a report from one prizewinning NRA member, A.P.Humphry, who had returned from a stay in Switzerland armed with all manner of information about local Rifle Clubs such as the number, 3,446, with a membership of 210,491, which had been steadily rising since 1874. The following year, the NRA could claim 211 Rifle Clubs affiliated to it, with more than 16,000 members, and that the movement had led to the construction of over fifty miniature and twelve new rifle ranges. Seventy further clubs were in the process of joining.

In that year, Queen Victoria died and an era was at an end. Since she fired the inaugural shot of the NRA on Wimbledon Common forty-one years before, she had never again visited the Meeting although her interest in the movement never waned, an interest which has flourished in her family ever since.

In 1901, after a singularly hot Meeting, the prizes were distributed by Field Marshal Lord Roberts, Commander-in-Chief, who had readily agreed to become a Vice-President of the Association. 'I consider the encouragement of rifle shooting of great importance, and everything I can do to foster the love of it in the Army will always give me much pleasure.' The war in South Africa had brought home to him, he said, the necessity of making soldiers good shots. 'However brave our men might be, however well drilled, however well set up, however well disciplined they might be, and however capable they might be of great endurance, or of riding across the most difficult country, admirable and desirable as all these qualifications are, the men would be valueless as soldiers if they were not experts in the use of the rifle.'

In 1902, as the Crown required the premises, the NRA moved its headquarters from Pall Mall East to 19 Charing Cross Road, intending to build and move into permanent offices at Bisley the next year. The war in South Africa not only seemed to inspire an increase in Rifle Clubs, it also encouraged donations such as one of £10,000 from William Waldorf Astor. 'The war in South Africa has taught the importance of training every able-bodied Englishman in the use of the rifle,' Astor wrote in a letter to the

Association, 'Beyond this, a remarkable feature in the life of an English country labourer is the absence of organised recreation, the spending of their Sundays and half-holidays, if not in the neighbouring taverns, in aimless wandering and lounging about.' Of the two trustees of the fund, it is interesting to note that one was a man who had served as a doctor in the Boer War and was the author of the celebrated adventures of Sherlock Holmes, Arthur Conan Doyle.

It was the year that Australia won the Kolapore for the first time against competition from teams which included Southern Rhodesia, Natal and the West Indies, while the British could console themselves with the fact that a team selected during Bisley fortnight went on to compete against Canada and the United States and win the International Match of the Palma Centennial Trophy held in Ottawa in September.

The following year, the Palma opened the Bisley Meeting on the Stickledown range which had been extended, with teams from France, Norway, Australia and Natal competing, besides those from Great Britain, the United States and Canada who led the field from the start. A team from Russia was due to compete, but failed to arrive in time. Apart from an improvement in their team coaching, the back-sight of the American service rifle which was adjustable laterally for wind allowance was believed to work dramatically in their favour, and so the Americans carried off the Palma. One of the first to congratulate the team was Mr Choate, the American ambassador, who had been watching the match with keen interest. That evening, he was among the 230 guests invited to the Trocadero restaurant in London for a banquet given by the Duke of Cambridge to celebrate the match. In fact, the Meeting of 1903, when there were well over 2,000 men staying on Camp, was heavily punctuated by a series of garden parties, receptions and entertainments given for the many foreign competitors by the new Chairman, Lord Cheylesmore, who had been Camp Commandant for many years at Wimbledon as well as Bisley and was one of the most popular figures in the Association's long history.

The banquet proved to be one of the final official duties carried out by the Duke of Cambridge. He died in the spring of 1904, having been the Association's President since its inception. Another stalwart from the first Wimbledon days was lost in the same year, Countess Spencer. The new President of the Association, the Prince of Wales (later George V), came to Bisley that year with the Princess of Wales (daughter of another frequent visitor to the Meeting, the Duchess of Teck) to watch the final stage of The King's Prize and a new Challenge Cup donated by Lord Roberts, and to distribute the prizes. Natal won the Mappin, New Zealand for the first time secured the Kolapore, while The King's Prize was won for the first time by a rifleman born in Canada, Private S.J. Perry, a twenty-four-year-old who came from Vancouver and worked as a pattern-maker in a shoe factory. He had volunteered for service in South Africa and fought at Paardeberg, and was thus greeted by one of the spectators, Lord Roberts, as a comrade in arms.

That year, the North London Rifle Club erected a clubhouse for its members, about a hundred trees were planted to form an avenue along the main road to the Camp, and a handsome pair of wrought iron gates, presented by Major John Barlow, were erected at the main entrance. Bisley was becoming smart as well as fashionable.

Bisley Fortnight in 1905 luxuriated in warm sunshine, and the Camp was adorned by as many pots of blossoming, fragrant flowers as it was visited by fair ladies in colourful costumes carrying pretty parasols, to the extent that, at times, the firing ranges looked like the lawns at Ascot. In the lazy, hazy hours between shooting, people relaxed or strolled round the grounds, listening to the music provided throughout the Meeting by a band of the Army Service Corps who were settled in the Umbrella Tent. For some, the rising temperature was extremely good for business—as one wag wrote, 'The local thirst seems to be getting lager and lager.'

But some of the ladies visiting Bisley were not just spectators. There were three ladies shooting on the range that year. Mrs Chapman, of the South London Rifle Club, who was noted as doing well in a new prize, the Conan Doyle; Miss Mabbs, daughter of a Quarter-Master Sergeant at Aldershot; and, among the party from Transvaal, which had sent a team to the Meeting for the first time, was Mrs Kitty Way, the wife of a Rand manager, a fearless rider who was renowned for her deadly accuracy with a rifle and who pitched her notably attractive pavilion tent close to the NRA offices. Mrs Way, who was also noted as an accomplished amateur actress, thought there ought to be competitions for ladies only at Bisley, as women should not have to compete with men on level terms.

Alas, the heat brought some problems. The camp of the Honourable Artillery Company was overrun with rabbits and then rats, while a number of people complained about bites from a plague of singularly odd insects which they nevertheless managed to catch, dead and alive, and exhibit before the Staff Captain, Captain Simpson. The Captain's Army training stood him in good stead. Faced with such an enemy, he issued an order that all blankets in the military camp were to be brought out at 8 a.m. the following day, shaken vigorously, and then left in the sun for an hour, weather permitting. 'If any were left alive after this ordeal the British Army are not so agile as they used to be,' reflected one wry observer.

Well over 2,500 people stayed on the Common, and more than eighty newspapers and Press agencies sent reporters to cover the Meeting from where they sent out over one million words. In addition, more than 26,000 letters were delivered and nearly 39,000 posted. There were several topics of note to write about: the prospect of a Boys' camp at Bisley for schools without a Cadet Corps, which was very much the idea of the Chairman, Lord Cheylesmore; Captain Fremantle's suggestion that the Association should start a collection of the various rifles that had been used in the principal competitions over the past forty-five years; and the growing fear that the War Office wanted to disband or at least diminish the Volunteer Force. 'Was he the Running Man?' queried one correspondent on the visit to the Camp by the much disliked Secretary of State for War, H.O. Arnold-Forster.

Quite a few of the words written concerned the visit to the Camp by King Edward VII, whose much beflagged train pulled into the Camp station at twelve minutes to two—two minutes ahead of schedule—on the final Saturday of the 1905 Meeting. Accompanied by the Crown Prince of Greece, the King was met by Lord Cheylesmore and members of the Council, and a population in the Camp which was thought to have doubled in the course of a few hours. After inspecting the guard of honour, the King was driven slowly along a route lined with Royal Marines and hundreds of boys from the Shaftesbury School. Lunch was taken in the Pavilion and, it was noted, the amiable Lord Cheylesmore engaged the King in animated conversation throughout the meal, while the Army Service Corps band left the Umbrella Tent for a while to provide the company with music.

After lunch, and posing for a group portrait taken by Mr Fry of Brighton, the King toured several of the Colonial camps and was then driven to the Stickledown range to watch the final of The King's Prize. By chance, he happened to be standing right behind the winner, Sergeant A.J. Comber, of the 2nd Volunteer Brigade East Surrey, who was immediately enveloped by a congratulatory crowd. The King, when told that Comber was probably the victor, laughed and replied, 'I hope he is, it would be hard if he were not, after all the shaking of hands.'

The King's Prizewinner was presented to the King, who stayed at Bisley just long enough to award Comber his Gold Medal at the prizegiving ceremony, and, again, to shake him warmly by the hand. While the cheers resounded round the Umbrella Tent, Comber left the platform and walked straight up to the place where his mother was sitting, to give her a hug and three affectionate kisses. The old lady had fainted when the news of her son's success was announced, now reporters were able to glean a little more information as she wept tears of joy. Comber, a thirty-six-year-old stone-mason born in Wimbledon, was a married man with six children. A member of the Southfields Rifle Club, he had served in South Africa and, since his return, had shot in The King's Prize five times, winning the Silver Medal four years before. He was a life-long abstainer from alcohol and tobacco, 'not strictly so, but practically,' he added, and was keen to point out that two of his brothers had made it into the final stage of The King's Prize. 'He has always been such a good boy,' sobbed his mother, 'I have never had the slightest trouble with him.'

Meanwhile, on the platform, Lord Cheylesmore welcomed the King in a brief speech and presented him with a gold medal, an exact replica of the one His Majesty had presented to Comber. The King, in his reply, cast his mind back forty-five years to recall how he had witnessed the shot that his mother, Queen Victoria, had fired on Wimbledon Common to inaugurate the NRA, and then fifteen years to when he had stood beside his wife, then Princess Alexandra, who fired the first shot on Bisley Common. He spoke of his 'deepest interest in the well-being of this most excellent and national institution,' and his delight in seeing so many competitors from the Colonies taking part in the rifle-shooting contests which could only help to bring the Empire closer together. ' ... Though intended for self-preservation, and to prevent the nearer approach of an enemy, still I hope it is, in its way, a peaceful occupation ... '

❧ ❧ ❧ ❧

A Miniature Bisley, with Service rifles fitted with tubes or adaptors, had been held at Olympia in April, 1903. It had run at a loss, but had otherwise been taken to be a great success. The Society of Miniature Rifle Clubs had joined in the event and, in 1905, there were discussions between the society and the NRA about an amalgamation as both appeared to be covering the same ground. The move came to nought as the NRA determined they would be contributing more in the way of finances to the marriage, and so the following year, again in April, the NRA organised its own Miniature Meeting which was held in Exeter.

That year, at Bisley, the weather was everything that could be desired throughout the Meeting, which closed with the presentation of prizes by the Duke of Connaught. The Lords and Commons Match was revived—the Lords winning the Vizianagram; a Miniature Bisley was held at the headquarters of the London Rifle Brigade; a permanent exhibition of rifles was opened in the Council offices; and, at the end of July 1906, Lord Cheylesmore's dream became a reality when the Boys' camp at Bisley was opened. The Chairman's enthusiasm for the venture was such that not only had he persuaded the King to donate fifty guineas to the scheme but he had also secured twenty-five guineas from the Prince of Wales, ten guineas from the Duke of Connaught, and, from numerous others, sums of varying sizes such as a donation of £100 from J.A.Mullens, whose prize in the main Meeting had been running since 1881.

A number of schools expressed interest in the scheme, but many preferred to wait and see how successful the venture would be. Nevertheless, in the first year, twenty-three schools took part which meant that on Monday, 30 July 1906 nearly 400 boys marched into Camp, accompanied by twenty-nine masters, for a six-day course, covering rifle drill and practice, physical and company drill, tent pitching and striking. Reveille was at 6 a.m. and the day ended with a Tattoo at 9 p.m., and Lights Out at 9.30 p.m., and when the prizes came to be presented at the end of the week by the Chairman's elder son, the Hon.H.O.F.Eaton, everyone involved agreed that the enterprise had been a huge success.

The 1907 Meeting had a chilly beginning. The Common was a cold desert inhabited by a bleak and bitter wind which put the range officers into their topcoats and sent shivering inhabitants scurrying around for eiderdowns, blankets and hot drinks. But then, after a few days, the sun came out and with it the summer muslins and the sun hats, causing one poetic correspondent to write, 'Bisley, the chrysalis of yesterday, is Bisley the butterfly of today.'

For Australia, it was the year she added 'the gem that was wanting to a tiara of successes,' when, after a close-run final, Lieutenant W.C. Addison, a thirty-two-year-old wheat merchant from Middleton, Southern Australia, snatched a victory and won The King's Prize. His broad-shouldered, six-foot frame in khaki uniform and slouch hat had attracted the attention of not a few admiring eyes. He was 'straight as a dart, and comely at that,' enthused the *Daily Telegraph* reporter, who also discovered that Addison's sixty-seven-year-old father hailed from South Staffordshire and had begun his shooting career at Wimbledon. But was he, enquired the correspondent in the perennial question which always concerned his readers, was he an abstainer, like the correspondent himself? Addison, unlike some previous winners who had chosen to prevaricate somewhat, was quick and adamant in his reply. 'No,' he said firmly, 'I'm neither a teetotaller nor a non-smoker.'

At the end of the year, a select band of the top British riflemen[1] had another opportunity to compete against Addison when the NRA sent a team on a tour of Canada and Australia, to take part in the Palma Trophy in Ottawa in September and the Empire Match in Sydney the next month. The team were given a rousing send-off at Euston Station on the morning of 9 August by a great party of friends and several members of the NRA

Council, including Lord Cheylesmore. Later that day, when they boarded the *Empress of Britain* at Liverpool Docks, Richardson, the team captain, noted that there were ninety-eight pieces of luggage—only one of which failed to arrive at its destination.

The ship arrived in Quebec on 16 August and, after some delay, docked in Ottawa at 11.30 p.m., where, despite the late hour, the team was met by a reception party from the Dominion Rifle Association. 'Colonials have always put us to shame in the many attentions they pay to us,' said Richardson.

Before the date of the Palma Match, the team had three weeks to practise in all manner of weather at the Rockcliffe range, three miles out of Ottawa, which they found 'very fair and open'. Richardson bemoaned the British rifles' weak bolt action and crude sights, and was not happy even when they changed to new rifles and ammunition. There was continual nickel fouling and, from the beginning, news reached the team of the amazing scores being made by the Americans with their peep-sights. The reports proved to be true and the British team were beaten by the Americans by 59 points and by the Canadians by 18 points.

No money had been spared to prepare the American rifles and ammunition, while the British were forced to use considerably inferior Service pattern rifles and ammunition which worked less well than at Bisley. It was a distinctly despondent team which joined the great banquet to which the President of the Dominion Rifle Association, Colonel Sam Hughes, and the Canadian Premier, Sir Wilfrid Laurier, had been invited. 'We have today learned not one lesson, but several. May we profit thereby! Britain has a reputation for muddling along, and for usually coming out all right in the end, even though it does mean a bit extra on the Income Tax! However, we have today come out all wrong. Rifle shooting is too exact a science to trust to a chapter of accidents,' Richardson reflected sadly.

But there was good news to be drawn from the enthusiasm of various states in Australia who were keen to compete against the British team. The schedule was rearranged to enable them to visit Queensland, New South Wales, Victoria, Tasmania, and South Australia, and, with a warm send-off, albeit at two o'clock in the morning, the team set off on a five-day rail journey across Canada in carriages which left a lot to be desired. Then, after

---

[1] The team, with Col. J.D.Hopton as Commandant, Major P.W.Richardson as Capt. and Capt. L.Lloyd as Adjutant, was reckoned to be the strongest that could possibly have been assembled, consisting of J.Fraser, E.L.Parnell, G.McHaffie, H.Ommundsen, J.A.Wallingford, W.E.Stephenson, A.J.Comber, F.E.Varley, H.Robinson, A.G.Fulton, A.J.Raven, W.Tatlow, J.E.Martin, J.H.Cowan and A.Lawrance.

a trip round the town with the Mayor of Vancouver, there followed a three-week voyage on board a crowded steamer. There were memorable stops along the way—Honolulu, with a trip to the aquarium; and Fiji, which included a comedy with Neptune involving a number of the team getting sprayed with blue paint and dumped into a large bath.

After twenty-three days of inactivity at sea, however, Richardson reported the pleasure in seeing on the horizon those strange Australian hills, the Glass Houses, in a blaze of golden sunset and experiencing 'a certain feeling of pride in being the first party of British riflemen to step on the hospitable shores of Australia.'

An enthusiastic welcome greeted the team in Brisbane, headed by the State Commandant, Colonel Lyster, and the President of the Queensland Rifle Association, Sir Alfred Cowley. Also in the party was Alex Ferguson, winner of The Queen's Prize at Wimbledon in 1880. The team enjoyed their week in Brisbane, with the temperatures up in the nineties, although they were nonplussed by the queer echelon formation of the firing points on the ranges, which made it look as if shooting was going on all over the place. They only heard of one accident, Hopton reported, and that was when a water-tank was emptied after being hit by a stray bullet. And despite the value of water in those parts, the owner expressed his complaints in the mildest of terms. Eight men, members of the North London Rifle Club, shot successfully against the Queensland Rifle Association, and other team members won prizes and were congratulated by the Governor of Queensland, Lord Chelmsford, and enjoyed a picnic lunch with Commander Pethebridge, secretary of the Commonwealth Defence Committee, on the river on board his launch.

The next stop was for the Empire Match in Sydney, where the team received 'every possible honour and attention from all concerned'. The highlight of the visit was a trip with the State Commandant, General Gordon, in a coach and six to an official reception given by the Premier of the State of New South Wales, Mr Wade.

As to the ranges at Randwick, a few miles out of the city, Hopton thought them 'very difficult', prone to a devastating wind dubbed the Southerly Buster, which caused him to remark in his diary, 'Our chances for the Empire match do not look rosy.' An initial loss of points to the Australians and the New Zealanders seemed to unsettle the British team and they never reached their form and so were beaten by the Australians by 52 points, and by 3 points by the New Zealanders. 'As we foreshadowed,' said the noble Richardson, 'Australia had the best team and every one is satisfied that the best team won.'

Still, the team were fêted lavishly, and especially enjoyed a 'great water picnic on the magnificent harbour'. Overwhelmed with invitations, the British divided into two parties to take part in more competitions and entertainments which included a song from the Premier of Tasmania. 'We wondered how our Prime Minister at home would feel if asked to imitate this example,' wrote Richardson. The two parties met up again in Melbourne, capital of Victoria, and continued on a winning streak which had returned to them immediately following the Empire Match. On their last day in Australia, the team were taken on a trip to Mount Lofty and Marble Hill where they had lunch in the bush and tea in a farmhouse and ended the day with a Smoking Concert.

The majority of the team sailed out of Port Adelaide for the journey home on 28 November, the Governor-General sending a farewell telegram, in which he expressed the hope that the trip would be the forerunner of many more. The others remained to explore more of the continent, while one of the team, the quiet and unassuming first-class shot, Comber, decided to settled there permanently as he simply could not face again the rough seas which would carry him home.

༄ ༄ ༄ ༄

The Bisley Stonehenge was erected in 1908. In fact, the edifice was simply a circle of flagpoles put up by the Council in honour of the representatives of the fifteen nations due to visit the Camp to compete in the shooting competitions of the fourth, recently revived Olympic Games, held for the most part at the Shepherd's Bush Stadium in London.

There was a total of thirteen events in the four sections covering Rifle Shooting, Miniature Rifle Shooting, Revolver and Pistol Shooting, and Running Deer Shooting, the most important being the International Match, between teams of six, using Service rifles, at six distances. There were riflemen from Canada, the United States, Australia, Holland, Hungary, Germany, Belgium, Norway, Greece, France, Denmark, and Sweden. The Italians failed to materialise, while the Russians were represented by a team from Finland who made up their own ammunition on the ranges. A wide variety of weapons and shooting positions was allowed.

The participants faced a mixed bag of weather during the three-day shoot which took place just before the Meeting. Blustery winds and heavy rains, which delayed the opening match by an hour and turned roads and pathways into running streams, didn't make conditions any easier for the Continentals who were mostly used to shooting under cover. Misunderstandings abounded among the markers and the bartenders, caused by the confusion of foreign tongues: one night, a Hungarian, searching in vain for his tent, approached a local and gesticulated his desire to find his bed by putting the side of his head on clasped hands. The Englishman, initially bemused, suddenly hit on the answer and drew a map whereby the Hungarian was able to obtain relief from a nearby chemist for his toothache.

By Saturday, the closing day, on which the International was held, the rain had lifted to be replaced by more gusty winds and ever-changing light. Despite the unsettled weather, an enormous crowd had turned out, and among the spectators was the Crown Prince of Sweden who had motored down from London to watch the event and to visit the various camps including that of the Malay States who were competing at the Meeting and who had assembled for the Royal visit dressed 'in their quaint Eastern garments'. The number of wires which had been sent daily to another keen observer of the Olympic events, the King of Norway, increased as the match progressed ...

The International was won decisively by the favourites, the Americans, with their new short Springfield. They had led at all but one of the distances. Behind them by 34 points came Great Britain; 59 points behind them, was Canada. The Americans' captain, General Drane, summed up the reasons for the victory: 'Good men, good teamwork, good rifles and good ammunition won us the match.' In addition to the high-velocity bullets and superior weapons, Lieutenant-Colonel Fremantle, captain of the British team,[1] pointed also to the fact that the Americans had adopted an aperture back-sight which gave them a huge advantage from the outset. And General Drane was quick to observe that if the weather had been better, the British and the Americans between them 'would have licked the world's rifle records', as the British team was the strongest he had ever encountered.

However, the Individual Competition for match rifles at 1,000 yards, was won by a renowned international shot, Colonel J.K.Millner of the Irish Rifle Association, whose score was five points above his nearest rival. And, at the end of the competition, Britain had won five golds, seven silvers, and six bronzes, their nearest rivals, the Americans, having managed only to take three golds, two silver and one bronze.

In April 1908, drawing from experiences in the Boer War, the War Office disbanded the Yeomanry and Volunteer Force and introduced the Territorials, a more strictly regulated defence body of men, to be trained on

---

[1] Members of the British team were Pte. A.G.Fulton; Ar.-Sgt. J.E.Martin; Sgt. H.Ommundsen; Ar.-Sgt. W.G.Padgett; Major F.E.Varley; and Major P.W.Richardson, who had captained the British team on its tour the year before.

military lines and who could be called upon, as required by law, to defend the realm. Combined with an Army Council directive on the ways rifle shooting practice should, as far as possible, approximate war conditions, it was thought this move could sound the death knell of the NRA which had pledged itself 'to give permanence to the Volunteer Force'. Instead, under the careful guidance of Lord Cheylesmore, the Association survived, accepting Territorial in place of Volunteer and increasing the number of competitions with a moving target. The Army Rifle Association, which used the Bisley ranges in the week before the Meeting, was the first to comply with the new proposals.

There was a good deal of disquiet among members of the Association about the War Office manoeuvres. Some of them felt the NRA, with its equal if not superior knowledge about rifle shooting, had not been adequately consulted about the changes but, ever the diplomat, Lord Cheylesmore was determined not to see the Association splinter in disagreement. While he pacified the more passionate members and dealt with the determined Government officials, he insisted publicly that there was no bad blood between the two. 'It has been the earnest desire of the Council,' he said, 'to assist the War Office in every possible way consistent with the knowledge gained by the practical experience of its members, than whom there are none more qualified to advise on all matters connected with rifles and shooting.'

Other changes, of a more acceptable nature, made inroads into the Camp that year: the electric light and cinematograph displays, the latter provided by the Kineto Company, which entertained the Olympic competitors as well as the visitors to the Meeting. While Lord Cheylesmore asked for a new invention, the Young's Army Rapid Potato Peeler, to be tried out in the Camp kitchen. There was a limit to progress, however, so members had to wait another four years until the telephone was introduced. Initially, it was thought that it would prove too great a nuisance with wives and girlfriends calling the main office all day to enquire about the position of their loved ones in the competitions.

The NRA's Jubilee Banquet of 1909, celebrating the first meetings of the Association held at Spencer House, was an impressive occasion. Held in the week before the Meeting began, on 8 July, at the Prince's Restaurant in Piccadilly, the Association's President, the Prince of Wales (later George V), and its Patron, the Duke of Connaught, presided over 300 guests, each of whom was presented with an illustrated history, its foreword written by Lord Cheylesmore. Among those assembled was the first Chairman of the Association, the Earl of Wemyss, who had been actively involved in its foundation, the Duke of Wellington, the Secretary of State for War,

R.B.Haldane, and two other former Chairmen, the Earl of Ducie and the Earl Waldegrave.

Seated at one of the long tables leading down from the top table were twenty winners of The King's or Queen's Prize, including Mr J.Wyatt, then in his eighties, who had won the prize in 1864.

The Prince of Wales, in his speech proposing the 'continued prosperity of the National Rifle Association, coupled with the name of Lord Cheylesmore,' outlined the Association's history, praising it for contributing to the development of the rifle, establishing strong links with the Empire, and encouraging a growth of interest in shooting in both young and old. In effect, for discharging 'a national duty in a truly national spirit'. Lord Cheylesmore rose to his feet to give his reply, and was greeted by loud and prolonged cheers. Once again, the Chairman took the opportunity to maintain that the Association had never criticised the War Office. On the contrary, it had only ever been desirous of helping and of serving its country, although, he added, 'there is no body of men who have received so little recognition as the men who are sitting round this table for the services they have done for the country.' But, he insisted, it was important to retain the bull's-eye because that was what helped to maintain an interest in shooting. It was a point which was greeted with loud cheers of deep-felt agreement.

The Earl of Wemyss recalled the inaugural shot fired by Queen Victoria: 'The echo of it rang over the Common and reverberated throughout the whole of the Empire.' He referred to the connection between the Association and the War Office, without whom, he reminded his audience, there would never have been an annual Rifle Meeting. And Mr Haldane, in his speech, went out of his way to emphasise the happier side of the relationship: 'The National Rifle Association has been the very foundation of interest in the rifle movement throughout this country, and long may it continue to be so whatever changes may take place in our methods, for in this world nothing will stand still. I am sure of this, that the relationship between the Department of State for which I am temporarily responsible and your Association, the tenure of whose life is much more durable, will continue to be cordial.' This was the first time in recent years that the War Office had raised some good-humoured laughter among the ranks of the Association and had come close to receiving an enthusiastic reception.

The Jubilee Meeting of the Association opened on 12 July. Bisley 1909, wrote Lord Cheylesmore, differed from the early Wimbledon years in that it had less of the picnic element and was essentially a business meeting. But in order not to discourage visitors, the Chairman was quick to add that 'a visit to the healthy, breezy common is the finest of tonics for the jaded Londoner and that during the meeting the gay colours of the ladies' dresses, the many-coloured uniforms, the rows of snow-white tents, and the heather-clad hills in the distance make up a picture as refreshing as it is pleasant.'

Bisley had certainly changed, even since the previous year. More trees had been planted and fresh gravel roads had been laid between the Council offices and the Century Range. And it had grown. The range staff consisted of ninety-three officers and 905 NCOs and men. About 4,500 targets were used, and, exclusive of Revolver and Miniature ammunition, the amount of Service Rifle ammunition expended amounted to 536,150 rounds. And, in its Jubilee year, the NRA welcomed teams from Canada, Natal, Transvaal, Southern Rhodesia, and the East African Protectorate, as well as individual competitors from Australia, New Zealand, the West Indies, Shanghai, Ceylon, Cape Town, the Orange River Colony, the Malay States, and the Straits Settlements. The Canadians shot particularly well, carrying off the Mackinnon, Kolapore, Jubilee, and *Graphic*, as well as the Prince of Wales's prize.

There was also a group from Serbia, whose country was destined to figure so prominently in the news, and the fate of Europe, within a few years. Members of the party, led by Major Borislav Pashtrovitch, had been shooting at a meeting in Hamburg and were overwhelmed by the size and the grandeur of Bisley. They were introduced to Field-Marshal Earl Roberts who expressed the hope that the party would make a return trip to a Meeting at Bisley. Yes, the Serbians all agreed, they certainly hoped they would.

The weather, though fine and fair, was not unduly sunny. However, on the rare occasions that the sun eased its way through the clouds, there were those who left the ranges to sun-bathe on the grass or the heather and enjoy the music from the band. However, the final stage of The King's Prize, for which there were more than 1,400 entries, was shot under wet and windy conditions. The winner was a popular figure on the ranges, Corporal Harry Burr of the London Rifle Brigade, who had won the Prince of Wales's prize three years before. He had also achieved the highest individual score in the Mackinnon, and yes, the thirty-seven-year-old surveyor who lived in Lewisham was very abstemious and 'only occasionally could he be induced to indulge in a cigarette.'

The Jubilee Meeting was tinged with sadness following the accidental fatal shooting of Armourer-Sergeant McCracken by a fellow Sergeant in the Royal Marine Light Infantry. Both had thought all the cartridges in a revolver had been spent, but it was not the case and the weapon was accidentally discharged after they had left the firing point. A fund was immediately opened for McCracken's child and nineteen-year-old widow.

But there was cause for celebration when, at the general meeting, it was announced that the King had conferred on Lord Cheylesmore the decoration of Knight Commander of the Royal Victorian Order, and made Members of the same order three men on the Council: Colonel J. Barlow, Mr Henry Whitehead, and Mr A.P. Humphry. The same honour was conferred on Lieutenant-Colonel C.R. Crosse, who was that year celebrating twenty-five years as the Association's Secretary, for which service he was presented with a carved oak grandfather clock, a carved oak writing desk and a pearl scarf pin which had all been bought out of money raised from more than 1,000 members and other friends.

One of the visitors to the Camp was the Duke of Connaught who couldn't help but notice the number of bloody noses and sticking plasters among the competitors. The reason was a popular new aperture sight which proved addictive as well as vindictive. 'What is a man's nose,' said one convert, the hardy Magpie in the *Military Mail*, 'compared with a string of bull's-eyes, which this sight seems to make an easy matter of?'

At 5.30 p.m. on the final Saturday, under a bright and sunny sky, the Prince and Princess of Wales motored into the Camp to present the prizes before a gathering of some 3,000, and, to mark the special occasion, Lord Cheylesmore presented the Princess with a souvenir, a rifle set with diamonds. But there was something else which caught the imagination of the Prince of Wales, the Duke of Connaught and numerous others, and that was an invention of Mr W.M. Mackintosh—a mobile coat-tent which, within minutes, could be transformed from an ordinary waterproof greatcoat for one man into a tent providing comfortable accommodation for eight. In fact, as the manufacturers proudly displayed, four coats could be turned into an Emergency Hospital. The impressed and beady-eyed Magpie in the *Military Mail* noted the enthusiasm of the Prince and of the accompanying general and staff officers. 'I hear,' he informed his readers, 'that arrangements are being made for an inspection of this clever invention, to take place at an early date, before the Army Council ... '

In 1910, the NRA lost one of its founders and an early Chairman, Earl Spencer, and another former Chairman, Sir Henry Aubrey-Fletcher. The urbane Edward VII also died, to be succeeded by his popular son, George V, who, following tradition, readily agreed to become Patron of the Association. The Coronation the following year was marked by the presentation of a gold, silver, and bronze medal to the competitors who made the highest score in the Service Rifle Competition, one of the events in the International Meeting held in Rome in June. (In the event, the gold and silver medals were won by competitors from France, the bronze by a Dutchman.)

By now, the Association had affiliated to it 2,083 Rifle Clubs, thirty-two of which were in the Dominions, with a total membership of 125,909, and 159 Air Rifle Clubs which had begun an affiliation in 1907. The new figure targets had been introduced and, in the early part of the year, a new firing point at 1,200 yards was made on the Stickledown Range, and there was an increasing demand to use the ranges throughout the year from Army Regiments, Territorial Battalions, Rifle Associations and Clubs, schools and colleges. The time had arrived, the Council decided, for the Association to have its own publication, a monthly journal to be delivered to members, free of charge, at a cost of one penny per month, or two shillings per annum. Circulation soon reached 5,000, and a postage charge was rapidly introduced.

The Meeting was preceded that year by the Empire Match, with teams from Great Britain, Canada, Australia, India, and Singapore competing for the shield in heavy rain and bitingly cold winds. In addition to the captain, the Hon. T.F.Fremantle, and the adjutant, Sergeant A.S.Bates, twelve men assembled on the ranges at Bisley a week before the match was due to take place and from these was picked the British team: Lance-Sergeant H.G.Burr; Private A.G.Fulton; Quartermaster-Sergeant R.Hawkins; Armourer-Sergeant J.E.Martin; Sergeant H.Ommundsen; Captain E.L.Parnell; Major T.Ranken; Sergeant-Major J.A.Wallingford.

The British team were leading on the short ranges by 7 points, but on the long ranges they faced a formidable Australian team and a Canadian team armed with a new pattern of Ross Rifle with its advantage of an improved trigger pull and a heavy barrel. Then the British captain had to be called away. Ranken, Wallingford, and Ommundsen took over the coaching, while the weather burst into storms of heavy downpours and strong winds, creating conditions to which a number of the competitors were totally unused. At 900 yards, the team began to increase its lead with high scores from Ommundsen, Burr and Parnell. At 1,000 yards, Ranken, coached by Wallingford, began with an inner and went on to make a remarkable 49. Wallingford himself made 47, and only one member of the team had a miss counted in his score. At the six ranges Wallingford had made a total of 284 out of a possible 300. Ranken made 280, while Fulton and Burr made 278 and 277 apiece. Thus Great Britain won a victory with 2,177 points, a lead of 72 points over the runners-up, Canada, and 132 points ahead of the Australians in third place.

The prizes at the following year's Meeting of 1911 were presented by Lord Kitchener, who had last visited Bisley on the occasion of its opening in 1890. He hoped to return within a few years, he told the assembly, to do a little shooting under the guidance of Lord Cheylesmore.

In that year, before the nightmare of the First World War began, the new Georgian Bisley was bathed in exceptionally dry, warm and fine weather. There was not even a drop of rain and the high temperatures soared on the final day to 90°F, the highest ever recorded at a Meeting. A Canadian, Private W.J.Clifford, won The King's Prize. The Church, meanwhile, which had always played a significant part in the life of the Meeting, took on an even bigger role that year. Divine Service on the Middle Sunday was conducted by the Bishop of Singapore, better known on the ranges as C.J.Ferguson-Davie, winner of the Silver Medal in 1904, and a match was organised between the clerical, medical and legal professions. The Bishop captained the clerics, scoring eight bull's-eyes out of ten. Against such competition, justice could not prevail and came third. The Church came first.

The Olympic Games of 1912 were held in Stockholm, and captain of the British team was Major P.W.Richardson.[1] Lord Cheylesmore gave a lunch for the men at the Trocadero restaurant the week before their departure, so that in the early hours of 20 June, there were no official farewells, only a small party of friends who gathered on the platform at King's Cross to wave goodbye. At the end of the month, they were followed by the Small Bore Team and the Pistol Team. For the Rifle Team, the journey from Hull to Göteborg took little more than a few days, and Richardson had four days to watch men practising on the Kaknäs range, about two miles out of Stockholm, before selecting the team.

The day of the International Match was hot and windless, and the light extremely bright which the riflemen found tiring on the eyes, and Richardson realised that such conditions placed the team at a disadvantage against the Americans who were using aperture sights. Among other things which made him unhappy was the Swedish disc system of marking which he thought inexact and inferior to the spotting system at Bisley. The outcome was a resounding win for the Americans, who carried off the Gold Medal with a lead of 85 points. Richardson was well pleased that under such adverse conditions, the British team picked up the Silver beating the Swedes by 32 points.

One thing that impressed Richardson was the interest the Swedes showed in rifle shooting. Not only did the Crown Prince make two trips to the ranges and the Government give the movement financial support, but in a population of five and a half million there were 148,762 active shooting

---

[1] As well as Richardson, the British team consisted of Sgt. H.G.Burr; Pte. A.G.Fulton; Sgt. H.Ommundsen; Capt. E.L.Parnell; Sgt. J.Reid; Mr E.Skilton.

members. 'We should have 1,300,000 in Great Britain to be in the same proportion,' he reflected.

The Small Bore team carried off two silvers, a bronze, and a gold in the Team Competition at fifty metres, in which Mr E.J.Lessimore made a score of 195, a result which was not equalled during the meeting. The Pistol team, due to a misunderstanding, arrived late and, in the three competitions they were still able to enter, they carried off three bronzes. One of the most colourful figures on the Pistol ranges was Walter Winans, an almost un-beatable revolver shot who had won the Revolver Aggregate at Bisley five years running. Winans, who lived in Kent and kept a luxurious hut at Bisley, was an American of diverse talents. He had been invited to shoot at the Tsar's bear preserves and was well known as a prize-winning horse-breeder. At the Swedish Olympics, however, his greatest achievement was the Art Prize for Sculpture, for a model of a trotting horse harnessed to a sulky. It was, said one critic, a masterpiece.

A week after the shooting competitions ended in Sweden, the annual Meeting opened and, as the *Daily Telegraph* put it, 'What has been termed the eternal woman question has come to stay at Bisley.' The problem was where to put them. They could visit the Camp. They could have their own rooms. They could be members of the Association. They could even shoot, sometimes considerably better than the men. They could organise their own shooting competitions, such as a recent one held by the Surrey Ladies, but still they were not allowed to stay in the Camp overnight. They lodged outside. And, as far as the shooting was concerned, they remained some-what of a novelty. 'There is nothing to weep for over all this,' said one man, philosophically, 'for if women shoot well, men must just push along and shoot still better.'

Something that was allowed into the Camp that year, and to stay, was the telephone, which was installed in the Refreshment Pavilion in time for the Meeting enabling visitors 'to communicate with London and the various Local Exchanges' and found to be 'a great convenience'. More space was demanded by the increasing number of shopkeepers who set up their stalls in the Bazaar, and while a new iron Exhibition Pavilion was erected, the Camp itself grew in size as the Association bought some land adjoining the Common at Cowshot.

Again the Meeting was blessed with fine weather, and a notable first was made when Private Arthur Fulton won The King's Prize, following in the footsteps of his father, George, who had won the prize in 1888.

∽ ∽ ∾ ∾

'I hope, with the Secretary of State for War, that our young men both here and in the Dominions will rise to the future before them, and by patriotism, loyalty, and steadiness make themselves feared by any who might come in opposition to them. I hope by their skill in shooting they will set an example to the world.' The year was 1913 and the words were spoken by Lord Cheylesmore at a banquet in London attended by the War Secretary, Colonel J. Seeley, and presided over by the Duke of Connaught, to welcome the teams taking part in the Empire Match held at Bisley the weekend before the Meeting.

By rights, the match should have taken place in the country of the holders of the trophy, but as Great Britain could not send a team to Sydney, the Australians decided to bring Mohammed to the mountain; also joining in the competition were teams from Canada and India. Once again, Colonel Fremantle captained the British team,[1] 'the finest one ever put into the field,' proclaimed the NRA *Journal*.

The match was shot at six distances, ten shots at each, with two sighting shots, compulsory and not convertible, and the British got off to a good start, dropping a fraction less than three points per man at the first distance, 300 yards. Fulton and Gray took top honours with 49. At 500, the favourite distance for the Lee-Enfield, things improved. With the first four men down Britain dropped only 3 points, while Halls and Ommundsen scored possibles. By the end of the first day the wind was playing havoc with the shooting, but Mann put on 50 to finish top scorer of the day—one point above Fulton who had scored three 49s.

The next day, the 800 yards proved to be the Canadian Waterloo, with one of the best shots scoring 5 0 3 0, and Australia settled into second position. But no one could reach the British who were in top form, despite the disappointing scores of Burr and Gray which they put down to the hide-and-seek light playing over the ranges and on their nerves. At the end, their scoreboard, decorated with thistles and roses entwined, showed Britain's winning result—2,210. The Australian score was 2,120; Canada, 2,073; India, 1,953.

In 1913, for the first time, civilians became eligible to enter for the Grand Aggregate, and in the Donegall there had been a magnificent score of 83 points by a lady, Mrs L. Alton of the Ham and Petersham Rifle Club, and a score of 82 made by another lady, Miss A. M. Sharp of the South London.

---

[1] The British team consisted of L.-Cpl. H. A. Mann; Pte. A. G. Fulton; Pte. C. W. Wirgman; Pte. W. Gray; Sgt. H. Ommundsen; L.-Sgt. H. G. Burr; Ar.-Sgt. J. E. Martin; Pte. W. A. Halls.

But the main topic of conversation that year concerned a War Office committee investigating the workings of the Association and every Rifle Club in the country. So far there had been no outcome, Lord Cheylesmore told the disquieted members at the general meeting in the Umbrella Tent, where the crowd shivered as much over the uncertain news as from a chill northerly wind whipping up the sides of the canvas tent. There was concern that the War Office was seeking to gain control over the Association, that Bisley would have to be surrendered, that ammunition and Army markers would be withheld, the consequences of which would not only reduce the Association to the status of a small Rifle Club but also bring to an end the annual Meeting. The worries and the doubts continued to grow, despite assurances from the Chairman that the Council, two of whom, Colonel Fremantle and Major Ranken, were sitting on the committee, would do all in its power to protect the interests of the NRA.

In October, 1913, the Army Council informed the NRA that assistance with the Meeting would cease unless Territorial competitions followed the Musketry Regulations. The War Office argument was that they gave half a million rounds of specially selected ammunition and, more valuable, the time of a considerable number of Army personnel to carry out various duties at Bisley, in return for nothing other than the knowledge that a band of men could take a leisurely shot at a bull's-eye. What they wanted was a rifle meeting organised along the lines set down in a circular issued by the Hythe School six years before, in which there were fewer stationary targets, fewer if any bull's-eye targets, and firing was done on a time limit. All conditions designed to approximate those that would be encountered on the field of battle. They underlined their threat by intimating that there was also talk of a rival Territorial Army meeting being set up.

The disquiet within the NRA and the Rifle Clubs which had rumbled through the year, erupted now in a deluge of anger and disbelief. As the very life of Bisley was threatened, rifle shooting in Britain made headlines and letters were written to *The Times*. Was Bisley to remain the home for sporting riflemen or was it to be run on military lines which would exclude a number of enthusiasts from taking part? They felt aggrieved: hadn't they introduced rapid-firing competitions more than thirty years ago? Were not two-thirds of the competitions in 1913, under 800 yards, shot at non-bull's-eye targets? As well as encouraging competition among weapon manufacturers to improve their rifles, hadn't the NRA also shown the value of the aperture sight, which was only recently being realised by the Army, although the War Office still wanted to put a stop to them being used at Bisley which would prevent a number of competitors from abroad, such as the Canadians, taking part as an aperture was now fitted to their Service rifle? And, as the NRA pointed out continually, all that they received in kind was something in the region of £5,000, an almost invisible sum in comparison with the sums of money and the extra grants, particularly for teams travelling to Bisley, donated by overseas Governments. Canada, for example, gave £3,000 in cash, and a large amount of free ammunition.

A Rifle Union was founded to express riflemen's opinions and to give support to the beleaguered NRA which found itself in an acutely vulnerable position. Rifle shooting was becoming more expensive and the new Territorials had less time and money than their earlier counterparts, the Volunteers, to outlay, and, as a consequence, the number of Territorial competitors had been decreasing over the years. Added to which, the NRA relied heavily on military assistance to keep going. As it was, they managed to persuade the War Office to modify their proposals and to give financial assistance to encourage Territorials to attend the Meeting.

It was agreed that all Territorial Army competitions, complying with War Office requirements, would take place in the first week of the Meeting along with the schoolboy competitions, and those involving the Regular Army, Match Rifle events, and the Small Bore meeting. The King's Prize would run along the following lines—in the first stage: ten rounds deliberate at 200, 500 and 600 yards. Second stage: five rounds deliberate, ten rounds rapid, and five rounds snap at 300 yards. Third stage: fifteen rounds at short distances at disappearing targets. The competitions in the second week, for 'All Comers', would be shot under rules similar to those of the year before and would include the big team events such as the Mackinnon and the Kolapore. A new event, the Imperial, run along the lines of The King's Prize, would be open to all British subjects.

The most important concession which the NRA wrought out of the War Office was that the implementation of the new rules would be postponed until July 1915, so that opinion abroad could be gauged. As it was, events on an altogether different scale interposed. One man who could not accept what he thought to be tampering with the very foundations of the NRA was the Earl of Wemyss. Nothing and no one could persuade him otherwise. He resigned as Vice-President, even resigning his membership of the Association, despite the pleas of Lord Cheylesmore, and in June 1914, at the age of ninety-five, one of the founders of the Association, its first Chairman, and always one of its most enthusiastic supporters, passed away.

As the storm clouds gathered over Europe that year, Bisley enjoyed a fine Meeting troubled with little rain and even less breeze, though the sunshine played hide and seek through the clouds. On the ranges, there were numerous competitors from abroad—India, Ceylon, Shanghai, Hong Kong, Perak, Cairo, Rhodesia, Khartoum, Jamaica and East Africa, as well as teams from Guernsey, Canada, and Australia. The King's Prize provided one of the most exciting finals ever witnessed, ending in a tie and then a shoot-off between Private Fulton and, the ultimate winner, Sergeant Dewar, while there was interest in the Bazaar in the automatic canteen which, on insertion of a coin, supplied hot or cold drinks instantly. An off-course and fast descending balloon containing three passengers caused some excitement and a ceasefire on the Century Range during the final stage of the Kolapore, and there was an abundance of congratulations for Ommundsen, the modest and popular crack shot, whose marriage to Miss Beatrice Lowrey was announced as taking place the week after the Meeting ended. The happy couple were then due to embark for Australia where the bridegroom was to shoot with the British team in the Empire. But events interceded in the honeymoon plans.

# CHAPTER FIVE

# *The War Years and the Winds of Change*

The outbreak of war meant that hostilities between the Association and the War Office ceased immediately, as attention was focussed on the defeat of the enemy abroad. Before the extent of the suffering in the trenches and of the appalling carnage was fully realised, patriotic fervour flourished, not least among members of the NRA, some of whom saw the First World War as 'the Grand Aggregate of national endeavour'.

Six days after Britain declared war on Germany, Lord Cheylesmore went to see Lord Kitchener, who had just been appointed Secretary of State for War in Asquith's Government. Kitchener, who had presented the prizes at the annual Meeting only three years before and had been among the guests at the opening ceremony in 1890, had served in the Boer War as Chief of Staff to Lord Roberts, an active Vice-President in the Association, and was more than familiar with the work that the NRA had done to help improve the standard of rifle shooting in the country. But he was not at all keen on Cheylesmore's idea of raising a battalion of the finest rifle shots in the world. 'Don't put all your best shots into one battalion,' he told Cheylesmore. But Cheylesmore had another idea. He proposed establishing a musketry camp for recruits at Bisley, the NRA providing the instructors. Kitchener jumped at the idea, but, within weeks, it became clear that more needed to be done, and quickly, and that Bisley was the place to do it.

The idea of a musketry camp was soon abandoned—instead a School of Musketry was to be established to provide Officer and NCO Instructors. As the scale of operations abroad expanded and the war rapidly consumed more and more men and resources, so the demand for qualified Instructors grew dramatically. The first request was for eighteen Officers and eighty NCO Instructors. By the middle of September 1914, the War Office were demanding another thirty-six Officers and sixty NCOs. The figures continued to rise, while the NRA School of Musketry, Bisley Camp, expanded its classes beyond rifle shooting.

From 1915, the School was authorized to give training in heavy and light guns, and range finding, and from 1918, there were classes dealing specifically with the revolver. Richardson and Captain H.Lattey gave lectures on sniping and the use of telescopic sights, which were published and sent to men serving in France and translated into French for use by the Belgian forces, and in a little over a year, the School undertook the calibration of more than 3,500 rifles. By the end of the war, the NRA School of Musketry had trained nearly 12,000 students, more than 4,000 Officers and nearly 8,000 NCOs. It was no wonder that when General Head Quarters sent Richardson to France in April 1917, to report on the Army sniping schools, he found that they were largely staffed by students from Bisley or by men who had been competitors during the NRA Meetings. While the NRA Blue Book, a training handbook on musketry regulations, ran through seven editions, and well over 35,000 copies. And it was not just in musketry instruction that the Association proved invaluable: at the Royal Woolwich Arsenal, Captain Hardcastle was helped in his inspection of all ammunition by a handful of NRA members—Maurice Blood, A.E.Rogers of the English Eight, Ernest Robinson, and young Arthur Fulton. 'If I had not got them I do not know how in the world I should get on with the work,' he told the assembly at the winter general meeting.

Initially, Major P.W.Richardson, the captain of a number of British teams on international tours who was appointed Chief Instructor, and his assistant, Lieutenant J.P.Somers, had incredibly limited resources. Their Instructors were a mixture of men they knew to be regular visitors to Bisley, personal friends, and members of Rifle Clubs, and they had nothing, in the way of guns and ammunition, other than what the NRA could itself provide. Fatigue duties were carried out by scouts or boys from a local school, while meals were provided, on a voluntary basis, by the North London Rifle Club and the Middlesex Rifle Association, whose manager and secretary, Mr John Dingley, also organised concerts in the Camp.

The School even had to search for its own students which it did by sending out hundreds of letters to secretaries of Rifle Clubs and to individual members of the Association. And yet, by November 1914, while some 5,000 men of the New Armies and the Territorial Force had spent three months in the Camp practising on the ranges, the School managed to fulfil its obligation to train for the 261 Battalions of the New Armies, seventy-seven Officers and 261 NCOs. Those who became Instructors represented every class of the community, the NRA noted in 1915, from schoolmasters to sanitary inspectors, pensioners to postmen, jewellers to joiners, blacksmiths to barristers.

By Christmas 1915, the School estimated that one and a half million troops had been taught musketry by men who had been trained at Bisley. A year later, it was also estimated that of the countrywide Rifle Club membership of 150,000, ten per cent had been killed or were missing, while thirty-five per cent had been wounded. In the first months of the war, the NRA lost some of its finest shots, among them Lieutenant H. Ommundsen and Sergeant J. Tippins who 'had no superiors with the rifle in any part of the world'. Ommundsen had won The King's Prize in 1913, and Tippins had in only a year trained a beginner to come within one point of a similar achievement. Both men were prolific prizewinners and famous Internationals. Tippins fell serving his machine gun. Ommundsen was killed by shell fire; he had been married but several months, in the week after the close of the 1914 Meeting.

Not surprisingly, the establishment of the School of Musketry meant changes in the Camp. All the Association's buildings, as well as the clubhouses and the private huts had been commandeered mainly for use as classrooms, and as early as 1915, the War Office had built forty large huts for accommodation. The following year, the huts had increased to some sixty and included stalls and sheds for horses and weapons. Where grass had grown there was now mud or bare sand. The earth was scarred and furrowed by troop manoeuvres. 'The Camp itself is still hut-covered like some great mining townships in Queensland or America,' the NRA noted in 1917, after three and a half years of war work, while the Siberia range had changed beyond recognition. Lord Cheylesmore told the Association's winter meeting: 'It looks like a river that is covered with Chinese junks and other well disguised objects, and you cannot tell anything about distance, the things do not look like targets at all.'

German prisoners-of-war worked on extending the Camp railway to Pirbright, Deepcut and Blackdown, and when the work was completed in the summer of 1917, the opening ceremony was carried out by the King and Queen. And, one afternoon close to Christmas that year, after her husband had inspected the School, Lady Murray, wife of General Sir Archibald Murray, the Commander-in-Chief at Aldershot, visited the Camp to open a recreation hut for the Women's Army Auxiliary Corps. Since the beginning of the war, the ranges at Bisley were open for limited use to the Volunteer Corps and to Rifle Club members who complained to Lord Cheylesmore about the exorbitant increase in the return railfare from London which had risen from a pre-war price of 1/6d to more than six shillings. On the intervention of the Association, the old cost was restored.

In 1917, because of the lack of attendance at the School itself, night classes for Volunteers were started at the Royal Courts of Justice in London, with additional lessons to be taken on Saturdays at Bisley. Despite the fact that about one in three Rifle Clubs had to suspend operations because of the war, the rest managed to survive. They opened their ranges to the Army, issued free ammunition to enlisted members, or lent their rifles to the police. Many recorded a significant increase in membership of boys under the age of eighteen and of women, some of whom became renowned Instructors, such as the members of the Bournemouth Ladies' Club. Nevertheless, while Rifle Clubs supplied numerous men for the Forces abroad, on the home front a great number of members were taken into the anti-aircraft defence units because of their marksmanship. The words of the late Lord Roberts began to take on a significant meaning. 'If the thousands of young men who pass their Saturday afternoons in watching football or cricket matches would devote some portion of their spare time and money to acquiring skill with the rifle, they would be fulfilling a sacred duty in preparing themselves for the emergency that may, probably will, arise.' What Britisher, added the Association, would not consider it an insult to be told that he is unable to or unwilling to protect his wife, his children and his home?

It was not Britons alone who felt the need to encourage rifle shooting skills in the country. In 1917, a South African, Colonel Raymond Schumacher, donated a sum of money to the NRA for boys' competitions to be held throughout the Dominions. More than 400 entered in the first year, among them Latymer School, Hammersmith, which entered twenty-four teams. In that year, Latymer also recorded that its old boys had received twenty-five Military Crosses, eight Military Medals, six Distinguished Service Medals, one Distinguished Service Cross, three other awards, fifteen mentions, and 400 commissions, as well as 140 casualties. Meanwhile, the Mullens prize which had been donated for the encouragement of shooting by Volunteers at unknown distances and at moving targets was given over to competitions for students at the School which, as far as possible, reproduced conditions that men might experience in the field.

The Camp was visited by numerous senior Army and War Office personnel. All came away impressed with the work being carried out at Bisley. In 1917, the United States declared war on Germany and by the spring of 1918, the Camp became even busier when American troops moved in to use the ranges and American Officers attended lectures. In June, they were followed by a detachment of Guards from Pirbright and, in the same month, King George V visited the Camp to watch the Military carry out light machine-gun trials.

By October 1918, the end of the war was in sight and the last class finished its training on 14 December. It was a time to celebrate. A shoot was arranged for all former members of staff, and six special souvenirs were presented to the winners. Despite the miserable weather, there were a number of entrants and, in the evening, about eighty former members of staff joined Lord Cheylesmore for a victory dinner. But the victory had been won at a cost. As the guests sang 'Auld Lang Syne', every one of them could count the loss of a friend. 'I hope we shall all meet again on the happy Common,' Major Munday said at the end of the spring meeting, earlier that year. 'When we do we shall miss a great number of our old friends, but there is this consolation, that they died for their country in a noble cause.'

ᔕᔕ ᔕᔕ ᔕᔕ ᔕᔕ

Those who had not visited Bisley for a while would scarcely recognise it, Lord Cheylesmore warned members in 1919 at the spring meeting in London, as the rural aspect of the place had been rather blotted out by the proliferation of War Office huts which had been built on the Common during the war for the accommodation of musketry pupils. One thing was for sure: the relationship between the Association and the War Office was now much more comfortable but, like so many others who had given so freely of time and finance during the war, immediately afterwards the NRA found itself short of funds. It was a problem which became increasingly acute in the immediate post-war years, with the number of shooting enthusiasts declining as, not unnaturally, weapons held an association for many which they preferred not to be reminded of.

Stalwart members of the NRA were sympathetic only to a degree with this feeling. What concerned them more was that men should still be prepared to defend their country, and that a general post-war apathy might lead to the demise of the NRA. 'We all want peace,' said Colonel Raymond Ffennell, 'but we have got to consider what is the surest way of getting it and of keeping it.' In 1920, Lord Cheylesmore warned members that the Association faced liquidation and an appeal was launched immediately. It was an appeal which was answered by the then War Office Minister, Mr Winston Churchill, who put his support in writing in a letter to the Chairman: 'I have read your Appeal with pleasure and fully appreciate the great value that the National Rifle Association has been to the country, not only in fostering the whole spirit of marksmanship which has been so long a national characteristic, but also in the consequent improvement in weapons. Nor is it possible to exaggerate the magnificent help that the Association gave during the Great War ... '

The rallying cry for funds, echoing the NRA's importance in national defence, was underlined in a strongly worded speech made at a banquet in London in 1925 by the NRA's President, the Prince of Wales (later, the

Duke of Windsor), a matter of weeks after the British Government recognised reluctantly the collapse of the monarchy and the permanence of the new Communist regime in Russia. 'Let us face the truth boldly, for once. Let us tell the world about ourselves fearlessly. We like rifle shooting. It really is our hobby. But it is something more. Each and every one of us knows that war has not ceased, that the continent of Europe is a seething pot of jealousy and distrust and envy and hatred, and that we may be fighting for our honour, our very existence as a nation, within a very short time. We love the rifle because it is a weapon and because it is not only the right but the duty of every citizen to be armed and trained in the use of arms. We are not just sportsmen. Let us emphasise that truth. Let us tell all our fellow citizens once and for all that we are not on the same plane as the golfer or footballer. We stand, with the Navy, the Army, the Air Force and the Territorial Army, between the vast mass of the unthinking, unarmed, and red ruin and disaster.' If the Association came to an end, said the Prince, it would be a 'calamity of Imperial dimensions that cannot be contemplated for a moment.' The appeal to the nation for funds was being made to enable the NRA to carry on with its work of inspiring a love of the rifle in the youth of the Empire.

Although the appeal eventually reached a sum sufficient to clear its £25,000 debt, the Association remained impoverished. Certainly, if it had not continued to receive its annual supply of some half a million rounds of ammunition free from the War Office, in addition to the Match Rifle ammunition supplied by ICI, the Meetings could not have continued. As it was, ranges and buildings needed renovating constantly, and, during the Meetings, there were always the additional expenses of the officers and men brought in to carry out range duties. In the 1920s, some 1,000 were needed; by the 1930s that figure had doubled. True, those forces came via the War Office and the various Service departments but the NRA still had to bear the cost of their working pay and allowances, Camp expenses, and what could be particularly costly, the travelling expenses. In all, said the Chairman, Lord Cheylesmore, in 1924, those particular costs, amounting to some £1,500, which had been borne out of the public purse would now have to be paid by the Association.

The NRA was not blind to the world outside the Camp. Post-war Britain was in an unhappy and unhealthy state: trade figures showed a depressing deficit, while unemployment was rising sharply. The Council had to watch everything that could affect its income, and no small matter was the cost of the railfare from London to Brookwood which had more than doubled its pre-war prices to become 7/10d for first class passengers and three shillings for third class. The Council fought long and hard, and in

1928 — the year the BBC
began regular, live broadcasts
on the final stage of The King's
Prize.

Miss Marjorie Foster, the first,
and to date, the only woman to
win The Queen's Prize, a feat
she achieved in 1930.

*Queen Elizabeth II visiting Bisley in 1960, to celebrate the NRA's centenary.*

*Prince Charles, Prince of Wales, who exercised his right as Duke of Cornwall to shoot in the Lords team in the Vizianagram in 1980. The Prince became President of the NRA in 1975.*

LEFT *An aerial view of Bisley.*    ABOVE *The NRA Offices on Bisley Common.*

BELOW *Sir Roland Gibbs (centre, facing), who became Chairman of the NRA in 1984.*

*Brigadier Peter Prescott, who became Secretary of the NRA in 1981.*

*Enthusiasts continue to use weapons from a bygone age at Bisley Meetings – and dress for the part.*

The military connection with Bisley is still strong, and the July Meeting is preceded by a week of competitions for the Services.

*Beating the Retreat — an annual ceremony which takes place on the first Tuesday in the July Meeting.*

*But all members of the family attend and take a keen interest in events.*

1922 won a reduction that entitled competitors to purchase a return ticket for the price of a single fare from anywhere in the country, a concession that continued until the outbreak of the Second World War.

Yet, despite its financial strictures, the NRA never forgot what it considered to be its duty: to train the young. In 1906, Earl Roberts initiated visits to Bisley for cadets from overseas, and reciprocal visits to Canada were begun for a team of British cadets, dubbed the Athelings, which translates from Old English to mean, the heirs to the throne. The Imperial Challenge Shield had been initiated in 1910, its competitions for miniature rifle shooting designed to encourage every boy of British birth between the ages of twelve and nineteen to learn how to use a rifle. Then in 1925, the King presented his own trophy to be shot for in team competitions, to which were added other prizes such as the swords of the Admiral of the Fleet, Earl Jellicoe and of Field Marshal Earl Haig, and, in the 1930s, as many as 40,000 youngsters a year were competing throughout the Empire.

The Victory Meeting of 1919, arranged of necessity in haste and with the knowledge of a limited availability of ammunition, was a short affair, lasting only nine days, but it showed signs of dramatic changes, not least in The King's Prize which was now open to anyone who had worn or was wearing the King's uniform, which thus entitled women to enter. And one did. She was Matron Gertrude Preston of the R.A.M.C., one of the nursing staff on Salisbury Plain, who also entered for the Queen Mary. She did not win or make it into the final 100, but the winner that year did break a record by becoming the first victor from New Zealand. Three Kiwis had made it into the last 100, and, on the day of the final, they had hung three horseshoes on the outside of their tent. For one, the horseshoe proved lucky.

Sergeant L. Loveday, who described himself as a 'bush boy' because his farm was miles from civilisation, was the son of a rifleman who had made two trips to Bisley to shoot in the New Zealand team. Sergeant Loveday was also on his second visit to Bisley. On his first trip in 1911, he had made it into the final 100. He had been a musketry Instructor during the war and had come to England, surrendering his stripes in order to get to France more quickly. But his talent with the rifle was soon recognised and he was awarded the Military Medal for reconnaissance work. Prince Albert (later George VI), pipe clenched between his teeth, drove down to the ranges from the clubhouse, to offer the victor his congratulations. The New Zealanders celebrated by taking down their flag and running up in its place, one of the horseshoes and Loveday's winning rifle.

More than 100 competitors came from Australia, Canada, New Zealand and South Africa, to compete in the Victory Meeting and in the fifth Empire Match held immediately afterwards, and the Australians announced their intention to build a clubhouse next to the Canadians'. The following year, another record was broken when The King's Prize was won for the first time by a South African, Sergeant Morgan of the Witwatersrand Rifles, who received a telegram of congratulations from his country's Prime Minister. And when a nineteen-year-old Canadian, Desmond Burke, won The King's Prize in 1924, he was promoted from Private to Lieutenant in the Governor-General's Foot Guards, showered with gifts by his old school who then declared a half-day's holiday, and welcomed home to Ottawa by a crowd of more than 10,000 headed by the Canadian Premier, the Minister of National Defence, and the Mayor and Corporation of Ottawa. Australian Rifle Clubs, the NRA *Journal* noted in 1938, were supported and maintained by their Government as part of the national defence system, in return for providing special guard duty.

Money, or lack of it, was a reason given constantly for not sending teams abroad to the extent that the Association had once been able to do. It was also the reason why a team was not entered for the 1924 Olympics at Châlons in France: while they did not approve of the development of the exclusively non-military target rifle, developed with the aid of the 'long purses' of the Americans and the Swiss, they admitted that they could not compete against it in the same way that 'a surgeon would not be expected to perform a delicate vital operation efficiently with a carving knife, even if he happened to be the best surgeon in the world.'

At some point in his life, every member of the NRA, particularly those who went on international shooting trips, came to realise just how much value was put on rifle shooting abroad, which induced not a little shame, anger, or frustration that the same respect did not hold true in Britain. 'Bisley is the heart of the Empire,' proclaimed a leading article in the NRA *Journal* in 1926, 'and the importance of Bisley is not to be measured by the number of overseas competitors who turn up for the meeting. More truly it can be measured by the thousands who have tried to win a place in a team, by the still larger number who would like to come, but who cannot afford the time, or who are not yet good enough, or have passed the day when they were good enough. It is to be measured by the keenness with which news of the fortunes of this team or that team, or this man or that man, is awaited in places which the home Briton has never heard of.'

'We have got to do what we can to keep up the reputation of the National Rifle Association which is, I may say, a historic and patriotic Association,' said Lord Cheylesmore, in launching the Victory Meeting. In 1919, the war was over but for the NRA the battle continued.

The Council of the NRA was not slow to recognise that certain things had to change if it was to continue to receive the support of the War Office, and in November 1919 a conference was organised to which were invited representatives of the rifle associations of the Army, Territorial Army, Royal Marines, and of the Royal Navy and Royal Air Force who, together with representatives from Canada, Australia and from South Africa, agreed to co-operate to produce a new framework of rules to bring the Association's operations 'into line to meet changed National requirements'. Following the Army's lead in 1922, the Services began to hold their Rifle Association meetings at Bisley in the same week before the NRA Meeting, with their own ultimate prize, The King's Medal.

The Association as a whole recognised the compliment paid it when in 1920 the War Office adopted the Bisley target, designed by its secretary, Major Etches, to replace the much disliked figure target with a flat base, black aiming mark, dubbed the 'tin-hat'. One change effected in the 1920 Meeting was the introduction of three shooting periods instead of two which, with two half-hour breaks at 12.20 p.m. and 4.30 p.m., meant that shooting was continuous from 9 a.m. until 8.15 p.m. Another introduction was that a Small Bore Meeting was held on two days during the first week, which in 1922 developed into the National Small Bore Meeting, organised by the NRA and the Society of Miniature Rifle Clubs in their first joint venture since 1904. The event proved to be increasingly popular over the years, as was the introduction of the Clay Pigeon ranges first constructed in the early 1920s. In 1920, rules were introduced standardising the different Service Rifles, which were now divided into four categories.[1]

In the face of competition from other sports, the Council was also aware of the need to provide more facilities and more creature comforts for competitors. A new brick Refreshment Pavilion was built in 1924, replacing the old wooden structure first erected on Wimbledon Common in 1871, with sufficient accommodation to provide 1,200 meals at one sitting, and dances held in it on Saturday nights after the shooting. Some of the more dramatically-minded clubs, such as the Stock Exchange, the Ibis, and the London and Middlesex, gave concerts in the Umbrella Tent, while the Camp was rarely without a regular band playing daily throughout the Meeting.

In 1922, the Sherwood Foresters, on duty in the Camp, drew large audiences on several evenings for a series of boxing matches, but that year a more enduring entertainment arrived—the wireless. Although demonstra-

---

[1] The S.R. (a) was the Short Magazine Lee-Enfield as issued; S.R. (b) the S.M.L.E. with aperture sight, windgauge and sling; S.R. (c) comprised any British Service .303 rifle with or without the aids used with S.R. (b). A fourth class, S.R. (d), included any rifle admissible in the previous classes fitted with telescopic sights.

tions were somewhat hindered by static in the first week, 'by the kindness of the British Broadcasting Company' listeners in Camp heard a talk on Bisley given by the Editor of the NRA *Journal*, Captain Ernest Robinson, and throughout the Meeting were able to tune in to hear the results of their shooting competitions broadcast in the news bulletins.

The BBC began regular broadcasts, live, on the final stage of The King's Prize, six years later, the running commentaries provided by Captain Robinson, who himself had won the prize in 1923 and was co-author with Ommundsen, the brilliant pre-war shot, on the standard text, *Rifles and Ammunition*. With only one break, in 1931 when all the stations followed the ceremony of the King opening the King George V Hospital, the BBC continued, and expanded, its coverage of Bisley, and among the team in Coronation year, 1937, was a young reporter whose voice was to become familiar to the whole listening nation, John Snagge.

The year before, due to circumstances beyond anyone's control, not least that of the BBC, listeners heard that the winner of The King's Prize was a South African, Sergeant J. E. Robinson. Except that he wasn't, and a special announcement correcting the error had to be made in the middle of the coverage of the tennis at Wimbledon. Needless to say, it was the weather which was the culprit. Gales between thirty and forty m.p.h. brought down the Umbrella Tent, thankfully unoccupied except for the entire collection of trophies, and blew three targets out of their frames. This meant that one rifleman, another South African, Sergeant Busschau, had to shoot on his own on a different and vacant butt which led to confusion in marking the final victory. And there was yet another delay.

When Busschau's score-card came to be claimed, it was found that the register-keeper on the first target had left the Camp to join his unit at the station. A messenger had to be despatched immediately, and he managed to catch the man just before the train left. Busschau, a keen, blue-eyed thirty-one-year-old clerk in the South African General Electric Company, admitted that he had very nearly missed the competition himself. He had made it only through the good grace of his fiancée who had agreed to postpone their wedding.

The Council realised that riflemen might be interested in other pursuits so, in the early 1920s, a putting green was constructed and two tennis courts. Norway maples were planted along the main road to replace the old elms which had to be cut down, a member of the Stock Exchange Club donated chestnut trees to be planted at the rear of the 600 yards firing point, and lime trees were planted opposite the Army Rifle Association hut. 'The club huts with their gay flags and their beautifully kept gardens delighted and surprised me,' wrote one lady visitor, on her first impressions of Bisley, 'wild flowers grow in abundance, and behind some of the ranges there are beautiful woods.' Thoughts entertained by some members of adding to the facilities by erecting a swimming pool, however, caused such *Angst* both in terms of cost and concern that the Camp would be invaded by hordes of scantily-clad girls, that Bisley remained, as it were, dry, at least in one respect.

Since Queen Victoria and Prince Albert attended the first Meeting on Wimbledon Common in 1860, one set of visitors the Association could be assured of, whether or not the Camp had a swimming pool, was the Royal visitor, particularly in the years between the wars. The Sovereign continued to be Patron of the NRA, but Royal interest stretched beyond attendance at Bisley or simply being a figurehead. 'There is no exaggeration in saying that the great hold which rifle shooting has in this country,' claimed the *Journal* in 1932, ' ... is directly due to the help and encouragement of the Crown.'

In 1920, before the British Rifle team embarked on its eighteen-week tour of Australia and South Africa, the whole party was given lunch at the Ritz by Lord Cheylesmore, then entertained at Buckingham Palace by the Duke of York who wanted to know about the men's experiences during the war as well as their prowess in the shooting world. On the team's return, their commandant, Lieutenant-Colonel P.W.Richardson, was once again summoned to the Palace to give an account of the tour to George V, which, as well as the matches and unbounded hospitality of their hosts throughout, had included a visit to Melbourne Cricket Club on 13 November when the team watched Hobbs make his century.

It cannot but have been an audience packed with amusing tales, for Richardson had a good eye for interesting detail as well as for shooting. In Southern Australia, for instance, the team had been taken on a tour of a vineyard which had involved a fair amount of tasting and had gone down a treat. 'We tasted several brands and found their quality excellent,' he reported. 'On enquiring why Australian sparkling wines were not exported in quantities to Great Britain, we were informed that the supply fell far short of the demand even in Australia. This is a great pity from the English point of view as we were much impressed with the delicious flavour of these wines.' Nevertheless, all but one railway line was 'dry', he noted, adding with a degree of bewilderment, 'and in the State of Victoria the mixing of mustard in the mustard pot is prohibited by law!'

King George V's obvious interest in the Association led him to institute the tradition of sending a telegram and a signed photograph to the winner of The King's Prize, a tradition which was carried on after his death by his son, George VI, and is continued to this day by the reigning monarch.

It was the Prince of Wales, who in his role as President of the Association had given the rallying cry for funds at the Special Appeal Banquet at the Mansion House in 1925. The Prince had presented the prizes the year before at the largest and most successful gathering since the war. In the morning, having watched the British Olympic team compete in a match on the Running Deer range, he himself decided to have a go. He borrowed the rifle of the team selector, Colonel Faunthorpe, and in six shots scored four bulls and an inner which entitled him to a prize of one pound, duly sent to him and duly donated to charity. At the end of the prizegiving, the Prince announced his support for the appeal because, as he said, 'Of all our National Festivals which draw our fellow countrymen to England from all corners of the Empire, this meeting of the National Rifle Association is in a position quite by itself.'

In 1926, the Prince was the host at a banquet given at the Hotel Cecil for the American and British teams who had been competing against one another in a match at Bisley in June. But it was not just British Royals who attended Bisley. Among the dignatories at the prizegiving of 1925 was the Raja of Vizianagram, grandson of the Maharajah who had donated the trophies which bear his name, and Earl Jellicoe prevailed on him to present the cups to the winners that year, the House of Commons. The following year, the crowds were treated to the spectacle of the Chairman, Earl Jellicoe, competing in the Vizianagram and taking part in friendly contests with the young Prince of Bhopal.

There were others apart from the Royals who considered the NRA as important: the City of London took the Association to its heart and, on occasions, to its coffers. In 1886 the Corporation had donated its own Challenge Cup, and every year since 1870, the Lord Mayor had welcomed the winning teams in the International competitions and their trophies, at either the Guildhall or the Mansion House. In the beginning the prestige of the occasion warranted a banquet. In later years, it fell to a luncheon, then to tea, and now a mere glass of sherry. But the enthusiasm was still strong, at times. In 1928, the Lord Mayor, Sir Charles Batho, was presented with the Empire Trophy, the National Challenge Trophy, the China Cup, and the Kolapore Cups of which he was asked to take especial care as they had a habit of roaming round the Empire. As a father, Sir Charles was proud to note his son's high score in that year's Ashburton, though his unmerited reward had been an attack of scarlet fever; while as Chairman of the City of London Territorial Association, he assured the teams that not only would their trophies be guarded securely, but just as important, they would be kept clean.

In 1932, the Prince of Wales's brother, the Duke of York, later to be

George VI, presented the prizes, repeating a role he had performed twelve years previously, just after the war, and noting the changes that had taken place in the meantime. 'The Association's task of revival after the Armistice was long and arduous,' he said, 'but it has been successfully achieved.'

∽ ∽ ∽ ∽

It was 'an epoch-marking event', according to the *Daily Telegraph*, when Miss Marjorie Foster won The King's Prize in 1930. The fact that a woman had won the accolade for the first time in the Association's history was flashed immediately all round the world, and, within minutes, rifle shooters in Canada, Australia, South Africa, India and New Zealand received the news in disbelief.

Initially, Miss Foster herself was equally taken aback by the information that she had achieved her long-held ambition. She had not realised just how close she was, although only two marksmen had separated her from her closest rival, Lieutenant Sandy Eccles, and, in scores, it was neck and neck until Miss Foster's final shot. She needed an inner to tie and a bull to win. She got the bull, and while the crowd around her went wild, she remained cool, calm and collected. She did manage a quiet smile, and a wave to her mother and Miss Blanche Badcock, her partner on her Frimley poultry farm, who were trapped at the back of the crowd which led her towards the Royal Pavilion where Princess Helena Victoria, who had been watching the match, offered her congratulations. And then another Royal stepped forward. Also keen to offer good wishes, the Sultan of Johore had other intentions—with Miss Foster's permission, he took a myriad of photographs of the slim, boyish figure, dressed in frock coat and breeches, whose hair was brushed back so severely from her forehead.

But the crowd were not prepared to wait for long. The heroine of the day was soon borne aloft and seated in the Prizewinner's Chair, to be carried round the clubhouses, including her own, the South London, and the North London and Middlesex. A reporter had offered her a cigarette which she had readily and gratefully accepted. And just this once, she told him, she thought she would have a drink as a club member offered her a glass of champagne.

Among Miss Foster's bearers were two men who had sat in the chair themselves in previous years, Arthur Fulton, twice a winner, and his father, George, who had won the prize more than forty years before, in 1888. It was George Fulton who had encouraged Miss Foster back to the ranges on a visit she made to Bisley some five years before. She had enjoyed shooting from the age of eight, she had told him, but her parents had advised her to give it up when she reached fourteen in order to concentrate on her studies. Fulton lent her his rifle and was so impressed by the accuracy of her shooting that he encouraged her to take up her hobby once more.

Miss Foster, a thirty-seven-year-old former driver in the Women's Legion, rapidly became known on the ranges for her shooting prowess and in 1929 had hit the headlines in most of the London dailies for being the first person to beat the new small bull's-eyes and get a full score, but her victory in 1930 focussed even more attention on her—not least from her local village. At four o'clock the news reached Frimley and a reception party was immediately got under way: a fire engine was sent from the local station, full of firemen, to collect the local girl and bring her back home. They had to wait, however, until Bisley had finished its own celebrations. Then Miss Foster was driven out of the Camp in the engine, a cavalcade of motor cars in its wake.

Meanwhile, Frimley Green was packed with men, women and children as it had never been before. Camberley British Legion Band, hastily summoned by telegraph from Reigate, had arrived and, as the fire engine came into view, the musicians began to play 'See The Conquering Hero Comes'. When the cheers died down, Miss Foster was welcomed, appropriately enough by Mrs Worsley, Frimley's only lady representative on the Urban Council. The speeches and the cheering eventually faded out and away, and Miss Foster was driven back to the farm to a little peace and quiet and home celebrations.

The locals in the little Surrey village did not forget their heroine, but celebrations continued in a much more gentle, rural way than those surrounding some earlier winners from abroad on their return home. In comparison with the grand receptions and the streets lined with fairy lights and bunting, some of Miss Foster's engagements appear rather prosaic. She attended a garden party in Frimley the following week, given by the Women's Institute of which she was a member, where she was presented with a telescope, while the Gold Medal and Badge, together with the telegram and signed photograph from the King, went on proud display in the window of a little shop in the village. Miss Foster may have been the first lady to win such a noble prize and the newspapers could flaunt the fact and 'carry-on' to their heart's content, but Frimley behaved as was right and proper and correct in England of 1930.

As did, it must be added, the National Rifle Association. Only two years before Miss Foster's win, the Duke of Montrose presented a Challenge Trophy for a competition, suitably named the Amazons, open to ladies only, while in 1938, Miss Foster's partner, Miss Badcock, broke another record by becoming the first lady to shoot in the Kolapore (her birthplace qualified her for entrance into the Indian team). And yet, the *Journal*, writing in praise of Bisley Weekends in 1932, had to remind readers about the dangers of bringing women into Camp. For just nine shillings a day, enthused the *Journal*, a visitor could get full board and lodgings and enjoy rifle shooting, putting green, tennis courts, and clay pigeon traps on the premises, or savour the delights of the nearby golf courses or go fishing on the River Wey, or, for alternative diversions, travel to Ascot or the Aldershot Tattoo. 'Just one point,' it warned, at the end of the promotion campaign, 'the Camp Regulations do not allow ladies to be accommodated in the huts; but if you want to bring your wife, there is the excellent and comfortable Brookwood Hotel. Rooms can also be had in Brookwood or Pirbright and food at the Pavilion.' And water, too, one assumes.

Despite her victory in 1930, nine years later when Miss Foster, in the Women's Auxiliary Territorial Service, applied to enter for The King's Medal, awarded to the best shot among serving members of the Territorial Army, she was turned down for reasons explained to her, in person, at the War Office by the Director General of the TA. It must have been particularly galling considering the fact that the medal was won by a man who had come eighteenth in The King's Prize that year, while Miss Foster herself had been beaten into second place, narrowly missing a second win and thus breaking another record.

Another newsworthy event in the 1930 Meeting, at least as far as a publication, *The Penguin*, was concerned, took place amidst a storm of wind and rain in the battle for the Junior Kolapore, a competition begun in 1926 for teams of four, and designed for countries unable to raise the eight necessary for the main Kolapore competition, with a Challenge Cup presented by the newspaper, the *Morning Post*. In 1930, the victory went to the team from the Falkland Islands which had been competing at Bisley for only two years.

The Governor, Arnold Hodson, was an enthusiastic rifleman, however, and the year before had presented the Association with the Falkland Islands Challenge Cup. He was not able to make the journey to Bisley in 1930 but, as *The Penguin*, the islands' only newspaper, reported, he was on the quay to await the arrival of the RMS *Orita*, along with the entire population—which according to the 1931 census was just under 2,400, not far off the size of the population of Bisley. Everyone downed tools to join in the celebrations. Schoolchildren were given a holiday, church bells were rung in an enthusiastic salute, and in the evening a victory dance was held at which the Junior Kolapore Cup was taken out of its box and displayed in triumph.

Another team from the Falklands competed at Bisley in 1937, the year of George VI's Coronation. Considering their own windswept habitat, they were not unnaturally among the few competitors totally unperturbed by the high winds on the ranges on one day, which enabled them to carry off the Junior Mackinnon. There were 150 overseas competitors that year, establishing a new post-war record, the figure including teams from Canada, Australia, India, Guernsey, Jersey, British Guiana, Trinidad, Gold Coast, Jamaica, Sudan, Burma, Sierra Leone, Federated Malay States, and Tanganyika. There was also a record number of entries, thirty-eight to be exact, competing in the Overseas .303 Full Range Postal Match, an annual match established three years before and open to teams of eight British subjects resident or stationed anywhere in the Empire.

The 16th National Small Bore meeting, held in the first week of the 1937 Meeting, also reported a record number of entries, as well as an increase in the number of visitors, undoubtedly due to the American team who had come to compete in the NSMB's Pershing Trophy, donated by General Pershing in 1931. The first match took place in that year and was won by Great Britain by just two points, a win they repeated in 1937, strangely enough, by the same margin. 'It was a good move to give a Sherry Party on the first day of the meeting to welcome the overseas teams and visitors,' enthused the *Journal*, not elucidating quite what was meant when it added, 'there is never enough of this.'

For the most part, Coronation Bisley revelled in fine and warm weather. Some riflemen complained about the vagaries of light and wind, but then, as Colonel Richardson had pointed out some years before, shooting men appeared to thrive on grievances, mostly imaginary. The sermon in the mid-Meeting service that year was preached by the Dean of Windsor, while there were evening concerts given by two of the clubs, and the Band of the Royal Welsh Fusiliers played twice daily in the central marquee. The BBC broadcast its regular running commentary on The King's Prize, which included a fifteen-year-old Devonian schoolboy in the final 100 but was actually won by a twenty-three-year-old Cambridge graduate, Officer-Cadet D.L.Birney, entering the competition for the first time. Birney also won the Silver Medal in the second stage, a rare achievement only accomplished on three previous occasions—by A.G.Fulton in 1931; F.R.Radice, an Oxford graduate, in 1910; and Major Pollock in 1892.

In the week following the Meeting, Great Britain, Australia, Canada, and India competed in the ninth Empire Match, after which the Chairman of the NRA, Lord Cottesloe, presented the winners, Australia, with the trophy. And in October, a British team of fourteen Service riflemen, captained by Commander D.S.Swanston, left Liverpool to embark on a 'long overdue' tour of South Africa, Australia, and, for the first time, New Zealand. A match for the Empire Trophy was included, as part of the 150th anniversary of the settlement of Australia, and brought home by the victo-rious British team.

In Canberra, according to Swanston, a Government minister who was representing the Prime Minister made a speech of welcome which 'kindly made us feel of some Imperial importance'. The feeling, and the hospitality, more often than not including a financial generosity which bore a great deal of the team's expenses, carried on throughout the trip. 'It must be evident to any one brought into direct contact with the Military Authorities, Rifle Associations, and Riflemen of South Africa, Australia and New Zealand, that rifle shooting is regarded as of the greatest importance in their organi-zation of defence,' Swanston concluded in his report on the tour. ' ... It may not be too much to hope that following the example set by Dominion Governments, the Home Government will be sufficiently interested to assist in financing future tours.'

Meanwhile, the face of Bisley was changing. Pressure from members meant that roads were improved in order to carry the increasing number of cars, which some riflemen blamed for the gradual decline in social activities in the Camp as more and more visitors scattered to the winds and the neighbouring villages in search of entertainment. Concrete pillars and posts seemed incapable of holding back the horsepowered wings of progress. The infernal combustion engines went everywhere, including the ranges. Really, it became too much and the Council was forced to impose restric-tions. The *Journal* reflected the general feeling of relief: 'The stopping of motor-cars rushing about all over the camp to the great inconvenience of those on foot proceeding on their lawful occasions to and from the ranges was a very great blessing and a distinct comfort.'

The recruitment drive for members continued throughout the years. In 1922 there were nearly 2,000 Clubs affiliated to the NRA, but twenty years later some seventy-five ranges had closed and the number of Clubs, due in some measure to amalgamations, stood at a little over 500. The cry for riflemen to encourage others to the ranges was made in 1922, but its message was repeated often in the pages of the *Journal*. 'The NRA can provide a Bisley Meeting, and prizes on a lavish scale, but it cannot manu-facture riflemen, nor can it take hold of them, when manufactured, by the backs of their necks, and fling them down on the neatly arranged mats on its firing points ... The nurseries of the rifleman are the County Associations and the County Association meetings, their birth-place is the Territorial Army units and the Cadet units and the O.T.C. units and the civilian Rifle Clubs. It is a hard struggle for a shot who has just been born, so to speak, when there is no nursery in which he can be brought up and educated.'

It was in November 1937 that a team of six NRA members visited Berlin, 'at the expressed wish of both the Secretary of State for Foreign Affairs and of our Ambassador in Berlin,' to take part in the International Shooting Championships. A request to the German Embassy for specific details, made by the captain of the British team, Mr C. Mackworth-Praed, resulted in a dozen of the actual targets being flown over within thirty-six hours. The British team took second place among the five competing nations which included Austria, Sweden and Portugal, and received an invitation to the prizegiving from General Goering. 'The most astonishing thing to us about it all was that this great lay-out is entirely concerned with sporting shooting,' wrote Mackworth-Praed, 'and, though a Government enterprise, has no direct concern with military matters at all.'

The *Journal*, which had assiduously campaigned for teaching the young to shoot, noted in the New Year issue of 1938 that seventy per cent of all German boys received training in the use of small-bore rifles and that, in the future, two boys from each Hitler Youth district would spend eight days on an intensified course at a new shooting school. In March that year, the prizes won by the British team were presented to them in London by the German chargé d'affaires, Dr Woermann. In his speech, 'in which there were touches of humour,' reported the *Journal*, Dr Woermann said that no matter how politicians disagreed marksmen would always be friends.

Only five years before, the then Secretary of State for War, Viscount Hailsham, had visited Bisley to witness the final stage of The King's Prize and to present the prizes. The day of the rifle and of the rifleman was not ended, he said in his speech: 'It is true now that automatic and machine guns play a big part—more than was the case 19 years ago, but I at least most firmly believe that the day of rifles is by no means over. The rifle is permanently a personal weapon which teaches a man confidence in himself, in his power, and in his capacity. It gives him self-reliance and courage, and I am sure that in the future as in the past, if the need arises, our British riflemen will show what they can do for the Empire.'

That need arose on 3 September 1939.

❧ ❧ ❧ ❧

'In thirty years of Bisley Meetings I do not remember a happier week or one with less grumbles,' enthused the Editor of the *Journal* in 1939.

At the beginning of the year it looked likely that the situation in Europe would put paid to the annual Meeting, but, as the months progressed, the position 'eased' somewhat. Lord Cottesloe described to members at the general meeting held in the central marquee at the Camp on Wednesday, 12 July, the turnabout which had enabled the event to go ahead, admittedly under reduced circumstances. Because of the international crisis, there was naturally considerable pressure on the Forces: if it wasn't the last thing on their minds, it was, nevertheless, the last thing they could do to guarantee their normal quota of well over one thousand men to carry out their regular duties on the ranges. As it was, almost at the eleventh hour, the Combined Forces did manage to supply several hundred men.

Surprisingly, that year, the number of foreign competitors was high. In fact, fourteen countries were represented: Canada, India, Jersey, Guernsey, Singapore, Uganda, Kenya, Jamaica, Trinidad, Burma, the Federated Malay States, Gold Coast, the Sudan, and Sierra Leone. Once again, Bisley's Stonehenge of fourteen posts, flying the flags of all the competing nations, was erected opposite the Council offices. And once again, visitors travelled into Camp on the little two-coached train, for a fare of threepence third class, on a six-minute journey from Brookwood where they were met on the green lawned platform by the station-master who also doubled, or quadrupled, his role by being booking office clerk, ticket collector, and porter.

Shooting was limited to two periods a day; more competitions than usual were compressed into each; and, although the military had taken away most of the tents, seventy-six schools still managed to send boys to compete in the Ashburton, as Rifle Clubs and neighbouring schools, such as Charterhouse, rallied round to provide the youngsters with alternative accommodation. The following week, a smaller meeting was organised by a member of the City Rifle Club in which a condition of entry was that every competitor had to take a turn at marking. The weather was abominable, but the novelty of everyone mucking in together created a bubble of joy. 'A happier, and at times more hilarious, affair would be hard to find,' recorded the NRA Secretary, Major-General Sir Alan Hunter, running his first Bisley Meeting.

There was a record number of entries for The King's Prize that year. The winner was Captain T.S. Smith, a forty-five-year-old brassfounder from Walsall, who received more than two hundred letters and telegrams of congratulations, some of which were thrust into his hands by hot and weary telegram boys who chased after him while he was being carried round the Camp. Not that Captain Smith remembered much of the occasion, other than having to hang on like grim death to his hat and his rifle and the chair, as somewhere along the line the chair-rest had gone missing. Then there was the odd celebratory drink, or three, along the way. 'Next time I win the King's,' he joked, 'I shall make sure of a real good meal before setting off on the round of visits to clubs.'

He nearly had not made The King's Prize that time round: the impending war had stepped up the orders at his works to such an extent that he had cancelled his entry, but a few days before the Meeting his name was restored, he came into Camp and went to hire a rifle. Not many months later, Smith was asking the NRA for a supply of rifles and ammunition for a Walsall Defence Force he had set up under the auspices of the Mayor and Chief Constable, weeks before the Home Guard came into existence, inspiring him to claim, in fact, that he was first Local Defence Volunteer.

Despite the high spirits which pervaded the 1939 Meeting, the NRA Council had not been blind to the need for the country to organise a home defence system. In December, 1938, it had submitted a scheme both to the War Office and to the Home Office offering to set up an organisation along the lines of which the Local Defence Volunteers, or Home Guard as they were rechristened, came to be based. The offer, however, had been turned down, and the Council, a little wounded, retired from the scene. But the moment Britain declared war on Germany in September 1939, the wounds were overlooked, if not entirely forgotten, and once again the Council offered the War Office the facilities at Bisley.

The offer was accepted and taken up immediately. The War Office called on the NRA to provide a number of Instructors in a Small Arms School set up in the Camp, and a King's Prizewinner settled in alongside a big game hunter. Most of the buildings were requisitioned, and a great number more erected. By June 1940, 100,000 men in the Home Guard had fired almost one million rounds on the ranges, mainly in rifle practice but also in the use of automatic weapons, and as well as recognising that range officers and coaches numbered 'many old Bisley Rifle-shots', the NRA estimated that it had lent out about 4,000 rifles. When the Home Guards were disbanded in the autumn of 1944, more than 400,000 men had fired on the way to three million rounds of ammunition, using 117,733 targets, while more than one million rounds had been sent out to units in the provinces.

The *Journal* carried on as a quarterly instead of a monthly during the years of the Second World War, continuing to report on the activities of local Clubs which managed to keep going, and on the endeavours of members. There were articles on weapons, the excellence of the large amount of arms and ammunition coming into the country from America, as well as reminiscences from old Volunteers and invocations to the Home Guard, many of whose units were run by Rifle Clubs, to 'make up his mind, from the first, that no matter what he is told to do he will do it with his whole heart and spirit ... After all, it is nothing less than our personal liberty, the lives of our families, and the whole structure of the great British Empire that we are defending.' And as the years progressed, more and more articles were devoted to life after the war and how it would affect the future of Bisley.

There were fears that there would be a return to the apathy prevalent in the years after the First World War, the 'years of the locusts', when the relief in a securement of peace took away all thoughts of continuing the country's defence. 'What I dread,' said Brigadier-General A.F.U. Green, in a letter to the *Daily Telegraph*, 'is that this greatest unpaid army that has ever existed may peter out in little sporadic groups of a sort of Old Comrades Association and that all they have done and learnt in four strenuous years may be wasted like water spilled on the desert sand.' When the Home Guard was disbanded, however, the interest in rifle shooting continued—at least in the short term, as 839 new clubs, 740 from the old Home Guard units, affiliated to the NRA.

The future lay to a great extent in encouraging youngsters to take up the rifle and, despite a decline in the number of entries, the NRA had continued to run competitions such as the King George V Trophy and the Imperial Shield throughout the war. In 1945, it began again to organise its 'postal' competitions such as the Overseas .303 Full Range, the East and West African Police Match (begun in 1927), and the Caribbean Colonies Police Forces Competition begun in 1934. Despite a deficit of more than £2,500 in 1945, the NRA looked to success in the future with more local Rifle Clubs, hopefully, able to adopt some of the many short ranges set up during the war and, in addition, continuing to expect reduced prices for ammunition from the War Office. With the 'nurseries' flourishing, the 'parent' could also prosper. The idea of a Meeting shortened to one week seemed a practical solution in the new post-war Britain in which fewer people could afford either the time or the money to spend longer away from work or home. There was even talk in the letters column of the *Journal* in 1945 of establishing huts to enable men to bring their wives and families to stay in Camp. The *Journal*, for one, with its feet still planted in a former decade, found the idea amusing enough to headline the correspondence, 'Squaw Camp!'

There was no time to organise a full-scale Meeting in 1945, but, with the help of the Small Arms School, a one-day event was held on 21 July. It was a fine day, though the gusty wind whipped up a fair number of the old grumbles among shooters. The crowd was small, a disappointing couple of hundred, but, reported one spectator, they cheered louder than a party twice the size when at the end of the main event, an aggregate shoot for silver cups presented by the Chairman, Sir Philip Richardson, F.J.Dorling of the City Rifle Club and H.E.Malpas of the Experimental Establishment Rifle Club stepped forward to receive their prizes.

As an expression of the co-operation and the goodwill which had existed throughout the war, on 13 October 1945, the Small Arms School presented the NRA with a purple beech tree. Like the tree, the NRA hoped sincerely that following the experiences of two world wars its importance in the line of defence as well as its appeal to sportsmen and -women would once again take root in the nation and in its people.

The North London Rifle Clubhouse.

Shooting, in the prone position.

*In the butts.*

*Competing for the Elcho Shield, 1986.*

*Shooting, in the back position.*

*Andrew Tucker, winner of the Grand Aggregate, 1986.*

*Belinda Moore, a young marksman tipped to be a future winner of The Queen's Prize.*

*Allan Martin, a retired farmer, who collects and shoots muzzle-loaders.*

*Roger Millard, who runs Fulton's, the armourers' shop at Bisley.*

*George Swenson (left) who designed the Swing rifle which won Geoff Cox The Queen's Prize in 1986, with his assistant, Eric McGibbon.*

RIGHT *The Elcho Shield, designed for a match which began in 1862 and was commemorated by Lord Elcho in this trophy.*

*The China Cup, reputed to hold 32 quarts, was presented by the Volunteers of China. Its great weight nearly prevented its entry into the country in 1866 because of a threatened import charge of 1/6d per ounce of silver.*

INSET *The medal presented to winners of The Queen's Prize, designed by Watt with the NRA motto* Sit Perpetuum.

Photographs of Bisley past, courtesy of the NRA collection (photographers: Tony Clark and Edward Younan); Bisley present by Harvest Productions and Paul Forrester.

# CHAPTER SIX

# *Bisley Today, and Tomorrow*

The face of Bisley, in post-war years, has changed. Time has not dealt kindly with some of its clubhouses, while disease has stolen trees from the lines of chestnut, lime and maple. The rows of gleaming white bell tents, which glistened in the sunlight when Lord Cottesloe visited the Meeting in 1912 as a twelve-year-old schoolboy, have been replaced by scores of rather unsightly caravans. The Bazaar of shops which once brimmed over with a range of goods and customers has long disappeared; now there is simply one small wooden stall selling souvenir T-shirts and mugs. The putting green has gone and so have the tennis courts. There are no dances in the Pavilion at the end of the shooting day, no entertainments given by the less shy members of the Clubs. No Jenny Lind. No cinema. And, other than the ceremony of the Beating of the Retreat on the first Tuesday, no music wafts over the Camp from the Umbrella Tent. The Bisley Bullet chugged along on its final journey between Brookwood Station and Bisley Camp in 1952. Competitions now fill out the day on Middle Sunday where once there was a place for Divine Service. And the BBC, which had covered the final of The Queen's Prize on radio and the prize-giving on television in the years after the war, has long since taken away its microphones and cameras.

The link with the Military has remained, with Bisley being the venue on more than one occasion for the CENTO meetings (the central area counterpart of NATO), but in recent years that link has weakened. The Services still hold their own combined meeting in the week prior to the main Meeting at which the Forces continue to provide a number of personnel, albeit considerably reduced, to assist in range duties. But developments in modern warfare and financial cutbacks have increasingly diverted the attention of the Ministry of Defence away from the ranges at Bisley, away from the purpose for which the National Rifle Association was formed.

But the NRA itself has not forgotten. In 1982, it could point to the men serving in the Falklands War and number among them half the Army shooting team, including two former Queen's medallists, and any number of units who had distinguished themselves on the battlefields in the South Atlantic as well as on the Surrey ranges. And memories of vital service in two world wars, which was in both cases immediately available and instantly taken up by the authorities, can not be erased easily.

Nevertheless, times have changed and, if a little late and slightly reluctantly, the NRA has seen the need to change with them. Shooting has become a sport, primarily, and, while the MOD continues to give support to the NRA, financial assistance now comes mainly from the Sports Council which provides about three-quarters of the funds necessary for overseas trips as well as about half or more of the cost of new developments such as the £95,000 Pistol range, the Melville, opened in 1983. The National Rifle Association is now concerned to turn Bisley into a national centre for shooting and is working towards this scheme with other shooting organisations such as the National Pistol Association and the National Smallbore Rifle Association which moved its headquarters to Bisley in 1979. And, as a member of the British Shooting Sports Council, founded in 1978, the NRA works to safeguard the interests of its members, battling particularly against restrictive legislation and increasing charges for firearm certificates.

The bond between the Royal Family and the Association, however, remains as firm as ever. In 1950, the Duke of Gloucester, President until his death in 1975, presided over the Jubilee dinner at the Park Lane Hotel in London, held to celebrate the sixtieth year of the Association at Bisley. Ten years later in 1960, when the NRA celebrated its centenary, the Queen paid a visit to Bisley during the Meeting, and was taken round the ranges by Lord Cottesloe. She sighed with regret that she could not shoot at the Running Deer (she is an ardent deerstalker), being dressed for a formal luncheon party to inaugurate the National Army Museum, and ended her tour by arriving on the 600 yards firing point to see the New Zealand team from the other side of the world win the Kolapore by equalling the total score of the British team with the higher score at the longest distance. By a strange irony, the weather behaved almost exactly as it had done a century before, when after days and days of heavy rain, the sun burst through grey clouds on the very morning of the Royal visit.

At the heart of every Meeting remains The Queen's Prize, and Her Majesty the Queen continues the tradition, instituted by her grandfather, of sending the winner of the Sovereign's prize a signed photograph of herself (or a memento such as a wallet, if they proceed to win it a second time). In 1954, the Duke of Edinburgh paid Bisley a flying visit, literally, when his helicopter touched down in front of the 1,100 yards firing point on the Stickledown, and he had lunch in the clubhouse of the English XX of which he is Patron.

In 1975, Prince Charles, the Prince of Wales, became the Association's sixth President and the Prince of Wales's Prize which had been in abeyance since 1936 was reintroduced. Five years later, Prince Charles shot in the Vizianagram on the side of the House of Lords. Good-natured objections from the House of Commons induced the good-humoured Prince to claim his right to shoot in the match if not as Prince of Wales then certainly as Duke of Cornwall. Notwithstanding, in the match between two sides, the Prince, and the Duke, found himself in the team which came second. It could be said that, in some way, the bond with the Royal Family has grown stronger since 1980. That was the year when Prince Charles married Lady Diana Spencer, whose distant antecedent, Earl Spencer, the NRA's second Chairman, had presided over the meeting in 1859 which led to the forming of the Association.

What role the children of the Prince and Princess of Wales will play in the life of the Association remains to be seen, but, as ever, young people are important in the eyes of the NRA. The number of schools competing in the Ashburton is growing once again: there were eighty-four entrants in 1986, four up on the previous year. While the popularity of the Inter-Services Cadet Rifle Meeting is also growing, as is the annual tour to Canada by the Athelings. Trips abroad and competing in international events such as the Commonwealth Games and the Olympics remain an important part of the life of the NRA. Every year teams are sent to Canada and to the Channel Islands, while more infrequent visits are made to the West Indies, Australia and New Zealand. The Palma Match continues to be held, as in 1971 when a team from Great Britain went to America to compete in the match and to join in the centenary celebrations of the NRA of the United States. But it is to Bisley, to the annual Imperial Meeting that riflemen desire to come above all other places. In 1986, among nearly 2,000 entries there were well over 200 visitors from twenty countries from as far afield as Australia, the West Indies, and Malaysia. The newcomers admitted that to them Bisley was the Mecca of the shooting world, and it wasn't hard to envisage that they would soon join the ranks of the 'regulars' who spoke of the place with considerable affection.

As ever, the funds of the National Rifle Association are limited. True, a lack of money has curtailed its activities in the past, but somehow the Association has always found a way round its problems, very often through the generosity of its more affluent members. Today, affluence comes in bigger packs and one of the ways in which the NRA is tackling its financial problems is through a Sponsorship Committee which is exploring the ways big corporations can fund competitions or events. Naturally, having a higher profile would help and the Association is rediscovering the value of publicity. The ancient ceremony of presenting the trophies won by England and Great Britain to the Lord Mayor of London which had dwindled over the years from a massive banquet to a glass of sherry, and then petered out altogether, was revived in 1978 by the then Chairman, Sir Ronald Melville, aided undoubtedly by the fact that the Lord Mayor was Master of the Worshipful Company of Gunmakers. 'Changes there will be, many of them difficult and unpalatable, but we shall, in one way or another, overcome them,' said the Chairman, Lord Cottesloe, in 1965. 'The Association and the Bisley Meeting will go forward into the future with determination and confidence, assured of their value to the nation.' The sentiments are as valid now as then; indeed, as they would have been even a hundred years ago.

Bisley may never return to the early days when it welcomed more than eighty members of the Press to the Meeting, but there are hopes for ventures in different fields. For the first time, in 1986 the NRA found itself the star of a BBC television documentary and with television's insatiable appetite, there is always the possibility that another sport which does not immediately appear to be a spectator-sport will get picked up, dusted down, and turned into a star watched by millions. Golf and snooker have received such treatment, and not suffered unduly as a consequence, so why not shooting which in Britain alone numbers more than one million active participants?

As long as the character of the place does not alter beyond repair, the face could be lifted without much ill-effect. But part of its charm lies in its ageing, or is it age-old, character. Perhaps the NRA do hoard and hide their recollections at the back of dusty cupboards and on the old wooden walls of crumbling clubhouses for longer than most, but that could be why Bisley still retains an air of the old, lost Empire.

That character, that atmosphere of a bygone age is best imbibed with a pre-dinner drink on one of the Club verandahs on a hazy evening in July during the Meeting. That is the time when the Camp, and the National Rifle Association, is in full bloom. Undoubtedly, there has been a downpour, this is the Bisley Meeting after all, but now the sun has come out and the chestnuts, limes and maples, and the forests of pine and heather surrounding the Camp, are sparkling with raindrops; the whole place looks as if it has been covered with thousands of fairy lights. Sunflowers lean languidly against the white clapperboard and brick buildings; the heads of geraniums and marigolds peep over the tops of scores of hanging baskets. Inside the Clubs, some people are finishing dinner. Outside, there are others having coffee or drinks. The dustbin and rejects wardrobe look which appears to be *de rigueur* for a number of men and women on the ranges has been exchanged for a smarter, cleaner form of dress. Dark Club blazers abound. Perhaps it is the last Saturday of the Meeting, when the crowd will follow the Prizewinner's Chair round the Camp, and the Canadians will fire their cannon to celebrate the victory—whomsoever's it is.

That is another thing about Bisley, and the National Rifle Association. A genuine pride is taken in the achievements of all of its members and of its visitors. It has been the case always, throughout its history. As you sit on the Club verandah celebrating the victor, you will be surrounded by talk of matches long past and of competitors long dead but there is something in the air which keeps their memories and names alive. Really, you need not have more than a wisp of imagination or a touch of magic amber fluid to think that this is how it has always been—at Wimbledon and at Bisley. *Sit Perpetuum.*

# CHAPTER SEVEN

# *Faces of Bisley*

## ∽ THREE CHAIRMEN ∾

*Lord Elcho (Chairman 1860–6, 1869–70)*
Francis Charteris Wemyss, Lord Elcho, who succeeded his father in 1883 to become sixteenth Earl of Wemyss, was born on 4 August 1818. He was, according to one obituary notice, 'one of the original and most potent figures in that Volunteer movement which has played so momentous a part in the military history of the country.'

Educated at the Edinburgh Academy, Eton and Christ Church, Oxford, he entered political life in 1841 when he became MP for East Gloucestershire, whose member he remained for five years before representing Haddingtonshire, a constituency he served until he moved to the Upper House. He was First Lord of the Treasury from 1852–5, but his political career was tempered by his independent nature which feared nothing for flying in the face of popular prejudice. It was this determination to stick to his principles which led to his resignation from the NRA just before his death when he disagreed with the proposals for change in The King's Prize and with what he saw to be the submission of the Council to the dictates of the War Office. Nevertheless, despite crossing swords with political enemies he managed to remain on good terms with them. He bitterly opposed Gladstone on some issues, but the House was often entertained by their witty exchanges which both contenders appeared to relish as well.

His move to the House of Lords, a place more accommodating to eccentrics and individualists, perhaps suited his nature more, especially in later life when his political and social conservativism was out of general fashion. He had supported Palmerston, but never joined the Conservative benches, his conservatism being more spiritual than political. In 1909, when he became Father of the House of Lords, he was presented with a portrait of himself by John Sargent, which had been commissioned out of a subscription fund raised from both sides of the House. 'Father of the House?' queried Lord Rosebery at the presentation ceremony, the Earl should be called the

House's son, he was so very youthful. Indeed, it was something noted in the newspapers. 'He looked a boy when he was a man, a youth when he was middle aged, and would pass for 55 when he was over 80,' the *Daily Telegraph* recorded.

He was an ardent horseman, a keen golfer, fond of the theatre, talkative and witty. He was tall and spare, and with his bewhiskered long, lantern-jawed face and confident gait, he cut an impressive figure in his Highland uniform of Colonel of the London Scottish. His first wife, Anne, daughter of the Earl of Lichfield, was much loved by members of the NRA for her care and support of her husband and the fledgling Association. She died in 1896, and, in 1900, the Earl married Grace Blackburn, daughter of a major and niece of a Lord.

It was Lord Elcho who commissioned the artist Watts to design the NRA medal; while the Elcho Shield remains to this day a memorial to this spirited, fearless man who never inspired malice, and never felt it. He died in June 1914.

## Earl Spencer (Chairman, 1867–8)

John Poyntz, the fifth Earl Spencer, was the second Chairman of the Association but it was he who chaired the meeting at Spencer House, his London home, which led to the formation of the NRA and, as lord of the manor, it was also he who was able to place Wimbledon Common at the disposal of the Council. He was, according to the obituary in the *Daily Telegraph*, a tranquil even phlegmatic man, a country gentleman with the tastes of the country. Born on 27 October 1835, he was educated at Harrow and graduated from Cambridge in 1857, the year he was elected MP for South Northamptonshire, but he served only eight months before he succeeded to the title on the death of his father.

He served as Viceroy of Ireland from 1869–74 and 1882–5 where he was involved, indirectly, with the infamous Phoenix Park murders in which two of his subordinates, Thomas Burke and Lord Frederick Cavendish, were hacked to death by a band of Irish extremists. Cavendish had declined an offer of a ride in Spencer's carriage, preferring to walk through the recreation park where a game of polo was in progress. By chance, Spencer took a detour from his normal route which would have led him to the scene of the crime, and possibly prevented it. He returned home and went into his study to read a book. He never forgot the subsequent events, as he told an Irish writer: 'I heard a shriek which I shall never forget. I seem to hear it now. It is always in my ears.'

Spencer also served as First Lord of the Admiralty from 1892–5, fighting, and defeating, Gladstone over cuts in expanding the Fleet. He was the

Prime Minister's first choice as a successor and it was on the tip of Gladstone's tongue to tell Her Majesty so but at his resignation meeting with her, he never got the chance. A determined Queen Victoria kept the subject on Gladstone's poor hearing and eyesight, straying from the subject only to draw comparisons between British and German oculists. Thus, it was the popular Lord Rosebery who received the Royal summons in March 1894, not Lord Spencer.

His thick red beard, ruddy nose, and a certain gauche carriage made the Earl a gift for caricaturists. With his irregular features, he may have looked rather like a rustic, said the *Daily Telegraph*, but his soft blue eyes, delicate complexion and gentle expression told readily of the sensitive nature beneath. He was a compassionate landlord, as the author Rider Haggard noted, and became President of the Royal Agricultural Society in 1898. Reduced circumstances forced him to sell the magnificent library at Althorp, reputedly one of the finest in the world, and, when needs arose, to let Spencer House. He never recovered fully from a stroke, or from the death of his wife, Charlotte, in 1903. It was a childless marriage, which perhaps accounted for the particularly strong bond between them. She had been a beautiful woman and a gracious one, supporting him in his work for the NRA and, on occasions, presenting the prizes. It was during their stay in Dublin Castle that she won sufficient affection to be called Spencer's 'Faerie Queene'. Lord Spencer died on 13 August 1910—the same day as Florence Nightingale.

## Sir Roland Gibbs (Chairman since 1984)

Sir Roland Gibbs was Chief of the General Staff (1976–9). He was commissioned into the 60th Rifles and commanded the 3rd Paras and the Parachute Brigade. He is Patron of the British Commonwealth Club. He took over the Chairmanship from Sir Ronald Melville, who had been Chairman since 1972.

'My first memories of Bisley go back to the Forties when I came with the Regiment's team. I was never all that wonderful as a shot, sort of on the edge of the team. The impression, which I think strikes anyone who visits the place, is its agelessness and its friendliness. Shooting and equipment is the talk and yet, it is all done with humour and a nice amateur professionalism. It is tremendous for a young shot to arrive at Bisley and find that people do help and give the benefit of their wisdom and experience.

'My aim is to try and carry on where my predecessor, Sir Ronald Melville, left off. That is to say, putting the place on a sound financial basis, trying to effect improvements in the infra-structure at Bisley, and also accepting that the NRA is not just Bisley, but has responsibilities throug-hout the country. It is important to remember that.

'But to return to Bisley, if I could take just one memory away to remember it by, it would be a picture of Century Range with every target engaged from 300 back to 600 yards. The whole range would be a mass of humanity, lying down and shooting. I think that is such a wonderful sight.'

## ∾ TWO NRA SECRETARIES ∾

### Captain E.H.St.John-Mildmay (1859–89)

Captain Edmond H. St. John-Mildmay was the first Secretary of the Asso-ciation. He was born in 1815, just a few months after the Battle of Water-loo, a year after the ending of the American War of Independence. Until he was twenty-nine, he served in the Hussars of the Austrian Army under Josef Radetzky, a much loved Commander who had fought against Napo-leon. Mildmay then became equerry to the Duke of Cambridge, and in 1850, to his successor, the Commander-in-Chief of the Army who was the Association's first President. He had also been Assistant Inspector of Foreign Legions during the Crimean War, and attaché to the Legation at Vienna. In 1859, Mildmay acted as British Commissioner to the Austrian Army in its campaign in Italy, and on his return home was actively con-cerned in the formation of the NRA, before taking on the job of Secretary.

It was actually Mildmay who suggested Wimbledon might be a suitable location for the NRA Meetings, when other sites such as Epsom, Alder-shot, Woolwich and Chobham were being considered, and he was certainly instrumental in persuading the Council of the need for a tramway in Camp to carry competitors to the ranges.

He was a quiet, well-built, diplomatic man. With his long sidewhiskers and normal garb of a light knickerbocker suit, he seemed like a figure from another age. He was a diplomatic man, popular with his staff and all who came into contact with him. When he chose to retire in 1889, the final year that the Association met at Wimbledon, more than £1,000 was raised from all the many friends he had made in his thirty years with the NRA. His departure marked the end of an era. He attended the opening of the New Wimbledon at Bisley which took place a month before his seventy-fifth birthday. He died in October 1905, aged ninety.

*Brigadier P.G.A.Prescott (Secretary since 1981)*
Brigadier Peter G.A. Prescott became Secretary in 1981. He was born in 1924, and 'turned into cannon fodder at the wartime Sandhurst'. He was commissioned into the 2nd Armoured Battalion, Grenadier Guards in 1944, and went over to Normandy, fighting at Caen and Caumont for which he was awarded the Military Cross. He was part of the regiment which fought for and took the Nijmegen bridge in the Arnhem campaign, and while on duty in Germany was wounded a month before the end of the war in Europe. After the war, he served with the Guards in Germany, North Africa, the Middle East, Cyprus, and the Far East. In 1966, he took over the command of the 2nd Battalion, Grenadier Guards in Germany and his Regiment for a year before going to Hong Kong for two years to command 51 Brigade. His last appointments, before joining the NRA, were as Deputy Commander North East District in York and then Deputy Director of Army Training in the Ministry of Defence.

'I am a sufficiently bad shot to have never got to Bisley, but did shoot for the battalion frequently—perhaps it was the others who let me down ... but I have, nevertheless, killed a stag from the back position. And while at the School of Infantry in '59–61, I was dabbling in the development of very small calibre, high velocity weapons.

'I intend to my bit to develop Bisley into the finest shooting centre in the world at which all disciplines of the sport will be able to take part to their heart's content, and I want to visit the Association at the grass roots as often as I can, because it is here that the sport is born and nurtured.'

## ∽ THE COTTESLOES ∾

The enjoyment of shooting appears to be hereditary, even a casual glance through NRA proceedings bears witness to that fact, but perhaps one family above all others should be singled out for its involvement with the Association. The family has an unsurpassable 101-year participation in the match for the Elcho Shield, and in two generations has provided two Chairmen equally committed to ensuring and safeguarding the future of the NRA. The name of that family is Cottesloe.

*Thomas Francis Fremantle*
Thomas Fremantle was born on 5 February 1862, and succeeded his father to become the third Baron Cottesloe of Swanbourne and Hardwicke in 1918. The title had been created for his grandfather and namesake, Thomas, whose father, also Thomas, had fought at Trafalgar and was held in the highest esteem by Nelson. Young Thomas took to shooting at an early age

and was in the Eton team which won the Ashburton Shield at the Wimbledon Meeting of 1880. At Balliol College, Oxford, he represented the university in each of his student years in the Chancellors' Plate and the Humphry Cup, when Oxford won seven out of the eight events. In 1884, his final year at university, he won a place in the Queen's Sixty when there were 2,200 competitors. He first shot for England in the Elcho Shield in 1885, and was in the team twenty-seven times, as well as being captain continuously between 1920–54.

He became assistant secretary to the NRA in 1889, and was closely and actively involved in the Association's move from Wimbledon to Bisley which he recalled in the *Journal*. 'There was a wet spell in the summer of 1890, when I went down to live in the camp about a month before the meeting opened. The noise of the croaking of the frogs was loud and continuous in the evenings.' He was also absorbed by an interest in ballistics, a passion he passed on to his son, John. It was a fascination which began in 1887 and involved work with Metford and the man who became his mentor, Sir Henry Halford whose home, Wistow, in Leicestershire was inherited by Thomas Fremantle. It was at Wistow that the three men shot up to 2,000 yards, testing the trajectory from a number of weapons, on what was said to be the longest range in the country, experiments which led to the replacement of the old muzzle-loader with the breech-loader.

In 1900, Thomas Fremantle became Assistant Secretary to the Secretary of State for War, W. St. J. Brodrick, and in that year was sent to report on the safety standard of rifle ranges abroad. He was captain of the successful British team in the match for the Palma Trophy at Ottawa in 1902, and in the return match at Bisley the following year. In 1909, he was captain of the Olympic team, and again captain of the British team which shot in the Empire Match in 1910. He shot on numerous occasions for the House of Lords team, and held an array of trophies for individual successes. In 1905 he became a member and latterly Chairman of the Small Arms Committee, on which he remained for more than thirty years.

Fremantle was elected to the Council of the NRA in 1891, and, after a spell as Vice-Chairman, served as Chairman between 1931–9. As did his son in later years, Thomas Fremantle donated several trophies to the Association, not least a Challenge Cup in memory of Halford and a Challenge Vase, a replica of one presented to Thomas Fremantle after the Battle of Trafalgar.

Thomas Fremantle held commissions in the Volunteers and then the Territorial Army, and was the author of several books on the rifle as well as co-author, with A. P. Humphry, of *The History of the National Rifle Association, 1859–1909*, to which this author is much indebted. He was also highly involved in local politics. He was Lord Lieutenant of Buckinghamshire (1923–54), and served as President of the County Councils Association. He last shot at Bisley in 1946 when he was eighty-four. He died in 1956, during the eighty-seventh Meeting, when he was ninety-four. When the news was broken to members, a minute's silence was observed in his memory. To his old friends, he had remained always Young Tom, a man of extreme modesty, integrity and wisdom, with a quiet humour and gentle, boyish face from which a smile was never far. He guided and inspired numerous public and charitable causes, said a friend of long standing, 'work all done in a quiet and self-effacing way that asked for no recognition.'

### John Walgrave Halford Fremantle

John Walgrave Halford Fremantle became heir to the barony on the demise of his elder brother, who died from wounds incurred at Flanders in 1915. Born on 2 March 1900, he was educated at Eton and Trinity College, Cambridge where he took honours in Mechanical Science in 1921. He was first taken to Bisley in 1903 and stayed with his mother on Cowshot Manor Farm at a time when ladies were not allowed in the Camp after 10.30 at night or before 9.30 in the morning. But on his second visit, as a twelve-year-old schoolboy in 1912, young John was allowed to stay in Camp in one of the bell tents. Although he shot at home, alongside both his parents, he did not shoot at Bisley until he came down from Cambridge in 1922.

That year, he rowed in the winning crew of the Oxford and Cambridge Boat Race, and then, within the space of one week, he rowed in the crew which won the Grand Challenge Cup at Henley, carried off the Albert at Bisley, the top prize for long-range shooting, and shot in the winning English VIII, alongside his father, in the Elcho Match. An outstanding year, but then John Fremantle has always been an outstanding man. Until he gave up shooting in 1980, he was also a remarkable shot. He shot in the English team for the Elcho on thirty-seven occasions, was captain twenty-five times from 1955–79, and remains its coach to this day. He also won the Match Rifle Championship six times, and, like his father, has countless trophies to his credit. He was elected to the Council of the NRA in 1932, and served as its Chairman from 1960–72 when, as a token of the great affection and respect in which he is held, he was created Deputy President.

But John Fremantle, like his father, has had interests away from shooting. He has been working Chairman of countless committees and boards, and that does mean working, among them the Tate Gallery (1959–60), the Arts Council (1960–5), the British Post-Graduate Medical Federation (1958–72), the North-west Metropolitan Regional Hospital Board (1953–60), and the Dogs' Home, Battersea (1970–83), to say nothing of his continued, regular attendance and speaking in the House of Lords. For nearly twenty years, he was Chairman of the Advisory Council and Reviewing Committee on the Export of Works of Art and is still closely involved in the battle to keep works of art in Britain through Heritage in Danger. As well as a love of art, Sickert in particular, like the first NRA Chairman, Lord Cottesloe has a love of the theatre. He was Chairman of the South Bank Theatre Board from its inception in 1962, overseeing the development of the immense project and, indeed, it is after him that the Cottesloe Theatre is named. It seems somewhat appropriate that the theatre specialises in new and experimental work: Lord Cottesloe's roots may be firmly embedded in tradition but he has not closed his eyes to present day thoughts or ideas which appear to belong to the future.

He is a tall, spare, gentle man, leaner featured than his father but with the same bright eyes. They penetrate but they don't punish and any sharpness is softened by surrounding lines of laughter and compassion. His knowledge is encyclopaedic in its depth and variety and to sit with him is like visiting the most magnificent library: there is much to learn, but it is for you to enquire. His sentences, as sound and intricate as the finest filigree metal, at times flash with an incisive wit. Always, he says exactly what he means. He has commanded the Association through turbulent waters which threatened to run it aground, but he steered it through into the modern age with a skill of which his naval forebear would have been justly proud. John Fremantle commands affection, even love, as well as enormous respect from many who know him but slightly. In its long and colourful history, the NRA can not have had a more valiant gentleman at its helm.

## ⤳ TWO QUEEN'S PRIZEWINNERS ⤳

### Edward Ross (1860)
Edward Charles Russell Ross was nineteen years old, soon to go up to Cambridge to study law, when he became the first person to win The Queen's Prize. He was a private in the 7th North Riding Regiment and had already picked up a few trophies at that first Meeting, immediately after which he joined a selected band of riflemen who shot a match against some of the Swiss visitors—and got the top score. He was in The Queen's Sixty, as it then was, three times, getting a Silver Medal in 1865, by which time he was living in London and was a member of the London Scottish. He shot in the Scottish Eight fifteen times, and was on several occasions in the Scottish Twenty.

He gave up shooting at Wimbledon, he said, to give others a chance to win prizes, although he took part in the last Meeting on Wimbledon

Common in 1889 when he was cheered enthusiastically by the crowds for carrying off three competitions. Even as a small boy, he was an expert with a bow and arrow, and he soon became noted as a singular shot and deer-stalker, a pursuit he continued when he retired from Wimbledon. But his interest in the NRA continued as did his love of ballistics and, as well as being an NRA Council member, he served on the Small Arms Committee which was responsible for the Army being issued with the Martini-Henry rifle.

He never practised at the Bar, for on leaving university he was appointed Secretary of Commissions to Lord Chancellor Cairns. In later life, he held a post on what was called the Lunacy Board, a position he resigned from some years before his death in 1896 at the age of fifty-five. He had been a strikingly handsome man, broad-shouldered and well over six feet tall, genial and sociable. Two bouts of flu had debilitated his normally robust health, which had been weakened further by a road accident in London the year before. He left a widow and several children, one of whom recalled that the family story went that he was knocked down in the fog by a cab he hadn't heard approaching, being a little deaf, an affliction which affects many shooters.

Edward Ross died just ten years after his father, Horatio, the remarkable parent of five outstanding sons. Horatio, at one time MP for Aberdeen and for Montrose, was the son of a large landowner and had taken his name from his godfather, Lord Nelson, whom his father had met while seeking his fortune in the West Indies. Horatio was an irrepressible soul, a real dare-devil throughout his long life. Bored by barrack-room life in the Army, he had retired as Captain from the 14th Dragoons to enter Parliament in 1831. He had won what is alleged to be the first recorded steeplechase in the country in 1826, which appears to have involved considerable horseplay along the way. He also won a sculling match over a seven-mile course between Vauxhall Bridge and Hammersmith, and once walked non-stop from the River Dee to Inverness, a distance of some ninety-seven miles. Against thirty top shots, he won the much-prized Cambridge Long Range Cup in 1867 and while he acted as second in sixteen arranged duels, he was proud to boast that he had prevented a shot being fired in every one of them.

Another story concerned a stay in Paris not long after Waterloo. He was keen to try out the pistol ranges in the capital. It was common knowledge that French officers used any excuse for a duel with an Englishman, and how much Horatio teased them is not, alas, known but he was one of the few people from whom they kept very well clear. A member of the first Council of the NRA, Horatio was for a number of years captain of the

Scottish Eight and, in 1863, shot in the team alongside three of his sons—Hercules Grey, Colin and Edward.

## Geoff Cox (1986)

Geoff Cox, a lecturer in computers and maths, began shooting small-bore when he was about fourteen and in the Air Training Corps. He represented his school and then about a year later, he met an ATC officer who also happened to be warden of a full-bore range near Nottingham. Young Geoff became bitten, and went to the ranges, regularly, on Saturdays throughout the year. He gave up shooting for a couple of years after leaving school, and began again, with small-bore, when he joined the Royal Air Force in 1962 at the age of twenty. The following summer he went to Bisley for the first time, and 'did quite well,' he admits modestly, by winning a Tyro trophy in the RAF Meeting, and went back for the Imperial Meeting.

'My first impression was surprise at how olde-worlde the place was. There weren't so many caravans as there are today, and we were living in tents. You could see the old railway line more clearly and I found that fascinating. As you can imagine, there were an awful lot of people around so, when I wanted a bit of peace and quiet, I used to wander off to an area between Bisley Camp and Pirbright and sit in the woods and read novels such as *Seven Days in May*, about an attempted military coup in the States.

'I enjoy shooting because you're always competing against yourself, as well as the elements. It requires a lot of concentration. If you once relax, you can be very easily caught out. When I won The Queen's Prize, I remember I was surprised although I knew I was in a fairly strong position. I felt a sense of achievement, not just for myself but for my Club, the RAF, who gave me a lot of support, I could hear them behind me. That's the other thing I like about shooting—the people, the good friends you make.

'If I could take away from Bisley just one thing to remember it by, it would be the old characters you see in their shorts. People such as Robin Fulton. I think it is so nice that they can still go along and take part. You see, shooting is something you can do for quite a long time. I hope to be back in ten, twenty and thirty years' time.'

## ∞ TWO GRAND AGGREGATE WINNERS ∞

## Thomas Kirk (1873)

Thomas Kirk won the first Grand Aggregate in 1873, receiving his prize from the hands of one of Queen Victoria's daughters, the Duchess of Teck. When the men in the country were seized with enthusiasm to join the new Volunteer movement in 1859, Kirk in later years would boast proudly that he had been the fourteenth man to join the Rifle Corps in Hull on 14 November 1859. He served in the corps for thirty-six years.

Kirk was reckoned to be one of the finest shots in the country during the 1850s and 60s. He won a place in The Queen's Sixty on five occasions, and won the Silver Medal in 1869. In his time he won many prizes, was a well-known shot at Yorkshire meetings, and shot for England in international competitions as well as being elected to the Council of the NRA. When he was about forty, he retired from his business as a gold- and silversmith in Hull, where he was born, and went into farming. He became a successful breeder and exhibitor of horses, and was a familiar sight at the London Hackney Show. He died at his home, Owstwick Hall, Holderness in Yorkshire in March 1906. He was sixty-five.

### Andrew Tucker (1986)

Andrew Tucker won the Grand Aggregate in 1986, the year he also won the Prince of Wales. Among numerous prizes, he was the winner of The Queen's Prize in 1979 and is reckoned to be one of the country's best shots.

He started shooting when he was about thirteen. His school gave him the choice of taking up one sport such as rugger, or squash, or rifle shooting. Not being particularly outstanding at the other sports, he was rather attracted to the rifle although he admits that it took him about eighteen months to get the hang of the thing. 'The principal problem is that you're wrestling with yourself, and that appeals to me.' His interest in shooting does not stop at the ranges, or at winning competitions. When he came out of the RAF in 1958 he thought he would try being a gunsmith for a year and has been in the business in Cobham, not far from Bisley, ever since.

He first went to Bisley with his school team to shoot in the Ashburton in 1951. 'My first impression was that it appeared to be like something in a time capsule and if there is one thing that sums up the place for me it is the feeling of tranquillity you get there, because when you are shooting you are concentrating incredibly hard. What is around you becomes irrelevant.'

## ∽ THE LADIES ∽

When Mr Punch visited the Imperial Meetings at Wimbledon his eye was often drawn away from the ranges by the sight of a pretty woman. Nowadays, Mr Punch might not know quite where to concentrate his field of vision as more and more women are taking up shooting. Unlike so many other sports, shooting puts men and women on equal terms. Physical strength does not ensure a good shot, concentration and determination can do, and neither is exclusive to one sex. Two women who are making a name for themselves on the ranges are Belinda Moore, who is tipped as a winner of The Queen's Prize in the not too distant future, and Piffa Schroder, a truly remarkable shot with the Match Rifle, who won the Cambridge Cup in 1986 with thirty-two consecutive bull's-eyes at distances of 1,000, 1,100 and 1,200 yards, breaking every record and arguably eclipsing Colonel G.C.Gibbs's well-publicised record of fifty-two consecutive bull's-eyes at 900 yards on a much larger target at the turn of the century.

## Piffa Schroder

'When I married in 1969, my husband Bruno asked his friend, John de Havilland (who has now succeeded Lord Cottesloe as captain of the English VIII), to teach me to shoot, which he did. Some years later, when he heard that I had taken up stalking, he suggested I visit the long ranges to see how easy it was to miss the bull's-eye by several feet. I fired a few shots and then one evening, after a few more visits, we were driving home and he said, "Oh, by the way, the Imperial Meeting is next week and you are entered for it. Don't worry, I've filled out the forms and Bruno has signed them." That's how I started.

'My first memory of Bisley was people in strange hats. An amazing amount of noise. Those incredible buildings. And everybody walking round looking as if they knew what they were doing. It was terrifying, absolutely terrifying. But then everybody was so sweet, so incredibly encouraging. You know, if you are out shooting a pheasant or something, as a woman you have to shoot as well if not better than a man to be accepted. But if you are shooting at Bisley, they accept the fact that you are there and you want to do the best you can. If you win something, everybody rushes round and says "Well done ... How wonderful" and you feel that they really, really mean it.

'I won the Edge Cup in only the second year I had been shooting. It was pure luck. Then I won another few trophies in 1975. That was the first year I won the Connaught Cup, which is for the highest score in the Hopton, and open only to the Irish competitors. In 1977, I was elected to the Cambridge Long Range Rifle Club. John Cottesloe, John de Havilland, Ronnie Melville, all the great and good shots have all been members and I thought, "I can go no further." Then I won the Cambridge Cup on my first time out, the first woman to win it, and now I have won it three times.

'I know when I started shooting my mother said to me, "Darling, you can't possibly shoot. I mean, all those men. So rough. Not a ladylike thing to do at all." I don't know what one says to encourage young girls to take it up. I mean, there is no reason on earth why they should not be as good as men, or, at least, have as much fun.

'If I could take just one thing away to remind me of Bisley, I think it would be my very old shooting jacket. It has been laughed at, rained on. I've wept in it. I've screamed with rage in it. I have been mortified in it. I have been absolutely over the moon in it. But I have had it ever since I started, and you get phobias about things, and so it goes on … '

## Belinda Moore

'We had a very good shooting master at my school at Woodbridge in Suffolk and some of my friends dragged me along one day. I managed to hit the target, and then the master put me on to the full-bore team. That was about 1982, when I was fifteen.

'I enjoy the challenge of shooting because, unless you get 50 all the time, and I certainly don't, you can always do better. You don't have to be superbly fit, although it helps, and age and sex make no difference. Women are in the minority, at the moment, which means you get noticed more if you do well but other than that you're treated the same—no, the older men are very gentlemanly, so really, you get the best of both worlds.

'I've got various medals, I've shot for Suffolk almost since I started shooting, and was the first girl to be vice-captain of the Athelings team. Then in 1986 I was seventh in the final of The Queen's Prize. I was amazed. To a lot of people it doesn't sound that brilliant, but if you know anything about it then you can understand why I was so pleased. I would love to win The Queen's Prize. It is the ultimate. I don't think there is any shooter anywhere who would not want to win it. I don't know that I would do anything afterwards, if I did win, probably just sit around pontificating … but, yes, I'd love to win it.

'I went to Bisley for the first time when I was fifteen with the school team. We were all overwhelmed by the place because it was so big and there were so many people. The Army was there and lots of other schools. It was very lively, and there were so many different people.

'I'm not sure that I would take away anything to remind me of the place—maybe add something, such as warmer accommodation. I have a hat which I wear for shooting and an old leather glove which I keep with me all the time, and a fluffy toy which my school team gave me when I went to Canada and now lives in my shooting bag. At the beginning, I didn't appreciate the history of the place but now it matters to me. The fact that you can go into somewhere like the North London and meet people in their sixties and older, still shooting. It gives a great sense of stability. Bisley seems to have been going on forever and it seems like it will go on forever, too.'

# CHAPTER EIGHT

# The Winning Rifles

At the beginning of the 19th century the gun, or flintlock musket, with its smooth, unrifled bore was an inaccurate and cumbersome weapon which took several minutes to load, a factor which severely limited its use in battle. Added to which, the flintlock musket was accurate at a range of no more than fifty yards. In fact, the archer could reach a distance four times further and with considerably greater accuracy, in addition to being able to load about four arrows to one bullet. But as the century progressed, so did the development of the rifled musket, and of the ammunition it used. Eight years before the NRA was founded, the British Government paid £20,000 to a Frenchman, Captain Minié, for his design of a bullet which expanded to fill the bore completely, a factor that is imperative for accuracy. The Minié rifle, used in the South African campaign, however, proved to be unreliable and it was superseded by an improved variation manufactured at the Royal Small Arms Factory at Enfield Lock, Middlesex. The Enfield, as the first official Army rifle came to be known, was used in the Crimea, and became the ultimate in muzzle-loaders.

The early Volunteers were armed with the long Enfield, relatively accurate at the shorter distances of 300, 500 and 600 yards, and competitors in the first stage of The Queen's Prize were restricted to using it. But for the second and final stage of The Queen's Prize, shot at distances of 800, 900 and 1,000 yards, the long Enfield was known to be insufficiently accurate and, after rifle trials held at Hythe in May 1860, the NRA Council decided to use the rifle designed by Joseph Whitworth, a mechanical engineer whose notable precision in his work revolutionised the development of the gun. It was significant, reported *The Times*, after the trials, that all the rifles sent to contend with Whitworth's had the bore and turn which he had adopted. Thus, the Volunteers, shooting at 300 yards in the standing position, and in the Hythe kneeling position for the longer distances at the first Meeting, used the Enfield in the first stage of The Queen's, the first twenty winning a Whitworth outright, the next twenty receiving one on loan, which qualified forty men to shoot for The Queen's Prize.

## ﮩ THE WHITWORTH ﮩ

(1860–7 except for 1865 when the Prize was won by a Rigby;
and 1866 when it was taken with a BSA)
Length: 49 inches
Weight: 7.5 lbs
Barrel: 30 inches
Calibre: .451 inches
Rifling: hexagonal
Operation: percussion
Feed: muzzle-loading
MV: c1100 f/s
Sights: 1,000 yards

Allan Martin is a retired farmer who lives in Dorset. He has collected, and shot with, muzzle-loaders for about twelve years, although his interest in guns goes back much further. Among his early memories are pictures of his father, a surveyor who worked in Africa and shot game to feed his native bearers, teaching him how to aim a rifle at the sparrows on the roof of their home. He went on to shoot with breech-loaders, but then an interest in the early weapons developed soon after he bought a few and began a collection. 'You must remember that the British Empire was built on blackpowder. I think every one of the weapons in my collection has a story to tell. They have so much more character than breech-loaders.

'The Whitworth has rifling called threepenny bit rifling because it is eight-sided. It used a bullet which was the same shape as the bore, and which was paper-patched. The paper helped keep down the fouling in the bore. Underneath the bullet, you loaded a greased wad which acted as a lubricant. When you fired, the grease cleaned and lubricated the bore, and took the old fouling with it. The Whitworth was very bad on fouling, particularly near the breech, and they had to make a special scraper on a ramrod to clean it. You see, the more the rifle fouls the harder it is to ram the bullet home. Sometimes, if it gets too fouled the bullet gets stuck and then you're in trouble because you can not fire a gun with a bullet lodged somewhere in the barrel. If you do, it will burst.

'The Whitworth is accurate to a degree, if clean, but it was somewhat of a hybrid and was never used in battle. Whitworth sold some to the United States for sniping and the like, but it was never taken up by the British military, although one or two of the smaller regiments were armed with them. Of course, the disadvantage of a muzzle-loader was that you couldn't load it lying down which is why soldiers and Volunteers were trained to shoot standing up or kneeling.

'We use eighty-six to over a hundred grains per charge nowadays, then a greased card wad, a little disc of tallow and beeswax, then the bullet on top. At the end of the day, I take out the barrel, scrub the bore with a bronze or wire brush to loosen deposits of black powder fouling, then put it in a bucket of water with a dash of solvent in it, and pour boiling water down the barrel. I clean it out with a rag attached to a cleaning rod, then wipe it out with a dry rag, and finally, wipe it out with an oily rag so that the barrel does not rust. You can use a chemical solvent, but I find that some of them take the finish off the woodwork which you can do without when you're talking of a rifle such as this which can be worth anything from £500 to £1,500.'

Twenty years before the rest of Europe, the Prussians had quietly taken to a new form of rifle, a needle-gun, developed by von Dreyse, whereby a bolt-action caused a 'needle' driven by a spiral spring to push through the base of the paper cartridge containing the gunpowder and strike a percussion cap, which would thus ignite the charge. Admittedly, in the early stages, the needle-gun was not as accurate as the later muzzle-loaders, because the needle was inclined to snap, but its firing rate—seven shots a minute instead of two, was naturally of great appeal to the military. Increasingly, it became apparent that a smaller calibre, or small-bore, breech-loading rifle helped to increase the speed of the bullet and maintain the flatness of its trajectory.

After trials at Woolwich Arsenal, a design for a breech-loader by the American, Joseph Snider, was recommended by the War Office Committee in 1866, partly as a cheap expediency because the system could be adopted for use on the muzzle-loading Enfield. Well over 40,000 rifles were converted, so that the Regular Army, the Militia, and ultimately, in 1871, the Volunteers were armed with the conversion rifle. More and more, Wimbledon became the place for inventors and gun manufacturers to try out their new weapons and their improved ammunition which was severely tested as, for a number of years, cleaning out the weapon between shots was prohibited.

In 1867, the War Office Committee, consisting of Earl Spencer, Edward Ross, Sir Henry Fletcher (members, or subsequently members, of the NRA Council), Colonel W. Mackinnon (Chief Instructor at the Hythe School of Musketry who became the NRA's Secretary in 1891), and Captain Rawlins, which had been instructed to examine the new breech-loaders, recommended the adoption of the Martini-Henry rifle. This weapon had a breech action developed by Frederich von Martini of Switzerland and a barrel designed by a respected Edinburgh gun manufacturer and enthusiastic rifleman, Alexander Henry, who is said to have sat up all night so that he would be the first man to enrol in his city as a Volunteer in 1859. Eventually, on the advice of the committee and with mounting pressure from the NRA, the Martini-Henry, with its seven-grooved rifling, was adopted by the military in 1871 and that year, for the first time, The Queen's was shot throughout with breech-loaders—the Snider-adapted Enfield in the first stage, while for the second stage the War Office issued the Volunteers with the new Martini-Henry.

## ᘓ THE MARTINI-HENRY ᘐ

(1871–96)
Length: 48 inches
Weight: 8.6 lbs
Barrel: 33.5 inches
Calibre: .450 inches
Rifling: 7 groove, l/hand
Operation: breech-loading
Feed: single
MV: 1350 f/s
Sights: 1,450 yards

According to Allan Martin, 'A Martini-Henry weighs nearly nine pounds so it is not too heavy. The only snag was that it had no safety catch, except in the sporting editions. The small bullet they used had a lot of power. The rifle does tend to kick back at you quite viciously, but it is not bad to fire and was quite accurate up to 1,000 yards, much more accurate than the Snider. The Martini-Henry was the rifle used against the Zulus at Rorke's Drift, and there are stories that one night, the battle raged so furiously that the breech of the Martini-Henrys got so hot that they actually glowed in the dark.'

By 1878 pressure from the NRA Council, in particular from Colonel Loyd Lindsay (later Lord Watage, and RNA Chairman from 1887–90) who was Financial Secretary at the War Office, on the Secretary of State for War, led to an increase in the number of Martini-Henrys issued to the Volunteers and, in that year, the War Office issued the rifles to competitors in the first stage of The Queen's Prize. By 1885, the Snider had been eliminated from competitions, except in the Ashburton because the aggressive kick back, or recoil, of the Martini-Henry was thought to be somewhat off-putting to youngsters. The conditions of The Queen's Prize also altered, and the competition was extended from two to three stages.

But it soon became apparent that the Martini-Henry was not the best breech-loader, particularly at long ranges, due mainly to the fouling which collected in the deeply-cut grooves of the rifle. As early as 1883, a new War Office Committee on Small Arms, which included an NRA Council member, Sir Henry Halford, was set up to examine the ways in which the Martini-Henry could be improved, and one development which they found of particular interest was the inclusion on the rifle of a magazine which carried a supply of cartridges and fed them individually into the chamber of the rifle.

Numerous weapons were tested at Enfield, but the one which survived extensive trials was the Lee Magazine Rifle, designed in 1879 by James P. Lee of New York, in which a metal case, carrying five cartridges inserted from the top, was fitted into the body of the rifle in front of the trigger guard by a detachable catch. The forward movement of the bolt fed the top cartridge into the chamber.

The Small Arms Committee were impressed with what they saw, and as a result of their recommendations, in 1888, a new weapon was designed at Enfield with a .303 calibre which incorporated the Lee magazine and a rifling pattern developed by William Metford, a keen shot who had worked as a civil engineer on the Indian railways. His design consisted of seven shallow grooves, with no sharp angles and, therefore, was less inclined to foul. This was called, simply, the .303 magazine rifle, or Lee-Metford, until the introduction of a similar, but shorter, rifle which came to be called the Short Magazine Lee-Enfield (or SMLE), and thus led to its earlier counterpart being termed the Long Magazine Lee-Enfield (LLE). It was the latter weapon which first won at Bisley in 1897, the year of Queen Victoria's Jubilee, the year also which saw the death of a distinguished shot, seldom unplaced in the English VIII, the man instrumental in the development of the new rifle, Sir Henry Halford.

## ↩ THE LEE-ENFIELDS ↪

(1897–1985)
**Long Lee-Enfield** (previously known as the .303 magazine rifle)
**Short Magazine Lee-Enfield** (SMLE)
**Rifle No 4**
Length: LLE 49.5 inches; SMLE 44.56 inches; No 4 44.43 inches
Weight: 9.5 lbs; 8.25 lbs; 9.103 lbs
Barrel: 30.2 inches; 25.2 inches; 25.25 inches

Calibre: .303 inches
Rifling: 5 groove
Operation: breech-loading/bolt
Feed: magazine
MV: 2440 f/s
Sights: open (LLE 'V' backsight, barleycorn foresight; SMLE 'U' backsight, blade foresight; No 4 aperture backsight, blade foresight)

Roger Millard runs Fulton's, the armourers' shop at Bisley, with his two partners. He was born on the Army's doorstep, in Farnborough. His father wanted him to have a trade and so, in 1946, sent him to train as an armourer at the Army Technical School, Arborfield. He travelled all over the world, working for units such as the Grenadier Guards, the Commandos, and the 5th Dragoon Guards. In 1970, after twenty-five years 'acting as mum' to his units' armoury needs, he was offered a job by Robin Fulton. 'I came out of the Army at two o'clock one afternoon and was working for Mr Fulton at 3 p.m.' The shop is open seven days a week, from 8 a.m. to 6 p.m., fifty weeks of the year, but Roger doesn't mind that. Not only is the shop right at the heart of where the developments are taking place, but it is also where the problems happen and 'face to face with the throbbing, anguished veins' of those to whom it is all happening. But Millard would not like to move from Bisley. 'There is no rat-race here. In general, shooting people are very nice. It must have been something like this back in the Victorian age, at Wimbledon, and I rather take to that.

'The Royal Small Arms Factory at Enfield made virtually all the weapons used by the military, and they found the .303 easy to manufacture, while for the soldier it was a much lighter weapon to carry. Initially, of course, the barrel was very long because the black-powder propellent was quite slow-burning, which made the rifle a little unwieldy. There is a story of the Mounted Infantry using them during the Boer War. After a skirmish or two with the Boers, they would leap up on to their mounts, slinging the rifles across the horses' backs and the barrels would be so hot that the horses would bolt. From that, so the story goes, the barrel needed to be surrounded with woodwork.

'Heat can affect the alignment of the barrel and the hammer blow in the breech when the propellent is ignited, which is a pressure something in the order of twenty tons and causes the barrel to vibrate, neither of which do anything for accuracy. George Fulton burned a lot of midnight oil trying to regulate rifles, to control the vibrations by making the woodwork fit as well as possible to the barrel. He couldn't do that much with the Long Lee-Enfield because the woodwork was so thin, but had a better chance with the

SMLE, the "Smellie", as it was nicknamed. The woodwork was more robust, as was the barrel, although the action was still very light. The vibrations in the Smellie were reduced further by the way the barrel was "bedded" in. And despite the standard U backsight, half-way up the barrel which obscured the target, it was a rifle that did shoot well. Arthur Fulton, George's son, used one and he was probably the best shot in the world, winning The Queen's Prize three times. During the war, he became known as a terrific sniper which won him the DCM. Arthur's son, Robin, then won The Queen's Prize with an SMLE at Long Range in 1958.

'The SMLE was a complicated rifle to make, but it's a beautiful weapon, almost hand-finished. They were issued in great numbers to the Regular Army in the First World War and they went over the top together, Tommy and the SMLE, at Ypres and the Somme, etc ... The Territorials were issued with the Long Lee-Enfield until 1920, but in the war they were often exchanged for SMLEs which the chap in the TA would pick up from the body of his dead Regular Army comrade.

'People get very fond of their SMLE. The woodwork was invariably walnut, the metalwork finished by hand. They can't be used in the Meeting now, but people who care for them like vintage cars come back here and use them on nostalgic shoots. And when the owner of the rifle gets too old to use it or can't fulfil the conditions necessary for a firearms certificate, they are almost in tears at having to part with them. For a long while we looked after Miss Foster's SMLE, which was the only one she would use. With the SMLE, bedding is all important. The sun can cause the woodwork to warp which naturally affects the shot, but it would go back to normal. Still, you had to do a lot of checking from muzzle to breech when the chap brought it into the shop after a bad shoot. If, after all that, however, you concluded that the rifle had cooled back to normal, you'd pop it into the "psychological" rack. The chap would come back to collect it next day, go out and shoot, and inevitably return to say "I don't know what you've done with it, but it is working marvellously."

'In the 1930s, the No 4 was introduced, and that really was the son of Smellie, just like it but for a few modifications. The barrel was heavier to reduce the vibrations still further, the action more robust, and the manufacturing had been simplified which made it easier for gunsmiths to work on. By this time, all sorts of bedding techniques were being developed.

'The Enfield rifles compensated for variations in velocity of the bullet. Nobody knew why, it seemed it was just luck in design. But whether the bullet was fast or slow, if the wind was right, you'd get a "waterline" shoot, right along the line of sight. Remarkable, when you remember as well that the bullet weight is only 174 grains (and there are 7,000 grains to the pound). The only adjustment shooters could do to improve the No 4 at this time, having had the bedding regulated, was to change the barrel regularly. People would change their barrels after 2,000 rounds or so, or at the end of each Meeting. The gas released by the cartridge would gradually erode the metal in the barrel and the bore would become enlarged. That used to be our bread-and-butter work. The NRA even used to sell a new rifle complete with a spare barrel. But now that there have been so many improvements in the manufacture of barrels the practice has died out.

'The Enfield rifles won every Sovereign's Prize up to 1985. In 1969 it was converted from .303 to 7.62 mm. It was a big upheaval. The new barrel was thicker and the woodwork had to be cut short to accommodate it. The twist of rifling didn't really suit the lightweight NATO bullet so barrelmakers introduced rifling with a slower twist which suited the new 146 grain bullet. Nobody has ever been carried down the hill from the ranges carrying anything other than an Enfield rifle, until this year, and I think that the superb ammunition played a part in it. Funny, though, in the early days of Wimbledon there were gunmakers such as Gibbs, Whitworth, then Government manufacturers took over completely. Now there are more private manufacturers coming back on to the scene—Schultz and Larsen, Grunig and Elmiger, and the 1986 winner, Swing. We seem to have come full circle.'

## ∾ THE SWING ∾

(1986)
Length: 48 inches
Weight: with 30 inch barrel, 11.25 lbs
Calibre: 7.62 mm
Rifling: 4 groove, r/hand
Operation: bolt
Feed: single
MV: 2925 f/s
Sights: Swenson Precision or Telescope

The Swing was designed by George Swenson whose lifelong interest in weapons developed into working in rifle manufacturing about fifteen years ago. He has worked as an engineer all over the world, including the Far East and Africa where he was an enthusiastic game-hunter, an interest he shares with his assistant for the past five years, Eric McGibbon, who did his hunting in India where he was born, brought up, and worked as an engineer on a tea plantation. George and Eric met at Bisley, and, although they are in the forefront of technology as far as rifle manufacturing goes, they like the place particularly for its atmosphere of bygone days. 'Bisley has an attraction for shooters from all walks of life,' says George, 'and they are all drawn together, consciously or unconsciously, regardless of age or sex, by the requirement for self-control and endurance.'

GEORGE: 'We've produced the Swing as a precision instrument for target rifle shooting. It is not an invention, it is a development, a design, because there is nothing new in rifle design—it's the most backward profession there is. The Swing's layout has been dictated by the NRA regulations which stipulate a bolt action of a design they determine to be conventional. It took the Council eight months to decide to approve mine. We've worked to achieve maximum accuracy, whereas with a Service rifle accuracy has always come second to reliability. At the moment the Swing has the fastest firing action of any target rifle, less than 1.7 milliseconds, while in the factory we've got it down to 1.24 which must be a significant advantage especially to nervous shooters. And it won't be long before we get it down to a millisecond.

'The most important, most unusual aspect of the Swing is the concentration on the importance of the trigger. A company once asked me to design a cheap rifle and I put twenty-five per cent of the cost into the trigger. They were horrified. But I think that has been the problem with rifle designers over the years, they've spent so much time designing the weapon they've almost forgotten that the thing has to be fired. When I sat down to design the Swing, I split the components up to give me a weight which would be well within the NRA limits of 12.01 lbs (five and a half kilos). The action was made as compact as possible, up to two and a half inches shorter than is standard, in order that any additional weight could go on the barrel which then becomes less sensitive to manufacturing processes and is actually a heat sink, a very important factor.'

ERIC: 'The basic length of a barrel for a long-range rifle is thirty inches, which we do in four twists. For the NATO bullet the ideal length is 1 in 14, but it really is a matter of personal preference. I like the 1 in 12 but Geoff Cox, this year's winner, chose a 1 in 14.'

GEORGE: 'I owe a lot to Major Hardcastle who worked at the Woolwich Arsenal and, after the First World War, made an examination of a number of military rifles from all over the world. Rifles got their stability from either horizontal or only one plane vertical lugs or supports; the lack of support in one always had disadvantages so I thought why not develop a rifle which has four forward-located locking lugs which assure all-round symmetrical support of the bolt head and two deep recoil lugs which ensure there is no torqueing, or twisting of the barrel action, when the rifle is fired.'

# CHAPTER NINE

# *The Glittering Prizes*

## ⟐ THE QUEEN'S PRIZE ⟐

As well as firing the inaugural shot at the NRA's first Rifle Meeting on Wimbledon Common in 1860, Queen Victoria expressed her support for the Association by instituting her own prize, the winner to receive the sum of £250—a figure, unchanged to this day, which, out of courtesy to the Monarch, sets a limit on the sum for any other prize.

Originally, the first stage of The Queen's Prize was five shots at each distance of 300, 500 and 600 yards. The final stage consisted of ten shots, fired from the kneeling position, at distances of 800, 900 and 1000 yards. The competition was open only to Volunteers until 1907 when the Territorials became eligible. After the First World War, King George V extended the rules still further to include anyone who had served in the war, which meant that women became eligible for the first time. After the Second World War, King George VI opened the competition to all subjects of the British Commonwealth.

Today, The Queen's Prize is competed for over three days. The first day at distances of 300, 500 and 600 yards, with seven shots at each distance. A special prize is awarded to the competitor making the highest score, in addition to the NRA Bronze Medal. The 300 competitors taking the highest places in the first stage go through to the second stage, again shooting at distances of 300, 500 and 600 yards, with ten shots at each distance. The competitor with the highest score receives the NRA Silver Medal. The third, and final, stage is open to the 100 competitors taking the highest place in the second stage. Shooting distances are 900 and 1000 yards, with fifteen shots at each distance. The three top scorers each receive a badge indicating their inclusion in the last 100. The third highest receives the NRA Bronze Badge; the second, the NRA Silver Badge. The Queen's Prizewinner receives the NRA Gold Medal and Gold Badge.

The Gold and Silver medallists have the initials G.M. or S.M., put after their initials in all NRA records. The winner of The Queen's Prize also experiences the thrill of being carried from the ranges in the wooden chair, donated to the NRA in 1883 by Charles Wainwright, at one time a member of the London Rifle Brigade, and then carried round the grounds to each clubhouse where he and all his bearers are offered congratulatory refreshment.

Many and varied are the stories attached to The Queen's Prize, but perhaps the most remarkable concerns the Fulton family—three generations of whom have won the prize. George won in 1888, and with his prize-money he gave up work as an engraver and established a business as a gunsmith, so pursuing a passion which, until then, of necessity, had been part-time. His son, Arthur, established a record, which has never been beaten, by winning the prize three times—in 1912, 1926 and 1931. Arthur's son, Robin, won the prize in 1958, while the firm of Fulton's, a name now synonymous with Bisley, carries out its business in a building which once housed the old Council offices and dates from the days of Wimbledon Common.

## ⟶ THE GRAND AGGREGATE ⟵

Among rifle shooters, this prize, introduced in 1873, is considered to be a greater test of skill than The Queen's Prize, because it is awarded to the person who achieves the highest score in ten of the competitions held during the Meeting. Initially, like The Queen's Prize, it, too, was open only to Volunteers, and was first won by Colour-Sergeant T. Kirk of the 1st East Yorks, who had been runner-up to The Queen's Prize in 1869.

The winner receives the Challenge Shield, presented in 1876 by the Dominion of Canada Rifle Association, who made their first appearance at Wimbledon in 1871 in the form of twenty members of the Ontario Rifle Association who went on to win prizes to the value of £100. The Canadians left the details of the annual competition to the NRA Council who decided to attach it to The Grand Aggregate. The Shield, which at its heart has a symbolic figure of Canada and is encircled by maple leaves and medallions of the arms of the various provinces, was actually handed over in the Canadian camp at Wimbledon in 1877 by Colonel C.S. Gzowski, President of the Canadian Association, to the Duke of Cambridge, President of the NRA.

The winner of The Grand Aggregate becomes distinguished with the initials G.C. The runner-up receives the NRA Silver Cross, the distinguishing initials S.C. The third prizewinner, the NRA Bronze Cross. Until recently, the record for the number of wins was three, a record held jointly by Ommundsen (1900, 1905, 1910) and Dr Kelly (1914, 1922, 1923), then in 1978 that record was broken by J.S.Spaight who had also won the prize in 1973, 1975 and 1976.

## ✌ THE ALBERT ✍

In the first year the NRA held its Meeting, Prince Albert, the Prince Consort, donated an annual prize of £100 to be open to all comers from all nations. After his death in 1862, the Association decided to commemorate their first patron by continuing his prize under the name of the Albert when it was won by Major Henry Halford who had worked closely with the gun designer, William Metford, and was later a member of the Small Arms Committee which introduced the Lee-Metford. At his home in Wistow, which he left to his friend and protégé, Thomas, Lord Cottesloe, Halford had built a long range and a rifle workshop, and was the popular host at frequent shooting parties. He went on to captain more than one British rifle team against the United States and Canada.

Until 1895, the Albert was shot in two stages. The final was open to the top forty competitors in the first stage. From that time, the Albert prize-winner was taken from the aggregate of scores at the three longest ranges—which was, in the early days, yet another method of testing the rifle and the ammunition, as well as the accuracy of the rifleman. Today, the Albert is shot at distances of 1000, 1100 and 1200 yards, with fifteen shots at each distance, but with no sighting shots permitted, and the winner receives a Challenge Bowl, presented in 1935 by the distinguished shot, Maurice Blood. The Albert is the premier prize for long-range shooting.

## ✌ THE PRINCE OF WALES ✍

The Prince of Wales's prize of £100, or a Cup of similar value, was introduced in 1861, and the Council of the NRA decided that it should be open only to prize-winning men. It was therefore confined to holders of 1st and 2nd Regimental and County or District Association prizes and to winners of prizes at the Volunteer rifle course at Hythe. In future years, in order to emphasise the competition's importance, the Council proposed that it should be open only to holders of medals given by the NRA to County and Colonial Associations. The prize, in abeyance since 1936, was reintroduced after the present Prince of Wales became the NRA President in 1975. The competition was shot at distances of 200, 500 and 600 yards, with five rounds at each range. Today, the competition is open to any subject of the Queen, and is shot for at one distance—600 yards, with fifteen shots.

## ∽ ST GEORGE'S VASE ∾

The St George's Vase, dating from 1862, is one of the most highly prized trophies in the NRA collection. Designed by Ortner of St James's Street, it was presented to the Volunteers, in order to encourage battalion shooting, by Lieutenant-Colonel the Hon C.H.Lindsay, on behalf of the St George's Rifles, which he commanded. Originally, the competition was held at 200 and 500 yards, with five shots at each distance. Today, it is competed for in three stages: the first at 300 yards, with fifteen shots, the winner receiving a Bronze Cross. The second stage is open to the 240 competitors with the highest scores from the first stage, and is shot at 600 yards, again with fifteen shots. The Silver Cross is awarded to the competitor making the highest aggregate score in the first and second stages. The third stage open to the 100 competitors taking the highest places in the aggregate of the first and second stages, is shot at 900 yards, again with fifteen shots.

The winner of the St George's receives a Challenge Vase, dating from 1891 (the original having been won outright under the terms of the competition at the time), the Gold Cross and the St George's Badge. In 1874, the St George's 100 was initiated, and in 1894 the St George's Badges were introduced and awarded to the first fifty in the final.

In 1865, a Dragon Cup was given to the winner of the first stage of the competition. Like the vase, the Dragon Cup was made by Ortner, under the direction of the Hon C.H.Lindsay. The *Illustrated London News* offers the most comprehensive description: ' ... The stand is surmounted by a bound laurel wreath, the stem of which is engraved with the words, "The Dragon Cup," and the base is adorned with floreated leaves. The bowl of the cup is ornamented in the Grecian style, and embellished with bunches of the rose, shamrock and thistle at intervals. On the front face of the cup appears a Norman shield, intended to bear the inscription relative to the successful volunteer in the contest. The lid is surmounted with a dragon grasping a scroll, upon which will be inscribed the year when the cup was won. The handles are formed of a pair of weirdlike and fantastic winged dragons, clinging to the sides of the cup with distended mouths. The cup is of sterling silver, and is embellished with gold reliefs.'

## ∽ THE ELCHO SHIELD ∾

In 1861 a match was decided upon between Scotland and England and Lord Elcho, the NRA President, proposed to perpetuate the match by awarding a trophy which the winning side would then exhibit in a public place such as Westminster or the Guildhall in London or Parliament House in Edinburgh. Lord Bury undertook to organise a team of eight Volunteers in England, Captain Horatio Ross to do the same in Scotland. Captain Ross included in the Scottish team his son Edward, winner of the first Queen's Prize, but two Rosses did not ensure a win, and England bore away the trophy for the first year, 1862, or at least a drawing of it, as the enormous and elaborately designed shield in wrought iron and gold was expected to take several years to complete. The design was also exhibited at Crystal Palace Prize meetings and at Wimbledon. An advance was made the following year: when Captain Ross went up to receive the prize on behalf of the Scottish team he was handed not a drawing but a plastercast model.

An extract from *The Times* of 1862 describes it thus: 'The shield is divided into compartments, in the most prominent of which Britannia, armed and erect, is represented, with the sea in the distance, and in the foreground her attendant handmaids, Plenty and Liberty, in the lap of Peace. A medallion, exquisitely drawn, of the Queen's head, separates the allegorical from the historical part of the shield, where miniature groups suggestive of Bannockburn and Flodden, Tilbury and Wimbledon, are introduced. Just above the point of the shield stand two figures, a Highland and an English Volunteer, shaking the right hand of good fellowship. These figures are among the best and most natural point of the design, a circumstance which is to a great extent accounted for by the fact they are studies from life … ' In one corner, it must be noted, into the design has crept a small spider which is, according to tradition, the creature whose persistence inspired a dispirited Robert Bruce to victory against the English at Bannockburn in 1314.

The Elcho Shield, when won by England, used to hang in the Guildhall in London, but the fate of the original shield is unknown. The one in the possession of the NRA is one of a number of copies which were made at an unknown date. Another copy, presented by the Ross family, hangs in the library of the Faculty of Advocates in Edinburgh.

In 1863 four members of the Ross family competed in the Scottish team, Captain Horatio and his three sons, Edward; Colin, a private in the London Scottish; and Hercules Grey, a member of the Bengal Civil Service who was known for his outstanding bravery during the Indian Mutiny. In 1869 the Canadians made a request to compete for the Elcho, but they were refused as the Council felt their entrance was against the original intention of the competition.

The Elcho Shield, its rules compiled jointly by Lord Bury and Captain Ross, began as a competition to be shot at ranges of 800, 900 and 1000 yards, with fifteen shots at each distance, between teams of eight ('the test of nationality shall be paternal descent'). Today, the distances are 1000,

1100 and 1200, although the shots at each distance remain the same at fifteen. Throughout its 125-year history, however, no sighting shot, not even so much as one shot at any distance on the day of the match, has been allowed.

On 19 July 1862 *Punch* published a poem, 'The Battle of Wimbledon', which celebrated the introduction of the Elcho Match, and England's victory, but more exactly what the match stood for. It ends thus:

Woe to a foe who dares our shore,
When, side by side, those rivals pour
On horses, guns, and men,
Such bolts of fire as those that tore
The air in Surrey's glen.

## ∽ THE ASHBURTON SHIELD ∽

The Challenge Shield, given by Lord Ashburton in 1861, was presented for competition to Public Schools with an unenrolled Volunteer Corps to have the effect 'not only of training our youth in early life to the use of the rifle, but be the means of giving an interest and stimulus to their drill, regular attendance at which should in all cases be made a necessary qualification for rifle practice.' The teams, consisting of eleven, shot with the rifles with which they were issued at school. Initially, the competition was held at 200 and 500 yards, with five shots at each distance. Three schools, Eton, Harrow and Rugby, competed for the Shield in the first year of the competition. Rugby, with their Hay muzzle-loaders, were the winners.

Today, the competition is also open to Cadet Corps. Distances are now 300 and 500 yards, with seven shots at each distance. The first prize is the Ashburton Shield. Second prize is a Challenge Trophy presented in 1947 by the O.T.C. Officers Club in memory of Major Montague-Jones.

THE SPENCER-MELLISH CUP: In 1861, the *Volunteer Service Gazette* and then later Lord Spencer, donated a cup to be competed for by the best shot of each school. In the first year, while Rugby carried off the Ashburton Shield, Howard of Eton, using a Hay muzzle-loader, carried off the cup. Today, the competition is open to one competitor from each school who has just competed in the Ashburton, Cadet Pairs, or Cadet Fours, and is shot at a distance of 500 yards, with ten shots. The Tankard now presented to the winner, was bought from an endowment made in 1926 by Lieutenant-Colonel H. Mellish.

THE ALLHALLOWS SALVER: In 1978 a special prize was presented by Allhallows School to commemorate their coach, Mr James Turner, who had led them to victory in a number of post-war competitions. This prize is awarded to the coach of the winning Ashburton team.

## ⚮ THE NATIONAL ⚮

The National began life in 1864 as the International Enfield, a competition between the Volunteers of Scotland and England which 'caused great excitement and interest in the two Countries,' according to the NRA's report of the proceedings for that year. There were twenty competitors on each side, shooting at distances of 200, 500 and 600 yards, with seven shots at each distance. In that first year, when England won, there was no prize other than an illuminated certificate for each of the victors.

Lieutenant-Colonel the Hon C.H. Lindsay, commander of the St George's, was put in charge of a committee to raise a fund to purchase a suitable trophy. Twenty-two silversmiths submitted designs, and the choice fell to Messrs Elkington and Co, and their artist Auguste Willms. The *Illustrated London News* on 8 July 1865, described it thus: ' ... this bold and pleasing piece of allegorical sculpture, adapted to the art-workmanship of the silversmith, is a very remarkable specimen of the art ... At each end of the plateau is an allegorical group—one illustrative of Peace, the other of War. Peace is typified by a representation of Minerva bearing the traditional olive branch, and standing in a car adorned with fruit and flowers. The car is drawn by oxen, harnessed with garlands, indicating the easy yoke of government in times of peace, and led by a youth who bears a sheaf as a sign of plenty.

'At the other end ... Mars, the god of war, rides in a car embellished with arms and laurels, drawn by horses, led by Valour in the form of a youth. The war god's shield displays the badge of the National Rifle Association, and his attitude full of majestic power shows that he is calmly awaiting the signal of attack. Somewhat similar is the expression conveyed by the figures of two volunteers, one in the English, the other in the Scotch uniform, who stand on each side of the pedestal against the column. They "stand at ease", yet are ready for action. The sentiment is made still plainer by the mottoes inscribed on the plinth, one under each of these figures:- "Si vis pacem, para bellum," and "Defence not Defiance".

' ... (there are) seated figures whose accessories indicate the essentials of a good rifleman—correct judgement of distance and precision of aim. Four allegorical groups occupy other portions of the pedestal. Of these one side shows the blessings of peace, represented by two happy matrons with their children, surrounded by the attributes of Commerce, Navigation, Science and Art. The evils of war are suggested by the figures of a woman who is

163

endeavouring to restrain her boy from following the god of war to the field, and a mother consoling her son, who has met with reverses, indicated by his broken sword and desponding attitude. The central column takes the form of a bundle of fasces (ensigns of authority), bound with wreaths of laurel, and surrounded by flags, emblematic of the various nations who are united by the British Crown. On top of the column stands the Genius of Patriotism, guarding the garlanded shields of England and Scotland.'

In 1865, the Irish competed for the first time for the trophy, although they were limited in their choice of men to those serving in Britain in the London Irish, because there was no Volunteer Force in Ireland. Their first victory came in 1873 when they were captained by Major A. B. Leech who became a driving force in instigating matches between the United States and Ireland.

The rules for the competition were drawn up by the National Match Committee, not the NRA, and the intention was for the following year's match to be shot in the victor's own country. But this caused problems in 1877 when the NRA, supported by Ireland, stated that such an important match should be competed for at the NRA's annual Rifle Meeting. The Scottish R. A. objected and withdrew entry in 1877 and 1888. At a meeting the following year, at which it was agreed that the Welsh be admitted to compete, a compromise was arrived at whereby the match would not be held away from Wimbledon for two years running. In fact, the National has been shot at Wimbledon practically every year since 1880.

Today, the competition is open to one team of twenty subjects of the Queen, from England, Scotland, Wales and Ireland, qualified and selected as directed by the National Match Council. They compete at distances of 300, 500 and 600 yards, with seven shots.

## ∽ THE DONEGALL ∾

The Donegall was first competed for as the Irish International Challenge Trophy in 1866, and was open to the best shots of the English, Scottish and Irish Twenties competing in the International Enfield (the National). Honorary members of the London Irish were considered eligible to shoot in the match, and national qualification was by paternal descent. Each competitor was to have seven shots at distances of 200, 500, and 600 yards. The competition ran along these lines for nine years until it was discontinued. For five years, the trophy became a prize in a match between the Volunteers and the Regular Army. This match developed into the United Services Match with a trophy of its own, subscribed for in 1880 by Regiments, Corps and the NRA, which is today competed for by one team of eight serving members of H.M.Forces, and any Dominion team from its permanent Armed Forces. The Donegall Trophy has been reinstated as a championship match to be competed for among members of Clubs. The competition is now shot at one distance, 300 yards, with ten shots.

The Donegall was presented by the Irish peer, the Marquis of Donegall, and was subscribed for entirely by Irish members of Volunteer Rifle Corps, and in the first year of the competition it was won by the Marquis' nominee, Lieutenant J.Hopkins of the 41st Middlesex. The trophy was made by Messrs C.F.Hancock from a design by Signor Modi. The *Illustrated London News* describes it thus: 'It ... consists of a handsome tazza-shaped vase, the cover surmounted by a group of figures representing the Irish King, Brian Boru, at the Battle of Clontarf, calling on his men to meet the invading Danes. At the feet are figures of Hibernia and Britannia. The former rests her hand upon an Irish harp and sits upon the Irish wolf-dog; the latter in one hand holds a trident and in the other her shield, the British lion crouching by her side. On the base are plaques for the winners' names, and two medallions, the one representing Erin welcoming the English galleys to her shores, and the other a rifle match. The ornamentation consists of various national and military emblems.'

## ☙ THE CONAN DOYLE ❧

The Conan Doyle, instituted in 1906, is competed for at 900 yards with ten shots allowed. When introduced, it was for service rifle tyros and civilians who achieved the highest score at 200 and 500 with ten shots. The trophy was presented to the NRA by Sir Charles Langham in Sir Arthur Conan Doyle's honour to commemorate his encouragement of rifle shooting among civilians. The story dates back to when the creator of Sherlock Holmes was serving as a young doctor in the Boer War, about which he wrote a celebrated and much translated pamphlet in 1902. Conan Doyle was working in the Langham Hospital, a military hospital financed by Sir John Langham, where he came to realise not only the destructive capabilities of the rifle, but also that in future wars the rifle would not always be in the hands of the professional soldier. On his return home, he had a rifle range built at his home, Undershaw (which is the word engraved on the plinth of the silver statuette), formed a rifle club with members of the local village, Hindhead, in Surrey, and promoted the idea so that within a few years there were village rifle clubs throughout the land.

## ∽ THE CHINA CHALLENGE CUP ∾

The China Challenge Cup, reputed to hold thirty-two quarts of celebratory liquid, was first competed for in 1865 in a competition entitled the Volunteer County Challenge Prize. The money for the cup was raised largely by Major Frederick Brine, of the Hong Kong Volunteers, who encouraged his fellow commanding officers of the Shanghai Volunteers, Edward Webb and Robert Antrobus, to raise a subscription for a silver cup weighing at least 2,000 ounces, to be presented on behalf of the Volunteers of China to the Volunteers of Great Britain. The cup was to be competed for by ten selected Volunteers from each county, at distances of 200 and 500 yards, with five shots at each, and then held by the Lord Lieutenant of the winning county. In the first year, the competition was won by Somerset but, for a while, there was no cup to display as it was still being made in Hong Kong.

The following year, in 1866, the cup was finished and then transported to the country, free of charge, by the Peninsular and Oriental Steam Company, an act of generosity which was not repeated at Customs who claimed an import duty of 1/6d an ounce on the imported silver. The NRA Council, not in a great hurry to pay in the region of £125, pointed out that the trophy was not for sale or private use and should be excused the duty. A word in the right ear led to the duty being dropped. On arrival, the China was taken to Wentworth, the seat of Earl Fitzwilliam, Lord Lieutenant of the winning county, Somerset, and went on display for the first time at that year's Meeting. 'It is,' boasts the NRA report, 'perhaps the largest piece of silver plate in this country, and does great credit to the Chinese workmen to whose care the manufacture of it was entrusted by Lee Ching, the silversmith at Hong Kong.'

*The Times* in its report on the Meeting was not quite so enthusiastic, although its opinion was perhaps clouded by the weather. At the 'dullest Wimbledon on record,' the reporter describes it simply as a 'very large dull silver vase'. The *Jeweller and Metalworker*, a fortnightly trade periodical, found much more to enthuse about: 'This vase, which is one of the prizes annually competed for at Wimbledon, is a massive and elaborate specimen of the silversmith's art, and cost three years' labour to produce. The vase, or cup, stands four and a half feet high, and is about two and a half feet in diameter and is the production of Lee Ching—one of the most celebrated workers in gold and silver in Canton. The cup was submitted for by British residents in China, and the amount raised was 5251 (guineas). For this sum the makers undertook to produce an appropriate work of art; but we understand that, in labour alone, before he had completed his task about one thousand pounds was expended. In this country a similar piece of work-manship could not be produced, we are assured, under two thousand pounds.'

There was a story in the early days which told of the execution of the artist, Lee Ching, by the Emperor of China for portraying so many dra-gons' claws on the cup. But a member of the fund-raising committee, on a visit to London thirty years later, refuted it. If the artist had lived in China in the early 18th century, he said, he certainly would have lost his head as the five-clawed dragon was an emblem only used by the Imperial family. The lesser the rank, the fewer the claws. But such severe restrictions had died out long ago.

Today, the China Cup is competed for by one Territorial Army team of eight from each Colonel's or Lieutenant-Colonel's command or from any Independent Sub-Unit and to equivalent 'Volunteer' teams from other Services. Each team is composed of a Captain, who must be one of the firers, together with five Riflemen, and two Light Machine Gunners, with one gun.

## ✃ THE CHANCELLORS' ✃

The Chancellors' University Plate was presented to the NRA in 1864 by the Earl of Derby and the Duke of Devonshire, respectively Chancellors of the Universities of Oxford and Cambridge, to be presented to the winners of a match between the two University Rifle Volunteer Corps. The competi-tion had actually begun two years earlier when among the members of the winning Cambridge team was Edward Ross, the first winner of The Queen's Prize. Eight competitors were allowed on each side, shooting at distances of 200, 500 and 600 yards, with seven shots at each distance, using the long Enfield rifle. Today, the competition has changed but slightly: distances are now 300, 500 and 600, ten shots at each.

## ✃ THE BELGIAN ✃

The Belgian was presented to the NRA in 1867 by the Chasseurs Eclaireurs of Brussels and the Belgians who had visited Wimbledon the year before. On 13 July 1867, more than 2,000 Belgians, including the Gardes Civiques under the command of Colonel Gregoire, were officially received at Wim-bledon by the Prince of Wales. Despite the fact that the whole ceremony took place amidst a torrent of rain, the welcome was warm as was the Colonel's response: ' ... This expression of goodwill, coming as it does from the heart of such a nation, cannot fail to bear the happiest fruit. Let us hope ... that it may be the destiny of England and Belgium long to journey side by side in the path of peace and progress ... '

Colonel Gregoire presented the Prince of Wales with the silver Belgian Cup and, in addition, a trophy presented by the Gardes Civiques of the City of Antwerp to the Volunteers of Great Britain. The trophy, states the *Illustrated London News*, consists of ' ... a cylindrical base of black marble, from which rises a shaft, decorated with flags and heraldic devices in bronze on one side, and on the other a bronze target encircled with laurel. It is surmounted by a flat cup or patera, also in bronze, with the names and arms of the provinces of Belgium inscribed around. Round the base are four standing figures of Belgians in uniform, beautifully modelled. The name of the designer is Hendrik Schaefels, and that of the sculptor Alphonse Bogaerts, both of Antwerp. At the upper part of the trophy are the words, "Fidelity, Force, Courage, Honour"; on the shaft are "King and Country", "Constitution and Liberty"; the date MDCCCLXVII, and a bas-relief representing Britannia welcoming Belgium to her shores; on the base is the inscription, "The Civic Guard of Antwerp—The Volunteer Force of Great Britain".'

Originally, the Belgian cup was competed for by volley firing by teams of 'Ten Efficient Volunteers from each Consolidated or Administrative Battalion,' at a distance of 400 yards, with five rounds. Today, the competition is an aggregate, open to any number of teams of four from Clubs affiliated to the NRA or Unit of H.M. Forces, and the Belgian Cup is awarded to the team whose members' scores in *The Times*, the *Daily Mail*, and the Wimbledon matches, make up the highest aggregate. The Belgian Trophy stands in the NRA offices, part of the Bisley Museum.

## ∾ THE SERVICE RIFLE CHAMPIONSHIP ∾

The Service Rifle Championship Challenge Cup began in 1866 as the Martins Challenge Cup, as it was given by the Association in acknowledgement of the 'liberal support received at the hands of Sir William, Lady, and Miss Martins, who at different times have made donations to its funds.' The competition was restricted to Volunteers who qualified as marksmen in the current or previous year. A competition which developed into the Service Rifle Championship was begun in 1905, and consisted of a single prize of £20 for the best aggregate score in the main Service rifle competitions in rapid firing and long and short ranges. The following year, the Service Rifle Championship was officially launched to include the scores from the Grand Aggregate, the Elkington and the Martins Aggregate.

In 1982, to commemorate the Sultan of Oman's visit to the UK, the

Omani Armed Forces presented a Challenge Trophy to be awarded to the highest placed competitor who is not a subject of the Queen.

## ∾ THE BRINSMEAD ∾

The defeat of the British by the Boers in South Africa highlighted the need for troops to be trained to shoot at moving, as opposed to static, targets, and in 1881 the Brinsmead Challenge Shield was presented by Messrs John Brinsmead and Sons for a competition between teams from any battalion of Regular Infantry, Militia Infantry, Rifle Volunteers, from any ship of the Royal Navy, and any division ot Royal Marine Light Infantry. The competition involved shooting at the figure of a man who appeared at intervals of fifteen seconds. Today, the Brinsmead is awarded to the team of four serving members of Her Majesty's Forces whose scores in the 'Imperial Tobacco' competition make up the highest aggregate.

## ∾ THE KOLAPORE ∾

Shortly before his death in 1870, the Raja of Kolapore sent to Lord Elcho the sum of £100 to be used to purchase a prize in the NRA Meeting, and an additional £10 as a subscription to the Association. The Council resolved to use the entire sum to purchase Challenge Cups to be awarded to the winners of a new competition to be competed for by teams from India, the Colonies, and a team from the United Kingdom. But in the first year, there was only one team from abroad, from Canada, who came second to the team from the UK. At first, the teams consisted of twenty to a side but from 1872 this was reduced to eight. The match is shot at distances of 300, 500 and 600 yards, ten shots at each distance.

## ∾ THE VIZIANAGRAM ∾

The first Vizianagram, the match between the House of Commons and the House of Lords, was held at the third Rifle Meeting in 1862. Its beginnings were rather inauspicious. On 15 May in that year, the House of Lords were about to adjourn when Earl Granville rose to inquire whether there was any truth in the rumour 'that this House is likely soon to be at war with the other House of Parliament?' The Lord Chancellor replied that he had indeed received a challenge to a rifle match from the Speaker of the House of Commons which he had accepted on behalf of their Lordships and returned an answer, 'that we would meet the House of Commons in honourable rivalry at any place, at any time, and with any weapons.'

Having accepted the challenge, he trusted that the Lords would 'enter the lists in a manner worthy of this House of Parliament.'

The following day in the House of Commons, Bernard Osborne, MP for Liskeard, asked the Speaker about a rumour circulating in the Lords which he considered to be 'a most unjustifiable hoax'. Before the Speaker himself had a chance to answer, Lord Elcho, NRA Chairman and MP for Haddingtonshire, stood to give an answer which included reading a letter from the Speaker to Lord Elcho which said he had heard of the Lord Chancellor's pronouncement 'with amazement'. Lord Elcho, according to the Speaker, had approached him with a roll of paper, saying that it contained a proposal for a rifle match between the two Houses, and asking for the Speaker's name. The Speaker said he was far too busy to read the paper, adding what he meant to be taken only in jest: 'The only part I could take would be to fire a shot with the Lord Chancellor.

'If you have made me party to a paper I did not read,' continued the Speaker's letter to Lord Elcho, 'and have been the bearer of a challenge to a rifle match to the Lord Chancellor from myself, putting me into conflict with that great dignatory, I shall have to request you to make an explanation to that noble Lord that you acted under a misconception—that, on my part, no such liberty had entered into my imagination.' Lord Elcho read this letter to the House and made his apologies. And the episode in the House of Commons ended with the Prime Minister, Lord Palmerston, hoping ' … that there never may be any other or more serious collision or conflict between the two Houses than that which is likely—if it be likely—a practical trial of skill … '

Despite the false start in the House, a match did take place two months later on Saturday, 5 July 1862. It was shot with 'any rifles', with eleven members a side at distances of 200 and 500 yards, with seven shots at each distance. Lord Elcho, Earl Grosvenor, Lord Bury, and Henry Hussey Vivian, MP for Glamorganshire (later created Lord Swansea and the grandfather of the present Lord Swansea, captain of the House of Lords team for many years), all using Whitworths, were among the team members shooting for the House of Commons. Lord Wharncliffe, the Marquis of Abercorn, Lord Vernon, and the Duke of Marlborough were among the House of Lords team which won the match quite easily, with a score of 411 to 349. The match was watched by an officer in the French Army in Africa, Jules Gérard, a celebrated lion-shooter, who recorded his enthusiasm for this competition and, indeed, the entire Meeting in a letter to *The Times:*

'Sir,—I propose, having been present during the whole of the Wimbledon meeting, to communicate to you my impressions concerning this national institution. In the first place, I found a well-chosen ground,

situated in an extremely pretty country; and, in the second place ... all the
innumerable details arising from so large an assemblage of men and things,
appeared to me to be well understood, and no less well carried into execution; and, lastly, I was astonished at the progress which the Volunteers of all
the regiments, but particularly the Victoria Rifles, had made in so short a
time ... But what impressed me the most during the meeting was the match
between the members of the House of Lords and those of the House of
Commons. It mattered little to my thinking, in which camp victory
remained; the importance of the fact entirely consists in the example set in
such high quarters ... With such examples before them, there is no fear but
that the young students of your universities will become men; no fear but
that the noble love of arms will spread to all classes of society. I conclude by
congratulating myself on having been able to witness so fine a sight ... '

In 1875, the Maharajah of Vizianagram donated £400 to the NRA to buy
a pair of silver parcel-gilt vases which are the trophy for the match. The
Lord Chancellor and the Speaker agreed to hold the trophy for the winning
side, and in that year, the Commons celebrated with a victory by scoring
313 to 220.

In the early years, the match became one of the social events of the
Meeting. In 1863, the NRA reported that the Prince and Princess of Wales
'watched the contest with keen interest'. A Lords and Commons Club was
formed in 1862, with Lord Ducie as President and Lord Elcho as Vice-
President, which met regularly for practice during the summer months,
but the early enthusiasm began to pale until, in 1888, there were only two
members on each side, and in 1889 the match did not take place at all and did
not resume until 1906, seven years after the NRA had moved to Bisley.
Bisley's MP for many years, Cranley Onslow, shot continuously for the
Commons team for twenty years, while the Duke of Cornwall, one of the
titles held by the Prince of Wales, shot in the Lords team in 1980.

Today, the rules for the Vizianagram state that the competition is open to
one team of not more than ten and not less than three from each House; the
number to be decided by mutual arrangement, with the helpful rider that
'outside' coaches are allowed.

## ∽ THE ALL COMERS AGGREGATE ∽

The All Comers Aggregate was begun in 1884, following the increase in
the number of Martini-Henry rifles issued to the Volunteers, to replace the
Snider. Thus the Council replaced the Snider and Martini-Henry
Aggregates with the Volunteer and All Comers'. In 1890, a Challenge Cup
was presented by A.Clark Kennedy, as a memorial to his father Colonel

Clark Kennedy, a member of the Council, who died in Egypt in 1867. It was Clark Kennedy, a Council member for many years, who had delivered the favourable report on the suitability of Wimbledon Common as a location for the NRA. Today, the cup is awarded to the competitor with the highest score attained from competing in the *Daily Telegraph*, the Alexandra, *The Times*, the *Daily Mail*, the Wimbledon, and the Prince of Wales matches.

# APPENDIX I

# *Winners of The Queen's/King's Prize 1860–1986*

*Note*: The abbreviations in brackets after some names indicate the number of times the entrant has won the Gold Medal and if he/she has previously received another award. *GM* = Gold Medal; *SM* = Silver Medal (runner-up to The Queen's Prize); *GC* =Gold Cross (winner of the Grand Aggregate); and *SC* = Silver Cross (runner-up to the Grand Aggregate).

| | | | |
|---|---|---|---|
| 1860 | Ross E.C.R. | Pte. | 7th North York |
| 1861 | Jopling J.M. | Pte. | South Middlesex |
| 1862 | Pixley S. | Sgt. | Victoria Rifles |
| 1863 | Roberts J. | Sgt. | 12th Shropshire |
| 1864 | Wyatt J. | Pte. | London R.B. |
| 1865 | Sharman J. | Pte. | 4th West York |
| 1866 | Cameron A. | Pte. | 6th Inverness |
| 1867 | Lane H. | Sgt. | Bristol Rifles |
| 1868 | Carslake J.B. | Lieut. | 5th Somerset |
| 1869 | Cameron A. *(GM2)* | Cpl. | 6th Inverness |
| 1870 | Humphries W. | Pte. | 6th Surrey |
| 1871 | Humphry A.P. | Ens. | Cambridge Univ. |
| 1872 | Michie W. | C.-Sgt. | London Scottish |
| 1873 | Menzies A. | Sgt. | Queen's Edin. |
| 1874 | Atkinson W.C. | Pte. | 1st Durham |
| 1875 | Pearse G. | Capt. | 18th Devon |
| 1876 | Pullman R. | Sgt. | South Middlesex |
| 1877 | Jamieson G. | Pte. | 15th Lancashire |
| 1878 | Rae P. | Pte. | 11th Stirling |
| 1879 | Taylor G. | Cpl. | 47th Lancashire |
| 1880 | Ferguson A. | Pte. | 1st Argyll |
| 1881 | Beck T. | Pte. | 3rd Devon |
| 1882 | Lawrance A. | Sgt. | 1st Dumbarton |
| 1883 | Mackay R. | Sgt. | 1st Sutherland |
| 1884 | Gallant D. | Pte. | 8th Middlesex |
| 1885 | Bulmer W. | Sgt. | 2nd V.B. Lincoln |

| | | | |
|---|---|---|---|
| 1886 | Jackson C.H. | Pte. | 1st V.B. Lincoln |
| 1887 | Warren R.O. | Lieut. | 1st Middlesex |
| 1888 | Fulton G.E. | Pte. | 13th Middlesex |
| 1889 | Reid D. | Sgt. | 1st Lanark Engrs. |
| 1890 | Bates H. | Sgt. | 1st V.B. Warwick |
| 1891 | Dear D. | Pte. | Queen's Edin. |
| 1892 | Pollock J. *(SM)* | Major | 3rd V.B. A.&S. Highrs. |
| 1893 | Davies W.T. | Sgt. | 1st V.B. Welch Regt. |
| 1894 | Rennie M.S. *(SC)* | Pte. | 3rd Lanark |
| 1895 | Hayhurst T.H. | Pte. | Canada |
| 1896 | Thomson J.L. | Lieut. | Queen's Edin. |
| 1897 | Ward W.T. | Pte. | 1st V.B. Devon |
| 1898 | Yates D. | Lieut. | 3rd Lanark |
| 1899 | Priaulx W.A. | Pte. | Guernsey |
| 1900 | Ward W.T. *(GM2)* | Pte. | 1st V.B. Devon |
| 1901 | Ommundsen H. *(GC)* | L.-Cpl. | Queen's Edin. |
| 1902 | Johnson E.D. | Lieut. | 1st London (L.R.B.) |
| 1903 | Davies W.T. *(GM2)* | Cr.-Sgt. | 3rd Glamorgan |
| 1904 | Perry S.J. | Pte. | Canada |
| 1905 | Comber A.J. *(SM)* | Ar.-Sgt. | 2nd V.B. E.Surr. |
| 1906 | Davies R.fF. | Capt. | 1st Middx. V.R.C. |
| 1907 | Addison W.C. | Lieut. | Australia |
| 1908 | Gray G. | Pte. | 5th Scot. Rifles |
| 1909 | Burr H.G. | Cpl. | L.R.B. |
| 1910 | Radice F.R. *(SM)* | Cpl. | Oxford Univ. O.T.C. |
| 1911 | Clifford W.J. | Pte. | Canada |
| 1912 | Fulton A.G. | Pte. | Queen's Westmr. |
| 1913 | Hawkins W.A. | Pte. | Canada |
| 1914 | Dewar, J.L. | Sgt. | 4th Royal Scots |
| | | | |
| 1919 | Loveday L. | Sgt. | New Zealand |
| 1920 | Morgan F.H. *(SC)* | Sgt. | South Africa |
| 1921 | Cunningham J. | Ar.-Sgt. | late R.A.O.C. |
| 1922 | Marchment A.F. | Lt.-Col. | 1st London |
| 1923 | Robinson E.H. | Capt. | late R.A.F. |
| 1924 | Burke D.T. | Pte. | Canada |
| 1925 | Smith A | Sapper | late R.E. |
| 1926 | Fulton A.G. *(GM2)* *(SM)(SC)* | Sgt. | late Queen's Westmr. |
| 1927 | Vernon C.H. | Capt. | late R.A.M.C.(T) |
| 1928 | Hale A.C. | L.-Cpl. | late K.E.S. O.T.C. |

| 1929 | Blair R.M. *(GC)* | Lt.-Col. | Seaforth Highrs., Canada |
| 1930 | Foster M.E. | Dvr. | Women's Legion of Motor Drivers |
| 1931 | Fulton A.G. *(GM3)* *(SM3)(SC2)* | Sgt. | late Queen's Westmr. |
| 1932 | Bayly C.F.H. | C.S.M. | late 4th V.B. Royal West Kent |
| 1933 | Woods D.E. | O.-Cdt. C.S.M. | Nottm. Univ. O.T.C. |
| 1934 | Barlow J.A. | Capt. | W.Yorks. Regt. |
| 1935 | French F.S. *(SC)* | Ar.-Sgt. | late Herts Yeo. |
| 1936 | Busschau L.D. | Sgt. | South Africa |
| 1937 | Birney D.L. *(SM)* | O.-Cdt. | late Camb. Univ. O.T.C. |
| 1938 | Barlow J.A. *(GM2)* | Capt. | W.Yorks. Regt. |
| 1939 | Smith T.S. *(GC)* | Capt. | late 5th S.Staffs. |

| | | | |
|---|---|---|---|
| 1946 | Willott C.C. | 1967 | Powell J. |
| 1947 | Bennett R. *(SM)* | 1968 | Parks A.A. |
| 1948 | Pavey P.A. | 1969 | Little F.G. *(GC2)* |
| 1949 | Brookes E. | 1970 | Arnold G.F. |
| 1950 | Greig R.D. *(SM)* | 1971 | Stevens R.M. |
| 1951 | Boa G.S. | 1972 | Rosling R.P. |
| 1952 | Kinnier-Wilson A.B. | 1973 | Pilcher K.M. *(GM2)(GC)(SM)* |
| 1953 | McCaw N.W. | | |
| 1954 | Twine G.E. *(SM)* | 1974 | Harriss F.O. |
| 1955 | Fenwick L.R. | 1975 | Trotter C.M.Y. |
| 1956 | Twine G.E. *(GM2)(SM)* | 1976 | Magnay W.H. |
| 1957 | Love J.R.C. | 1977 | Friend D.A. |
| 1958 | Fulton R.A. *(SC)* | 1978 | Graham G.R. |
| 1959 | Mallabar L.W. | 1979 | Tucker A.St.G. |
| 1960 | Westling G. | 1980 | Marion A. *(SC2)* |
| 1961 | Beckett N.L. *(SM)(SC)* | 1981 | Ayling G.M. *(SC)* |
| 1962 | Hall P.W.M. | 1982 | Peden L.M. |
| 1963 | Pilcher K.M. *(SM)* | 1983 | Marion A. *(GM2)(SM)(SC2)* |
| 1964 | Harris A.D. | | |
| 1965 | Allen J.A. | 1984 | Richards D.F.P. *(SC)* |
| 1966 | Hampton R.W. | 1985 | Bloomfield J.P.S. *(SC)* |
| | | 1986 | Cox G. |

# APPENDIX II

# *Chairmen of the NRA Council*

| | |
|---|---|
| 1860–1866 and 1869–1870 | Col. The Rt. Hon. The Lord Elcho |
| 1867–1868 | Col. The Rt. Hon. The Earl Spencer KG |
| 1871–1874 | Col. The Rt. Hon. The Earl of Ducie |
| 1875–1879 | The Rt. Hon. The 1st Earl Wharncliffe |
| 1880 | The Rt. Hon. The Earl Stanhope |
| 1881–1883 | Brig.Gen. The Rt. Hon. The Earl Brownlow ADC |
| 1884–1886 | Col. Sir Henry Wilmot, Bt, VC, KCB |
| 1887–1890 | Brig.Gen. The Rt. Hon. The Lord Wantage VC, KCB |
| 1891–1896 | Lt. Col. The Rt. Hon. The Earl Waldegrave, VD |
| 1897–1902 | Brig.Gen. The Rt. Hon. Sir Henry Aubrey-Fletcher, Bt., CB, MP |
| 1903–1925 | Maj. Gen. The Rt. Hon. The Lord Cheylesmore KCMG, KCVO |
| 1926–1930 | Admiral of the Fleet The Rt. Hon. The Earl Jellicoe GCB, OM, GCVO |
| 1931–1939 | Col. The Rt. Hon. The Lord Cottesloe CB, VD, TD |
| 1939–1946 | Lt. Col. Sir Philip W. Richardson Bt., OBE, VD |
| 1946–1952 | Major E.G. Monro, CBE, TD |
| 1952–1960 | Marshal of the Royal Air Force The Lord Tedder, GCB |
| 1960–1972 | The Rt. Hon. The Lord Cottesloe, GBE, TD, DL |
| 1972–1984 | Sir Ronald Melville, KCB |
| 1984– | Field Marshal Sir Roland Gibbs, GCB, CBE, DSO, MC, DL |

# APPENDIX III

# *Bibliography*

*Bisley, Past and Present* by Sir Ronald Melville (NRA, 1984)

*Chronology of the Modern World, 1763–1964* by Neville Williams (Barry and Rockliffe, 1964)

*A Dictionary of Modern History: 1789–1945* by A.W.Palmer (Penguin, 1963)

*Dictionary of National Biography* (Oxford University Press)

*Europe Since 1870: An International History* (Weidenfeld and Nicolson, 1973)

*The Gun and Its Development* by W.W.Greener (Arms and Armour Press, 1910)

*A History of Wimbledon and Putney Commons*, edited by Norman Plaistow (Conservators of Wimbledon and Putney Commons, 1986)

*The Illustrated Encyclopaedia of 19th-Century Firearms* (Salamander Books)

*Illustrated English Social History* by G.M. Trevelyan (Longmans Green, 1960, Penguin)

*The Lee Enfield Rifle* by Major E.G.B.Reynolds (Herbert Jenkins, 1962)

*The National Rifle Association 1859–1909* by A.P. Humphry and Lt.-Col. The Hon. T.F.Fremantle (Bowes and Bowes, 1914)

*NRA Jubilee, Official Souvenir* (Gale and Polden, 1909)

*New Cambridge Modern History Volume X: The Zenith of European Power (1830–1870)*, edited by J.P.T.Bury (Cambridge University Press)

*The Oxford Companion to English Literature*, edited by Margaret Drabble (OUP, 1985)

*The Story of Bisley* by Howard N. Cole (Gale and Polden, 1960)

*Tennyson: The Unquiet Heart* by Robert Bernard Martin (Clarendon Press, Faber and Faber, 1980)

*Who Was Who* (1897–1916) (A. & C. Black, 1920)

*Who's Who* (1986) (A. & C. Black)

## Newspapers and periodicals

*The Camp Magpie* (1879)

*Daily Graphic* (various editions)

*Daily Mail and Graphic* (1895, and various editions)

*Daily Mail, Toronto* (various editions)
*Daily News* (various editions)
*Daily Telegraph* (1859 onwards)
*The House Magazine* (November 1985)
*Illustrated London News* (1860 onwards)
*Jersey Independent and Daily Telegraph* (1860 and various editions)
*Jeweller and Metalworker* (various editions)
*Mid-Surrey Gazette* (1878)
*Military Mail* (various editions)
*New York Tribune* (1875 and 1882, and various editions)
*Punch* (1860–1890, 1934 and others)
*The South London Press* (1869 and others)
*The Surrey Comet* (1879)
*The Times* (1859 onwards)
*Weekly Mail, Toronto* (various editions)
*Wimbledon Times* (1889 and others)
*Wimbledon, Tooting and Merton Temperance Gazette* (1886)

## Other
*NRA Journals* (1910 onwards)
*NRA Proceedings* (1860 onwards)
*NRA Rules of Shooting and Programme, 117th Annual Meeting* (NRA, 1986)

And always, always, *The Shorter Oxford English Dictionary*

# INDEX

# Jowett

ADVERTISING THE MARQUE

# "The CURFEW tolls—"

At least, the buzzer blows, and the road is filled with crowds of Jowett men. Their loitering feet and backward glances show very plainly they are loth to leave the scene of their labours.

And well they might be.

In this factory they make cars which are **'nulli secundus'** (see footnote).

A Jowett car was the first to cross Africa, West to East. The first to climb Park Rash. It will take 5 people 200 miles for less than 4/- each, petrol, oil and tyres.

It will do anything any other light car will do, but just a bit better. You can try one for nothing.

Prices from £135.                                              Tax £7

**N.B. (This means second to none; we got it out of a quotation book. Probably Greek!)**

## JOWETT CARS LTD. IDLE, BRADFORD

# Jowett

## ADVERTISING THE MARQUE

NOEL STOKOE

TEMPUS

*Frontispiece:* 'The CURFEW tolls–'. This 1932 advert shows what humour Jowett placed in their adverts. The text is full of grand words on how Jowett workers were loth to leave their place of work. The picture shows two workers sprinting out as soon as the hooter blows!

Other titles by the same author:

*Images of Motoring: Jowett 1901 – 1954.*
ISBN 0 7524 1723 1

*My Car was a Jowett.*
ISBN 0 7524 2796 0

First published 2005

Tempus Publishing Limited
The Mill, Brimscombe Port,
Stroud, Gloucestershire, GL5 2QG

British Library Cataloguing in Publication Data.
A catalogue record for this book is available from the British Library.

ISBN 0 7524 3535 3

Typesetting and origination by Tempus Publishing Limited
Printed in Great Britain

# Contents

# Foreword

I have always had a soft spot for the Jowett motor car, (although I have never owned one), and I suppose that is partly because Benjamin and William Jowett shared the same philosophy as my own hero, Sir William Austin. Their policy of providing dependable, down-to-earth transport which represented excellent value for money, and which appealed to the no-nonsense, cloth cap, working-class thrift market at which their cars were aimed, was akin to that of the Austin with the Seven.

If the Jowett was uncompromisingly individual and proud of its Bradford roots, however, Jowett advertising – particularly that which followed Gladney Haigh's appointment – was more so. As I wrote in *Automobilia* (Batsford, 1979):

> Their advertising had none of the high-flown classicism of Cadillac's 'Penalty of leadership', and yet, portraying a bluntness of character totally in keeping with the car's provenance, and a down to earth honesty, each homily they issued had a classic quality of its own.
>
> No other manufacturer has managed so successfully to combine straight talk with the lyricism of Laurie Lee and the psychology of Ned Jordan, and they made every word count.

I was equally enthusiastic when in 1976 I ghosted a book called *Any Colour So Long as it is Black - The First 50 Years of Automobile Advertising* (David & Charles). That the company were so successfully to change their image after the Second World War, without losing any of their individuality, is little short of a miracle.

In 1979 I wrote 'A full collection of Jowett advertising has never been published between two covers, but the seeking out and compilation of such a collection would prove a rewarding experience'. Now, albeit twenty-five years later, that collection has been brought together, and I can think of no one better suited to the task than Noel Stokoe, who has been publicity officer for the Jowett Car Club for as long as I can remember. I am delighted to be associated with this book.

Mike Worthington-Williams

# Introduction

My first memory of a Jowett was in the shape of a Javelin which was owned by my English teacher, Harry Watts, who was a good friend of my father, Norman Stokoe. The car he owned was a Golden Sand example, which as I remember, was very old-fashioned looking through a schoolboy's eyes, as Ford Zodiacs and the like were the new cars by then. This would have been in the early 1960s.

My father was a real car enthusiast, and owned fifty cars during his lifetime; he would wax-lyrical about the Jowett marque, but he never owned one. One of my most treasured possessions is a Jowett Jupiter sales brochure of my father's, with various calculations he had written on the back of it, regarding extras. He never bought the Jupiter, but I was too young at the time to know the reason why. I would guess that, as he was a married man with five children, this would have been a factor in his decision!

In May 1974, the Jowett Car Club held its National Rally on York Racecourse; by this time I was married to Jane and living at Riccall near Selby. My Mum and Dad were still living in York, as were Jane's parents. So we had a trip over to York, Jane went to see her parents and I took my Dad to look at the Jowett display. I remembered the Javelins very well, but it was the first time I had seen a Jupiter, and fell in love with them! Sadly, my Dad died four months later.

It was not until 1984 that I felt I was in a position to own a classic car, and the obvious choice for me was a Jowett, as they were cars with character. I am proud to be a Yorkshireman and wanted an example of Yorkshire's only mass-produced car. I joined the Jowett Car Club and the Jupiter Owners Auto Club in August 1984, and bought my first Jowett, a 1952 Jupiter registered JBE 4, in February 1985, which I still own. I have owned several Jowetts since, and at present I also have a 1952 Javelin and a 1953 Bradford Utility. I have been Press Officer and Librarian of the Jowett Car club for twenty years, and have also been Press Officer of the Jupiter Owners Auto Club for about fifteen years, posts I enjoy very much.

I have always been interested in how Jowett Cars Ltd tended to do things their own way, as they were away from the main car-producing area in the Midlands, so had a different approach to going about things. This was certainly the case when it came to advertising their cars. From the early 1920s the mould was set, and remained basically the same up to the outbreak of the Second World War.

The adverts would nearly always occupy a full page, and featured in the leading motoring press at the time, such as *The Motor, The Autocar* and *Light Car and Cyclecar*. They would be in a floral border with text inside; some had details of the cars, but many others extolled the virtues of Yorkshire and the Yorkshire way of life! They were also very prolific, and this collection is far short of the definitive one that Mike Worthington-Williams referred to in his very generous foreword.

I do hope that you will enjoy reading this selection as much as I did in putting it together – it has been a very enjoyable task.

Noel Stokoe,
July 2005

# Acknowledgements

First and foremost I need to thank Harry Mitchell and Gladney Haigh, and others at Jowett Cars Ltd, who wrote these wonderful adverts in the first place; without these there would have been no need to write this book!

I would also like to thank all the members of the Jowett Car Club and Jupiter Owners Auto Club, who have sent me copies of Jowett adverts over the years, in particular: Colin Bishop, Eden Lindsay, Geoff Boston, Geoff McAuley, Ted Miller, Dave Burrows and Ian Priestley.

Also my long-suffering wife, Jane, who is a constant source of help and encouragement to me in all matters Jowett! Also to my children, Jonathan, Jessica and Ben, who have grown up with Jowetts over the last twenty years.

I would also like to thank Campbell McCutcheon of Tempus Publishing for sanctioning this book. This is now the third I have written on the marque, and his continued support is greatly appreciated.

*one*

# The 1920s

The little engine ... with the big pull.

7 h.p. JOWETT £300 complete.
Wide Dickey Seat £10 extra.
De Luxe Model £335.

" Simple, Straightforward, Sturdy

**JOWETT CARS LTD. IDLE, BRADFORD**

It has already been well documented that Ben and William Jowett built the first Jowett car in 1906. It was used and tested by the Jowett brothers for around four years, prior to putting the car into production. Between 1911 and 1916 a total of forty-eight cars were built; at that time all car production ceased to assist in the war effort.

A larger purpose-built factory was constructed at Five Lane Ends at Idle on the outskirts of Bradford, which enabled car manufacture to commence again by early 1920. At this time, the Jowett brothers took on more clerical staff and increased the factory shop floor workforce. Two important appointments in respect of publicity and advertising took place at this time; the first was Harry Mitchell, who started as works manager. At the time of his appointment he had been working for ABC Motor Cycles Ltd. He was a very sociable person and produced Jowett adverts and sales brochures, and arranged publicity events. The second appointment was Gladney Haigh, who came in from a Bradford

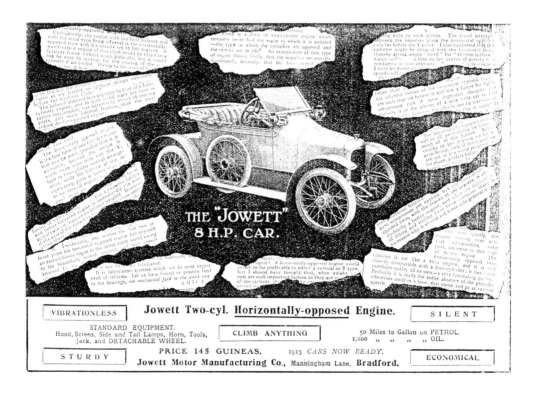

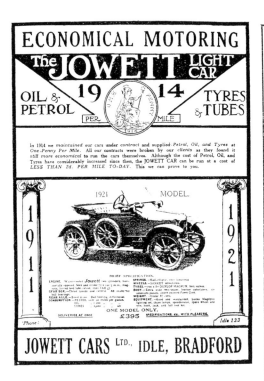
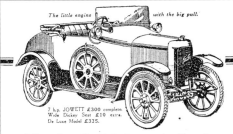

garage selling Karrier commercial vehicles. He was appointed as a buyer but in 1927 he took over writing sales booklets and adverts after Harry Mitchell left the company.

From the very start of their advertising, the main theme was to extol the fact that the cars were sturdy and strong and above all, cheap to run and maintain. The style in which this was done was unique as far as I am concerned. As mentioned in the Introduction, many adverts never pictured the cars at all, but asked the reader to send for a sales brochure. Another popular theme was to extol the virtues of Yorkshire and, if possible, take a swipe at Lancashire at the same time! I think it would be fair to say that it was Harry Mitchell who started this wonderful style, but was carried on to great effect by Gladney Haigh from 1927.

The Jowett brothers also liked free publicity whenever they had the opportunity. A good example of this came about in 1924, when a new sewerage system was to be opened between Bradford and Esholt. The mayoral party wanted to lay the last brick, which required a journey of three miles down a narrow sewerage tunnel in cars. Needless to say, they accepted the challenge and laid on four long-fours for the ceremony, which made the trip without incident.

It was as early as 1923 when one of Jowett's best-known slogans was first penned, 'The little engine with the big pull'. A typical advert from December 1923 extolling the strength and performance of the Jowett is one of a long-four, under the heading 'The car that stands out', which reads:

> So numerous are the points of superiority of the Jowett four-seater that it can be said to be in a class apart – ahead! When we say 'ahead' we mean it. Since 1906 it has remained the car with the smallest horse-power rating, and has won for itself a world-wide reputation as a high performance car.
>
> The world discredited our opinion when, in 1922, we staked our reputation on the capacity of a 7hp engine to haul a full-sized four-seater. But could we afford to risk a reputation so dearly won? Not a bit of it, we knew there was no risk, and so won as usual. Since the Jowett paved the way, look how the others follow. It was ever thus, and will be, since we intend to remain in front.

Another theme adopted by Jowett was the personal endorsement, particularly if it was from overseas, and better still, from the Colonies. These testimonials were regularly published in little booklets under the title of *Readers Opinions*; they were also used in sales booklets and advertisements. A nice early example appeared in *The Motor* on 2 September 1924 written by Commander C. Elliot RN, regarding his 1923 long-four in Lagos, Nigeria. This advert shows him sat in the car, complete with pith helmet, together with his wife, looking very glamorous in a large hat and long dress. Their black servant in shorts and wearing a fez is seen standing to the rear of the car.

The heading of the advert reads: 'Why 14 When 7 Suffices?'. The text reads:

The 7hp Jowett performs wonders in the far places where roads are mostly conspicuous by their absence, and conditions anything but favourable, except that the sun often shines. Across Africa East to West, the little engine with the big pull, is daily adding to its laurels.

How easily then will it conform to your more reasonable demands? Why 14 when 7 suffices and costs but half as much?

The following week, 9 September, *The Motor* published another advert, which clearly shows how Jowett utilised humour in their adverts. This shows a short-two in a country setting with two chaps in tweeds sat at the front of the car. The text reads:

'When are you going to sell it Jack?' 'Sell it! – Why should I sell it?' 'Because I want to buy it old man!'.
Had there been a brick handy, Jack would have shied it at his pal. There wasn't and the milestone was too big. Instead, Jack led him round to the local agents were he also bought a 7hp Jowett. So would you if you knew more about it. May we tell you? At the new price of £150 our two-seater is unrivalled, as was the four-seater at £170. Prices operative September 5 1924.

This style continued in 1925. Here are a few typical examples:

*GET THE JOWETTING HABIT......A 30 mile spin after an early lunch, a chat and a smoke, then home for a cup of tea before*

# THERE WILL BE A GREATER OLYMPIA THIS YEAR.

## BECAUSE THE JOWETT WILL BE THERE.

## VISIT STAND 16 AND SEE THE MOST COMPREHENSIVE RANGE OF ECONOMY CARS BUILT BY THE PIONEER ECONOMISTS.

At Show time the Technical Press usually classifies all cars on a price basis, to enable the public to decide which cars come within its purchasing power.

Do not forget, however, that The Jowett car, although well inside the £200 class, is equipped and finished in a manner usually associated with a £300 car.

At the prices quoted, each model is complete with Leather upholstery, Aluminium panelling, Speedometer, All-weather equipment, 5 Dunlop steel wheels and cord tyres, oil gauge, grease gun lubrication, full kit of tools, pumps, jack, etc., etc.

The tax is £7, and the cost of running is considerably under $\frac{1}{2}$d. per passenger mile. Everybody agrees that no car has a better performance than the Jowett.

May we be honoured by a visit at our Stand No. 16.

**2 Seater £168.**
Dickey Seat  -  -  extra £2.

Electric starter on all models - £10

**4 Seater £192.**

*Get your name on our waiting list for the new catalogue now in the press.*

# JOWETT CARS LTD., IDLE, BRADFORD.

the fall of the evening mists! That's Jowetting and it costs less than a bus ride. The annual tax is only £7, that saves you £5 anyway. Our literature tells how to motor and save money. May we send it, gratis?

OH – IT AIN'T GONNA RAIN NO MO'.......But if it does – what odds! There is all-weather comfort for the family in the new Jowett light four-seater. And the rhythmic beat of its vibrationless engine, with the bouyant feeling engendered by the fresh clean air of the countryside, just makes the kiddies want to sing all the songs they know. They are happy. So you can buy happiness! And it is cheap the Jowett way.

GOING UP? RATHER, WE'RE JOWETTING......Way up there in the hills there are a number of delightful little spots for picnic-ing and ne'er a char-a-banc all day. The Jowett will take you there every time. If you want to go where a Jowett won't, you'll need a windlass. Every Jowett is expected to perform prodigies – and does! That is why only the best materials can be used in their construction, and are!

ECONOMISE – THIS WAY......By shopping in the best market, instead of 'just round the corner,' you can easily save at least five shillings a week. Shopping by Jowett makes this possible, and the saving thus effected pays for running your Jowett nearly 80 miles. Jowetts are cheap to buy, economical to run, and sell for most when selling time comes A very important factor nowadays.

   You have probably read about our new catalogue. Everyone agrees it throws a new light on the subject of economy motoring. May we send you a copy free?

ON ILKLA' MOOR B'ART......Our caption is a bit of real 'Yorkshire.' So also is the Jowett car. 'Kullos' says it contains 'all the best of Yorkshire except the pudding.' 'The little engine with the big pull' goes everywhere.

SPRING OPENS THE DOOR......To what? If your car is a Jowett, to countless hours of joy, and endless miles of care-free motoring, at a cost you never dreamed possible. Including 'the little engine with the big pull,' and 'everything that makes a car a pal.' Two seater £168. Four seater £192.

THE RAIL WAY, 1d a mile, third class excursion. 'Catch-as-catch-can' for seats.

THE REAL WAY. Less than ½d a mile for 1st-class Pullman door to door travel. 'Jowetting' for four adults costs little more than third-class fare for one person. Take the family to the coast four times as often for the same cost as once by rail. Buy health, the Jowett way!

   And health means longevity, just as the provision of big, healthy components, sturdy design, and the incorporation of such items as real leather upholstery, hair stuffing, hand

*enamelled rustless aluminium panelling and a truly vibrationless engine, ensure that remarkable longevity which is a characteristic of all Jowett Light Cars.*

*IN SYLVAN SURROUNDINGS......Far from the madding crowd. Forget-me-nots and roses bloom not where 'charas' invade. Steal away to the glens and the glades off the beaten track, on a JOWETT CAR one-sixty eight pounds. You cannot motor for less than it costs on a Jowett car. Less than ½d a passenger mile. Investigate the Jowett, it saves money.*

*THE LAST WORD......The only thing that can beat a woman at her own game is the echo. There is no echo to the Jowett programme; it is the last word in economy motoring.*
*Has it ever occurred to you that the use of bus, tram, or rail is not the cheapest form of travel; that they are not the most comfortable of conveyances; that there is a vast difference between the 'shamway' and the real way?*
*If this line of thought has never struck you, may we suggest that you take the first step towards an introduction?*
*There are all too many instances where men have missed their mark by not taking the first step surely. If your mark be the freedom, joy and comfort of the real way of travel, then send for our catalogue, THE BIG PULL – it's the last word.*

*A YEAR OF PROMISE......The ensuing year is going to be a happy one for those who decide on the new Jowett.*
*A chassis, which while retaining all the features of the Jowett which made the car the most reliable light car in the world, has adopted such improvements as detachable heads, submerged oil sump, valves operated direct from the camshaft etc. Bodywork which has achieved the almost impossible task of improving upon last year's.*
*We say definitely that the Jowett is the cheapest light car to run, and that it is excelled by none in reliability.*

To further boost overseas sales, two booklets were produced in 1925 giving details of expeditions carried out by Jowetts. The first was called *Where there's a way the Jowett will go,* and describes the 840 mile trip from Alexandria across the Libyan desert to Siwa, and back via Gara. The party included one 1924 Jowett short-two and three American cars. The little Jowett proved to be far superior to the other cars as it never became bogged down, and never needed to be pushed or towed. It averaged at 47mpg, which was almost three times better than the American cars, a point that was not overlooked in the write-up! The second booklet gave details of a similar trip, with equally impressive results; this journey was from Cairo to Siwa and back on a previously unused route covering 930 miles.

As detailed in my earlier book *Jowett 1901 – 1954,* in 1926 Frank Gray, the former MP for Oxford, threw down a challenge to the car manufactures in the UK, to produce

TRY NOT THE PASS THE OLD MAN SAID

UNTIL HE SAW THE CAR WAS A
## JOWETT,
THEN HE ASKED FOR A LIFT.

He got it, of course, because
that's characteristic of Jowett
ownership, and, incidentally, of
the car's capacity to take a full
load where other cars take the
alternative route.

Not only is the car capable of
a high performance, but its first
cost is very low, and running
costs less than any other car.
The 2-seater, complete - £168
The 4-seater, complete - £192

### NO OTHER PERFORMS SO WELL.
May we post you Catalogue and full details?
JOWETT    CARS,    IDLE,    BRADFORD.

A JOWETT *IS* A JOWETT

*The 7-17 h.p. JOWETT "FULL FOUR." Price £192.*

AND WHEN  WE  SAY  JOWETT  WE  MEAN  IT.

A's ENGINE
B's GEARBOX
C's AXLES
D's CHASSIS
E's BODY

DO  NOT  MAKE  THE  CAR  YOU  WANT.
*THAT'S WHY WE MAKE ALL OUR OWN.*

No other engine is capable of the wonderful
performance, the unfailing reliability and
economy of "the little engine with the big pull."

The gearbox, axles and general chassis
work are of equal excellence.

Our bodywork has always been famous for
its roominess.  We make it of English timber,
panel it in aluminium, and upholster it in
leather.  It pays you  in  the  long run.

BUY THE CAR THAT'S BUILT TO SAVE YOU MONEY.
Fullest particulars, all models, on request to
### JOWETT  CARS,  IDLE,  BRADFORD.

a car capable of crossing Africa unaided. This was a trip that had never been attempted before, as for most of the journey there were no roads of any description. The Jowett brothers, however, realised the advertising potential such a trip would create and agreed to prepare two cars – each car would have to tow a trailer as they would need to carry their own water, petrol and supplies.

Gray would drive one car and a wealthy neighbour of Gray, Jack Sawyer, would drive the other. It should be noted that Sawyer could not drive but would learn on the trip! At a press conference prior to the cars' departure for Africa, a reporter asked Ben Jowett if the cars had any real chance of completing such an arduous journey, to which he replied, 'Wait and See'. Gladney Haigh heard this and ordered the two cars to be sign-written on each side one 'Wait' and the other 'See'!

The crossing was to be from Lagos in the West to Massawa in the East. There were various problems on route but neither car had any major mechanical problems, and the expedition reached Massawa sixty days later on 14 May, which represented only forty-nine driving days. In all, a total of 3,800 miles were covered – they even had time to rescue a slave girl and transport her 120 miles to safety!

The press loved this story of British endeavour and Jowett Cars received a considerable amount of publicity. The two cars went on tour, calling at Jowett agents around the country, so the general public could inspect them. These events also generated great

# MAKE A NOTE OF STAND 40.
## You Must See The
### 7 h.p.        JOWETT        Tax £7

The first
Light Car
and still
unequalled.

THE WORLD-FAMOUS TWO-SEATER.        Price £150
Earned the well-known slogan—
"The little engine with the big pull."

You cannot
motor for
less than on
a Jowett.

THE NEW LIGHT FOUR MODEL.        Price £160
Built to supersede so-called "Chummies."
"There's more room in the rear."

Why pay
for 12 or
more when
7 suffices ?

THE FAMOUS FULL FOUR - SEATER.        Price £170
The car that amazed all Africa.
The 7 that passes a 17 like a 70.

IF COMING TO OLYMPIA, ASK FOR
YOUR LOCAL AGENT ON STAND 40.
If not, write for Catalogue to

## JOWETT CARS, IDLE, BRADFORD.

GOES
EVERYWHERE
AT
HOME
&
ABROAD

*The 7-17.h.p. Jowett*
*Light Four, Price £160.*

*Fitted with "the little engine*
*with the big pull," it makes the*
*MILESTONES S'MILESTONES.*

# JOWETT CARS, IDLE, BRADFORD.

THE NEW REPRESENTATIVE

OF THE HOUSE OF JOWETT.

Elected by popular vote, the premier of its class.

As a member of the Jowett range, it naturally stands for true economy.

Buy the Jowett Light Four and ensure five years and more of care-free motoring.

With Dunlop Balloons £165-5-0
With Standard Dunlops £160-0-0

JOWETT CARS LTD., IDLE, BRADFORD.

interest in local papers, as the cars were battered and dirty, as they were left just as they departed Africa. Jowett Cars Ltd went on to produce a lovely forty-eight-page booklet called *Across Africa by Car in Sixty Days*, which gave a full account of this epic journey.

A full-page advert also appeared in the motoring press under the heading, 'Not an inch to spare', which shows 'See' being manhandled across wooden trestles over a river. The text goes on to say:

*The Trans-Africa Jowetts were frequently in tight places, with not an inch to spare. Here is one such; where a trestle bridge had to be rigged up to get the car ashore after crossing the White Nile by steamer. I always thought the Nile was black – with bullrushes.*

*There's geography 'without tears' as well as an amazing story of hardships overcome, in the 48-page book Across Africa in Sixty Days. May we send a copy gratis, along with the equally interesting 'This Freedom?'*

**Slogan sent by an owner, JOWETT'S HAVE MADE THEIR WAY BY THE WAY THEY ARE MADE.**

The cars ran on Dunlop tyres, so Dunlop were also keen to extract as much publicity as they could from the event. They placed an advert in the motoring press, saying,

> 'The Jowett Car involved behaved just as one expects a Jowett to do, and there can be no higher praise. The Dunlop Tyres stood up to the amazingly arduous conditions in a wonderful way, and the romantic trip afforded yet another testimonial to the durability and all-round excellence of Dunlop Cord Tyres.

Dunlop presented Frank Gray with a silver tea caddy in the shape of one of the cars to commemorate this achievement. This trophy is now owned by the Jowett Car Club, and is on permanent display, with other club regalia at the Bradford Industrial Museum.

1927 started off in a similar way with full-page adverts, mostly with text, with no pictures of the cars being offered for sale and no technical details about the cars either! A couple of typical examples are detailed below:

*B.B.C......We believe we are the only British Manufacturers to issue a folder giving running costs of the car produced.*

*This, coupled with experiences of Jowett owners, proves conclusively that the Jowett car can be run at a cheaper cost than any other car in the world. The Jowett Trans-African expedition and other feats of a like nature maintained our reputation for unfailing reliability, and we are reaping the reward of twenty-one years' fight for economy motoring.*

*Our scheme of deferred payments, devised and financed by ourselves (ensuring strict secrecy), allows you to take delivery of a Jowett on a first payment of £35, which includes tax and insurance for one year.*

# NEARLY EVERYBODY KNOWS ALL ABOUT The JOWETT.

But, in case you do not, we append details of their characteristic features, although we prefer you to read our catalogue which we will send free on request, and which describes minutely

| THE 2-SEATER | THE LIGHT FOUR | AND FULL FOUR |
|---|---|---|
|  |  |  |
| 7 17 H.P. TAX £7 | 7-17 H.P. TAX £7 | 7-17 H P TAX £7 |

**THE 2-SEATER**

This model has earned an enviable reputation for ultra reliability and economical service in the hands of private owners since 1910.

*" The little Engine with the big pull."*

Length over all   -10 ft. 0 in.
Width   -   - 4 ft. 6 in.
Height (hood up) - 5 ft. 6 in.
Wheelbase -   - 7 ft. 0 in.
Weight   -   - 8½ cwts.
Petrol consumption 40 m.p.g.
Oil   -   1,500 m.p.g.

Fitted with metal frames, side curtains, leather upholstery (hair stuffed), aluminium panelled and hand coach enamelled, full kit of tools, jack, etc.

**THE LIGHT FOUR**

Introduced this year, to supersede the so - called Chummy. We call it a Light Four because it seats 2 adults and 2 youths in comfort, not agony.

*" There is much more room in the rear."*

Length over all   -11 ft. 3 in.
Width   -   - 4 ft. 6 in.
Height (hood up) - 5 ft. 9 in.
Wheelbase -   - 7 ft. 0 in.
Weight   -   - 9¼ cwts.
Petrol consumption 38 m p.g.
Oil   -   1,500 m.p.g.

The rear side curtains may be used to form an effective rear screen. Entrance to rear seats is through wide door in front seat, no folding seat.

**AND FULL FOUR**

One of the roomiest bodies made, and will take four full - grown passengers and luggage anywhere, and maintain an average of 30 m.p.h.

*" Passes a seventeen like a seventy."*

Length over all   -12 ft. 0 in.
Width   -   - 4 ft. 6 in.
Height (hood up) - 5 ft 10 in.
Wheelbase -   - 8 ft. 6 in.
Weight   -   - 10 cwts.
Petrol consumption 36 m.p.g.
Oil   -   - 1,500 m.p.g.

A glove and newspaper rack is fitted in the rear compartment, and three capacious side pockets. Ample accommodation for cameras and accessories.

# JOWETT CARS, IDLE, BRADFORD.

B.B.C. is a decoration for Jowett, meaning 'Britains Best Car.' Shall we send you a range of interesting literature?

SWEET AND LOW......We imagine that out of the millions who have sung or listened to this pretty little part-song of Sir Joseph Barnby's, there are few who appreciate how neatly the above words apply to the running of the Jowett. For the running of the Jowett is certainly sweet and the cost of running is indubitably low.

We feel sure that the writer of the song had a Jowett in his mind when he penned the words, and yet, bearing in mind that the song was written before the Jowett was thought of, we must admit there is room for doubt. Be this as it may, there is no doubt that the Jowett is the cheapest car to buy, and the cheapest to run.

Its reliability, economy and general excellence are world-renowned. And look at its second hand value. Much above that of any other car. No wonder we are behind with orders, but we have made arrangements to remedy this.

'The little engine with the big pull.'

In early February a new series of pictorial adverts were sent to the motoring press. I should point out, however, that they featured a wide range of topics, but pictures of the

WARWICK
CASTLE.

*Jowett Cars never wear out.*
*They are, like castles, left*
*to the next-of-kin.*

*The*
# JOWETT
## LIGHT  CAR
## TWO-SEATER

*Compound in East Africa, where
Jowett cars earned undying fame.*

16

## Idle thoughts
### of an
## Idle fellow

You can buy other cars at a little more money than a Jowett. They appear to offer better value. But *do* they?

You can buy cars which *claim* to be more economical to run than we can *prove* the Jowett to be. But they are *not!*

Read our running costs and folder — and remember we were the first, and for years the only firm, to publish such figures. We may be still the only firm. Such is our confidence in our car.

You rarely see more than one or two Jowetts advertised for sale in the second-hand columns of the Press.

This is because a man buys a Jowett and keeps it. He knows a good thing. If he *does* decide to sell, there is no need to advertise. It sells itself.

The second-hand price of a Jowett is quite 20% more than other cars of similar first cost and equivalent age.

The Jowett saves your money every time. Decide on a Jowett now.

Short two, £139.   Long two, £150.   Chummy, £145.
Full four, £150.   Saloon, £185.

Dunlop Balloons and Stewart Speedometers standard

### JOWETT CARS LTD., IDLE, BRADFORD

---

## More "Idle" thoughts.

If it be true that "Contentment is better than Riches," the Jowett owner is in a very happy position. He has a car which makes him contented for the following reasons :—

His tax is only £7 per year. His running expenses are less than any other means of motoring. At the present price of petrol, the four passengers in a Jowett are carried one mile for a cost in petrol of one-twelfth of a penny each. The cost in oil is infinitesimal, while letters from friends show that their tyres have a life of 20,000 to 30,000 miles. The Jowett's reliability and performance are excelled by no car of anywhere near a like price. There is every reason for, and none against, the purchase of a Jowett. Although the cost of our car is low, we are just as pleased to deliver under our Hire Purchase Scheme (devised and financed by ourselves), whereby a first payment of £35 allows you to take delivery.

Short two, £139.   Long two, £150.   Chummy, £145.
Full four, £150.   Saloon, £185.

Dunlop Balloons and Stewart Speedometers standard.

### JOWETT CARS LTD., IDLE, BRADFORD

---

## Rays of Comfort.

| CHAMPIONSHIP TABLE — 30/6/27. | | | | |
|---|---|---|---|---|
| | P. | W. | L. | Per cent. |
| Lancashire .. | 14 | 7 | 0 | 75·89 |
| Notts .. | 12 | 6 | 1 | 71·87 |
| Derby .. | 10 | 5 | 1 | 71·25 |
| Leicester .. | 11 | 4 | 1 | 63·63 |
| Surrey .. | 11 | 5 | 2 | 63·63 |
| Yorkshire .. | 15 | 7 | 3 | 61·66 |

We are very much upset about the position of our County in the cricket world, but we folks in Yorkshire have our compensations. · For instance, the Astronomer Royal and thousands more had to come to Yorkshire for the finest view of the eclipse.

Again, thousands have already come to Yorkshire for the Jowett, the finest light car obtainable, and thousands are still coming and will continue to come, for while the eclipse was a matter of seconds, the Jowett continues to give satisfaction for years, and years, and years.

It is built that way.

The cheapest to buy and to run.

Our private system of deferred payments is the fairest ever devised. Please ask for catalogue.

Short two, £139.   Long two, £150.   Chummy, £145.
Full four, £150.   Saloon, £185.

Dunlop Tyres and Stewart Speedometers standard.

### JOWETT CARS LTD., IDLE, BRADFORD

---

## "The (W)Ringer."

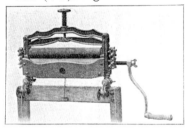

What Mr. Edgar Wallace thinks about the Jowett has not, so far as we are aware, been placed on record.

We are certain, however, that an author with such a consistently good output can have nothing but admiration for a car with such a good output as the Jowett.

A few of its good points :—

It makes bad roads—good roads.

Any road with any load.

First in 1906, still at the top.

Provides the cheapest form of motoring.

The cheapest to buy, the cheapest to run

"The little engine with the big pull."

May we send you our unique Catalogue and particulars of our private deferred purchase scheme?

Short two, £139.   Long two, £150.   Chummy, £145.
Full four, £150.   Saloon, £185.

Dunlop Balloons and Stewart Speedometers standard.

### JOWETT CARS LTD., IDLE, BRADFORD

cars were few and far between! These are a selection of them:

*HOW LOVELY!* (Picture shows a robin feeding from a person's hand)
*How lovely to have a car, which, to quote an opinion, has the appetite of a canary. (The Jowett has also the pull of an elephant). A car which is so docile, that it will, so to speak, eat, out of your hand. A graceful car. A car which covers distances with the smooth and perfect sense of flying...Effortless ease. There are no bad roads to a bird, and a Jowett makes bad roads into good ones. The car backed by 21 years' experience. The cheapest to buy, the cheapest to run.*

*BLACK AND WHITE* (Picture shows a team of Shire horses ploughing, they are all dark, except for one white one)
*We make no claims for the Jowett car which are not fully substantiated in black and white in actual letters from users. Consider this: "Mileage 40,000, three of original tyres still in use and engine untouched except for decarbonisation twice. Petrol consumption 48.7 mpg.*

*The Jowett is right because it is designed right and built right of right materials. The cheapest to buy. The cheapest to run.*

*SEA NYMPHS, BATHING* (Picture shows two elephants bathing in a large lake)
*This beautiful picture, which hangs in the National - Mong Dew - Carraba - hang it - it's the wrong one!*

TIME TELLS.

"*During the past week I have completed 200,000 miles, running on my 1913 Jowett car (shown above), and take the opportunity of expressing my satisfaction with the wonderful running and lasting properties of your production. During the twelve years this car has been in constant use by myself I have only had two stoppages—one owing to an encounter with a cow, and one due to a fractured ball race. The total cost of replacements has been under £15. The car is still in daily use and likely to increase the mileage considerably.*"

The above letter amply bears out the statement which was made several years ago by Kuklos of the "Daily News," i.e. that Jowett cars never wear out —they are left to the next of kin.

May we send particulars of this remarkable light car, fitted with the engine with the big pull?

SHORT 2, £139.  LONG 2, £150.  LIGHT 4, £145
FULL 4, £150.        SALOON, £185.
ALL models can be had on our own Hire Purchase Terms.
*Dunlop Balloons and Sin-car Speedometers standard.*

JOWETT CARS LTD., IDLE, BRADFORD

## Costs less than Tram-fare

Gone is the day of frenzied scrambles for a seat in 'bus or tram. Today, in your very own car, you can purr along smoothly, comfortably and speedily, sure that your Jowett will take your whole family wherever you want to go at less than the cost of tram and train fares. The Jowett is the car for the man who can't afford a car—all-in costs *for four people* are less than 2d. per mile.

The Jowett Saloon will easily climb a gradient of 1 in 4.

Real leather upholstery, hair stuffed. Dunlop Balloon Tyres, Speedometer, Electric Horn, Screen Wiper, Five-lamp lighting set, and Starter, Number Plates, License Holder, etc.
7 h.p. Engine.  £7 tax.

# JOWETT
PRICES
LONG CHASSIS MODELS—Two Seater - £150
Full Four   - £150  Saloon   - - £185
SHORT CHASSIS MODEL—Two Seater - £139
Easy Hire-Purchase terms, financed by ourselves, can be arranged.
SEND TODAY for FREE Literature. "This Freedom" (the catalogue-") "Across Africa in Sixty Days," "Running Costs," etc.

The secret of the ample leg-room in the Jowett car is the small space occupied by the engine. Compare these diagrams.

**Jowett Cars Ltd** <sup>Dept.</sup> **Idle Bradford**

# A JOWETT NEVER WEARS OUT

## It's left to the next of kin

Light though the Jowett is, and therefore cheap in petrol and tyre costs, it is built to last. We have numerous instances of cars running 200,000 miles without trouble. The Jowett will do everything a big car will do—at less than a quarter the cost. ¼d. per mile per person is the all-in cost (including depreciation) of a Jowett. It is therefore the car for the man who can't afford one. It's cheaper than tram, bus or train—more comfortable, healthier, and enjoyable. It's easy to drive and in tax costs only £7. You can afford this car if you take advantage of our private hire-purchase terms.

# JOWETT
## "The little engine with the big pull"

### PRICES

| Coachbuilt body-work. Real leather upholstery, hair stuffed. Dunlop Balloon Tyres, Stewart Speedometer, Electric Horn, Smith's Mechanical Screen Wiper, Five-lamp lighting set, Starter, Number Plates, License Holder, etc. | LONG CHASSIS MODELS<br>Two Seater ... £150<br>Full Four ... £150<br>Saloon ... ... £185<br>SHORT CHASSIS MODEL<br>Two Seater ... £139<br>Easy Hire - Purchase terms, financed by ourselves can be arranged. | SEND TO-DAY for FREE Literature, descriptive of the Jowett, the most economical of light cars: "This Freedom" (the catalogue), "Across Africa in Sixty Days," "Running Costs," etc. Fill in coupon below to-day, cut out and post now. |
|---|---|---|

*Fill in and post to-day for our FREE literature.*

Name _____

Address _____

JOWETT CARS LTD. Dept. A IDLE, BRADFORD

Equally with the elephant, the Jowett is noted for its power, but the Jowett is also as graceful as they make 'em, here it has the pull over the elephant. Still more are they divergent in their cost of upkeep, for the Jowett's appetite is that of a canary.

A Jowett gives you motoring at a cheaper cost per mile than any other car. Less than ½d per mile per passenger. The cheapest to buy, the cheapest to run. Change to Jowett and keep the change.

AND THEN MY HEART WITH RAPTURE THRILLS AND DANCES WITH THE DAFFODILS (Picture shows a bunch of daffodils)...... Wordsworth wrote of a scene in the Lake District, and the call of nature becomes instant. No matter where the "daffies" are a-blowing the Jowett will take you there, easily, comfortably, cheaply. Start on a fresh Spring morning, a happy, care-free day in the woods or by the sea, horning in the twilight, everything seems in tune. But – your car must be in tune also, and the car that most nearly reaches perfection is the Jowett. It will serve you faithfully for a longer time than any other light car. When, regretfully, you decide

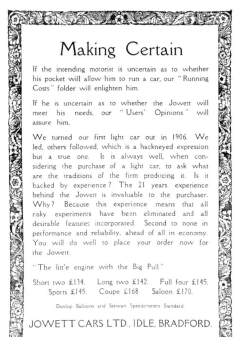

to change it for a new Jowett, it will command a higher second-hand value than any other car. Will you write for our literature?

THIS FREEDOM! (Picture shows a chick that has just broken free from its egg)......The chicken from the egg enters into a new world and so does the man who buys a Jowett. He receives not the Freedom of the City, but freedom from the city, the freedom of the countryside, the seaside. The Jowett owner has freedom from breakdowns because the Jowett design ensures reliability. He has freedom from financial worries because Jowett design ensures economy. The cheapest car to buy and the cheapest to run. There is no skimping. Real hair, real leather, aluminium panelling, Smith's automatic wiper; where will you find these on a car at anywhere near the price? Shall we send you our catalogue 'This Freedom'? A post-card will be sufficient.

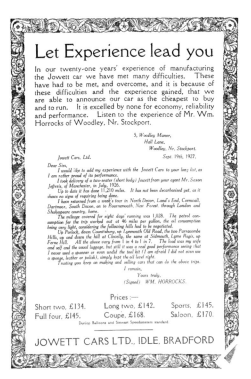

TWINS (Picture shows two Alsatian dogs on a lead)......Opinions are divided on the subject of Alsatians. They are treacherous, they are loyal, they are fierce, docile, cowardly, and brave – it is, in fact impossible to get a unanimous opinion on them.

There is no difference of opinion on the merits of a Jowett. It is safe, reliable and economical. The equipment leaves nothing to be desired, and the letters we receive daily from enthusiastic Jowett owner's offer striking testimony to Britain's Best Light Car. The Jowett offers motoring giving a maximum of pleasure at a minimum of cost.
**Send for our unique literature.**

READY FOR ANYTHING (Picture shows five young children on the seashore)......Up with the lark, and off to the sea. Listen to the delighted cries of the kiddies. How they enjoy the run! Even the Jowett's contented purr suggests that the car is enjoying itself. And then the arrival at the sea! Shoes off, socks off, and into the water. Happy, healthy, care-free joy – And later the journey home. The prattle of childish voices dies away, heads begin to nod, and soothed by the song of the Jowett, the children fall asleep. And you, your heart warms to your car and already you are planning next week's outing. This happiness can be yours tomorrow, but your car must be a Jowett. 'The little engine with the big pull.'

ANOTHER 'FRUITY' ONE (Picture shows an apple and an orange)......Dear Sirs, Re your advertisement in last weeks "Light Car," it may interest you to know that my 1925 Jowett pulled a greengrocer's cart loaded with twelve hundredweight's of crated oranges and bananas up the Snake Hill out of Glossop which is about three miles long and about 1 in 10 or 1 in 12. This was in addition of my wife and a large dog, and we created much amusement with passing motorists, many with much larger cars.

  Yours faithfully, Sidney Carter.

  Excellence of design, plus excellence of materials produce the excellence of Jowett motoring which is excelled by none. The cheapest car to buy and the cheapest car to run. Make your choice a Jowett and taste to the full the delights of economical motoring. **'The little engine with the big pull'**

A SONG TO SING (Picture shows a bar of music with the words 'I have a song to sing, O') Dear Sirs, You will be interested to know that this car has now run over 20,000 miles, during which time it has given absolute

## House, girl and car.

What of the man? Pooh, he doesn't count. We may admire the house, we may admire the girl (discreetly), but the man, he's only the insignificant being who pays the bills. We're bound to admire the Jowett, for where is the car that can hold a candle to it as regards economy, reliability and efficiency? The man who pays the bills has an easy job, for he finds his Jowett will almost run on the exhaust of the average car. The chances of it doing so, however, are few and far between, as the Jowett is generally in front! A typical Jowett log.

| | | | |
|---|---|---|---|
| Mileage | .. | .. | 17,000 miles. |
| Petrol | .. | .. | 49 m.p.h. |
| Tyres | .. | .. | Still in use. |
| Replacements | .. | .. | 1 Valve at 2/6 |

If you want economical motoring you'll have a Jowett sooner or later, and it might as well be sooner.

Prices from £134.     Tax £7.

*Shall we send you our literature?*
Dunlop Balloons and Stewart Speedometers Standard.

JOWETT CARS LTD., IDLE, BRADFORD

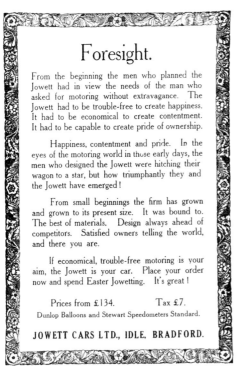

## Foresight.

From the beginning the men who planned the Jowett had in view the needs of the man who asked for motoring without extravagance. The Jowett had to be trouble-free to create happiness. It had to be economical to create contentment. It had to be capable to create pride of ownership.

Happiness, contentment and pride. In the eyes of the motoring world in those early days, the men who designed the Jowett were hitching their wagon to a star, but how triumphantly they and the Jowett have emerged!

From small beginnings the firm has grown and grown to its present size. It was bound to. The best of materials. Design always ahead of competitors. Satisfied owners telling the world, and there you are.

If economical, trouble-free motoring is your aim, the Jowett is your car. Place your order now and spend Easter Jowetting. It's great!

Prices from £134.     Tax £7.
Dunlop Balloons and Stewart Speedometers Standard.

**JOWETT CARS LTD., IDLE, BRADFORD.**

satisfaction, so much that I intend to keep it for another year. Previous to having a Jowett, I always changed cars every year, but now I see no advantage to be gained by doing so. I know you are not in a position to need praise, but when I do get extra good service, I like to **make a song about it**.

Yours truly TPC......Denbighshire.

The Jowett is always in tune with its owner. Everything on the car is in harmony. Its performance and reliability are fortissimo, shall we say great, while in running costs it is double piano (very low). Dare we quote a certain and say of the Jowett.

'The more we are together
The merrier we'll be.'

WHAT IS THIS? (Picture is a square of grainy mass)......It is a section of Jowett crankshaft, the magnification being 200. We do not consider it sufficient to buy the finest of steels it is possible to produce, but we regularly have these micro-photographs taken to assure ourselves that the very vital process of heat-treatment has been carried out correctly. In this case the structure is perfect. It is by working on these lines that we are able to produce in the Jowett car, which above all others bears the name for long life and reliability. The Jowett design ensures economy and performance, and justifies a new dictionary reading for the word perfection, i.e. Jowett.

We hope we have not bored you by this departure from our usual style. We haven't? Thank you. Jowett's provide the cheapest form of motoring, also the happiest.

Another nice humorous personal testimonial that appeared at the end of April, this was a text-only advert that takes a bit of believing!

WE WILL REWARD the owner of the Jowett mentioned in the letter below, if he will send his name and address.

Dear Sirs, I thought I would drop you a line and tell you this. On Monday when I was motoring round Gloucestershire and Worcestershire I pulled up at the top of Fish Hill, and to my surprise, there was a Jowett car at the top of this hill, which I should think is one of the steepest hills in the country, and there were **eleven up**.
I do not know if this is a testimonial to the goodness of the car or otherwise, but it rather tickled my fancy, and I thought I would just drop you a line to tell you.
Yours faithfully S.J. of Birmingham.

Although **slightly** overloaded, what striking evidence of the unbounded confidence every Jowett owner has in his car! "Any road with any load" is evidently our friend's motto. It is certain that Jowetts with their superior design and materials are daily doing work which would be a task for many cars of double the price. Make your choice a Jowett.

During May, June and July several adverts appeared, which did feature cars in interesting locations, the first of which featured a Long-Four, which they referred to as a Full 4, parked in front of the leaning tower of Pisa. The advert reads:

BALANCE......The Leaning Tower of Pisa is a marvel of balance, the top being more than sixteen feet out of the perpendicular. The Jowett engine, a horizontal twin, is even more marvellous in its balance. It exceeds a "four" in this respect and approaches the smoothness of the "six."

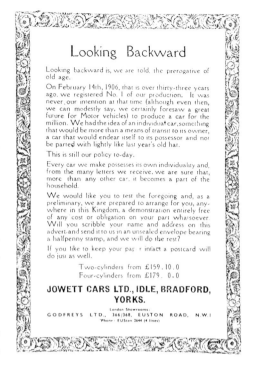

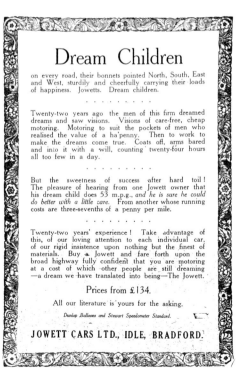

# ANTICIPATION.

It is a fact of life that a large percentage of the sum total of enjoyment derived from pleasures is accounted for by anticipation, but unless anticipation is followed by realisation life is void.

Thousands of potential motorists have remained in anticipation because they are afraid of the three motor Bogies—First Cost, Running Cost, and Maintenance. If some kind person would only show them the Jowett Running Cost Folder, or if they would write to us and ask for it, doubts would disappear.

For true enjoyment anticipation must culminate in realisation. We do not ask you to take our word for it that the Jowett is the cheapest car to buy, to run and to maintain, but a glance at our booklet "Owners' Opinions" will convince you that our statement is true; a copy awaits you at the address below.

Our catalogue is a straightforward collection of facts and can be had for the price of a post-card.

Hesitate no longer; learn more about the Jowett, the cheapest real car in first cost, in running cost and in maintenance.

## Prices from £134.

*Dunlop Balloons and Stewart Speedometer Standard.*

## JOWETT CARS LTD., IDLE, BRADFORD.

Consider what this smoothness means to you. Negligible wear, long life, freedom from irritating repair bills. In fact, one of the many reasons why Jowett motoring is cheaper than any other kind of transport. If happy, care-free, economical motoring is wanted, the car must be a Jowett. Send now for our unique literature.
Short 2 £139, Long 2 £150, Light 4 £145, Full 4 £150 & Saloon £185.

The next advert I am detailing shows a Saloon, sideways on, parked in front of a stately home. Jowetts were clearly very proud of this model, as several adverts featured it over this period. We now know this model as the Greenhouse Saloon, due to the amount of glass in it! The advert reads:

DECEPTIVE APPEARANCES......The appearance of the Jowett Saloon suggests a price of at least twice what it actually costs namely £185. Real antique leather, real hair stuffing, aluminium panelling, Smith's Automatic Wiper (the best of its kind), etc., provide equipment usually associated with cars at treble the price. There is no skimping on a Jowett, but it has its cheap points.
It is cheap to buy, cheap to run, inexpensive in upkeep. It provides the cheapest and, at the same time, the happiest form of motoring. Our range of literature is as unique as our range of cars. A p.c. will get you the former.

The next advert, which appeared a week later, featured a long-four, showing the full side view of the car. It was parked in front of a large country house; two chaps are with the car and are talking to a couple of young ladies who are on the front lawns. This one reads:

THERE'S NO HURRY!......These happy Jowett owners know their car will take them to the appointed place at the appointed time. That is one of the many happy characteristics of this wonderful car. Its ability to perform all task with an entire lack of fuss that makes the most difficult job look (and feel) simple. Its wonderful acceleration which enables it to get round the corner, or through the traffic, and away again while the other car is thinking about it. Of course, everything about the Jowett is just a little better. Even our literature, which a p.c. will bring to you.

This next advert also featured a Greenhouse Saloon, parked sideways on at the side of a Bowling Green. Two young ladies are playing bowls on the green in front of the car. The advert reads:

BOWLING ALONG......Dear Sirs, Just a few lines to assure you that I find your claims for the Jowett Saloon are too modest. In the course of a week's holiday, just completed on June 14th and on June 17th, I did 208 miles and 206 miles, the running times being 7 hours

# CRINOLINES!

Fancy a lady in crinolines in a light car, or riding pillion! Would the light car have killed the crinoline or vice versa?

They certainly needed space in those days, and, although to-day our ladies are more rational, they don't like squeezing.

(This statement requires a qualification, but we do not intend to pursue that line of thought.)

Do you want a car that is a tight fit for its passengers, or do you want to travel in comfort with roominess in plenty? There are many light cars of the former type, but only one of the latter —the Jowett.

The Jowett, as you can prove for yourself, is the roomiest light car made. It is also the most reliable, the most economical to run, and the most completely equipped.

All very good reasons why you should buy one.

Prices from £134. Tax £7

*Dunlop Balloons and Stewart Speedometer Standard.*

## JOWETT CARS LTD., IDLE, BRADFORD.

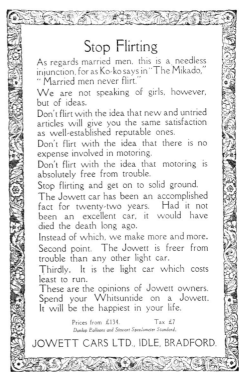

*45 minutes in each case and the consumption being 42.6 miles per gallon. I was not hard on the car at any time. The run was Corbridge-on-Tyne to Spalding (Lincs). The*
*Route was through the very hilly part of Durham via Allansford and West Auckland. The return journey was the same route except via Sleaford to Newark instead of via Grantham. Total mileage in 10 days 1023. Total petrol 24 gallons. Load in car 462 lbs.*
*Yours very satisfied, (signed S.H.P of Glasgow).*

*The Jowett Saloon gives you every comfort and its price is only £185. Better value cannot be found. And so cheap to run. May be had under own private deferred payment scheme.*

This type of advert continued right through 1927. These are a few more from October through to December:

*THE JOWETT SALOON......The Saloon is the Jowett car converted into poetry. It is the right answer to those who have arrived at the stage when a touch of luxury in motoring is welcome.*

*Well there you have it. Note the exceptional height of the roof. And the screen which is so helpful to the driver in times of mist – that is a boon. The windows give all the light and air that anybody could need and the view is unrestricted on both sides.*

*Inside there is a beautiful travel room to add to your home, giving you freedom in winter and summer, sunshine and storm.*

# Mount Everest

We wish to contradict the absurd rumour that a Jowett four-seater in climbing Mount Everest, boiled. We state definitely that the Jowett did not boil. The cooling system is so efficient.

Do you want further proof?

Here it is.

A Jowett has never made an attempt on Mount Everest!

So much for rumours.

Now for some facts.

The Jowett makes mountains into molehills.

It costs least to run and to maintain.

Its equipment is better than that of any other car of a similar cost.

It was the first car to cross Africa from west to east.

Every car has twenty-two years' actual manufacturing experience behind it. That is to say, we are not experimenting at your expense.

The Jowett absolutely satisfies.

Prices from £134.            Tax £7

*Dunlop Balloons and Stewart Speedometer Standard.*

## JOWETT CARS LTD., IDLE, BRADFORD.

Big, deep, delightfully sprung seats, and pillowy seat-backs, finished and trimmed in a way worthy of a boudoir, but in tough, serviceable, deep-ribbed Bedford Cord, or, if you prefer it, real leather. Look round for all kinds of fittings beloved of My Lady. Truly a most civilised car. And she will give you an average of twenty-five mph on a day's run.

THE PULL OF AN ELEPHANT (same sideways-on long four photo as used in There's no hurry)......Dear Sirs, Re 1925 Jowett full four 'I am proud to tell you that on Sunday last with my '25 full four I towed my friend's 2-seater, which I believe is a much heavier car, all the way from Beachy Head (Eastbourne) to North London which is a fairly hilly road most of the way. Incidentally, I have convinced the owner (who was sceptical) of the pulling power of the Jowett. I think his next car will be one of your production, and for a certainty my next car will be a Jowett again.'

A car with twenty-one years' experience behind it merits your attention, because experience counts very heavily in motor car production. The Jowett gives maximum performance at a minimum expense.

Its reliability is world-renowned. Allow us to send you our literature, including running costs folder, which tells you exactly how you stand.

OVER 50 MILES PER GALLON (same picture of a saloon as that used in Deceptive Appearances)......Read what Mr. Bruce has to say re the Jowett Saloon:

Dear Sir, - I thought you would be interested to know that we had returned from touring Devon and Cornwall in our 7hp JOWETT Saloon car. I was a bit dubious, as you will remember, before starting, whether the hills in that part of the country would be too much for her, but she took them all well with four of us up and luggage.

I thought the performance of my previous 2-seater JOWETT wonderful, but I consider the performance of the saloon is even more wonderful – you wonder where the power of the Little Engine comes from; and unless you knew when riding in her, one would think it was a high Horse Power Car.

I had no trouble whatever on the journey. I was much surprised with the petrol consumption, it worked out to over 50 miles per gallon and the small amount of oil used was also surprising, our journey covering over 1,000 miles.

Yours sincerely W.T. Bruce

Place your order for a Jowett now, and have no vain regrets.

WINTER COMFORT (shows a side view of a Coupe on a chilly winter morning with a young lady in a fur coat and hat stepping inside)......The Jowett Coupe at £168 provides cosy comfort for winter motoring, and by reason of its well-thought-out ventilation is free from stuffiness in the hottest weather. The design and colour-scheme never fails in its appeal to the fair sex, while its economy and reliability endears the Jowett to the man who generally has to foot the bills.

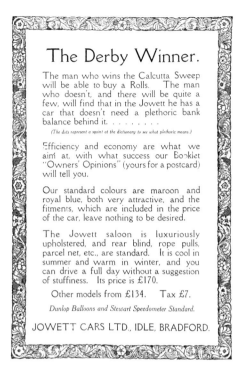

*If you prefer a car of larger seating capacity, allow us to send you details of our latest model, a well-designed fabric saloon with rounded corners. A car that makes an instant appeal. First-class travelling at less than third-class rail fare.*

*JOWETT'S GOOD YEAR ......We have received more praises this year from Jowett owners than ever before. So well has every model performed that we have decided to make no changes for the coming Show, so that all cars now being delivered may be said to be Show Models. Read the following letter and hesitate no longer. Order a Jowett now, confident that no car can approach it for reliability and cheapness in running.*

*Dear Sirs, I took delivery of a full four model during the week before August Bank Holiday, and on the Sunday (July 31st) I ran from Pevensey to Linton, Cambs, via Blackwell Tunnel. The distance, according to the A.A. and speedometer, is 110 miles from door to door. My wife and I have been over the journey so many times that there is no question on the mileage.*

*On leaving Linton in the evening I had to fill up, and much to my amazement-also the garage owner's-* **the tank overflowed before 2 gallons** *had put through the pump. Over a pint was wasted, and as I had not filled the tank so full before starting, you will have a good idea of the petrol consumption: over 60 m.p.g. I estimate. The load consisted of wife and self with a fair amount of luggage and a hilly ride to London.*

*Please use this letter if of any use. The Jowett puts up a better mileage than you claim.*
*Yours faithfully, W.M. Kidman. Pevensey, August 4th 1927.*

1927 was rounded off with a New Year message which read as follows:

THE NEW YEAR......The directors and staff of Jowett Cars Ltd. Extend to all motorists their best wishes for a Happy and Prosperous New Year.

In the case of present Jowett owners they are certain that their wishes will come true.

You get happy motoring all year round with a Jowett. Start the year right by buying a Jowett.

1928 carried on in a similar vein; here are a few examples from January through to March:

A 'FABRICATION (shows side view of a greenhouse saloon with a lady stepping in)...... But it is no fabrication to describe the new Jowett Fabric saloon as one of the smartest cars on the road. The fabric is a lovely shade of blue. Rear corners are nicely rounded. Interior fittings to match, the seats and back cushions being pleated, and the proud owner, parking his car, has the satisfied feeling that among the cars assembled his Jowett is equal to the best and better than the majority. A landmark in Jowett history. A proof that Jowetts can supply the beautiful as well as the serviceable. In fact, with this model, beauty and service go hand in hand. No stropping, no honing. Sorry. No drumming, no groaning. Place your order now for early delivery. Price £170.

JOYS TO COME (shows a small girl and boy picking daffodils with a long-4 parked in the distance behind them)......Easter will soon be here, to be followed, let us hope, by "a summer of roses and wine." The demand for Jowetts increases daily, for the motorist who is anticipating tasting these joys to come is placing his order now and making sure of prompt delivery. There is no motor joy like Jowetting. With a petrol consumption between 40 and 50 miles per gallon, negligible oil consumption, and tyres which seem like Tennyson's brook "to go on for ever," the Jowett owner experiences satisfaction in full. Known throughout the world for its reliability, a fair owner suggests the following motto, 'THE JOWETT NEVER LETS YOU DOWN'

Decide now and cut out vain regrets. May we send our interesting literature?

ROADMENDERS (shows a greenhouse saloon overtaking a steamroller working on a city street)......The Jowett is the best roadmender. Its well-sprung chassis, its deep seats and backs with best coppered springs and real curved hair (no fibre used) damp out the shocks on the worst road, and give the Jowett owner a sense of physical well-being.

Just as important is his mental well-being, and in this regard the owner of a Jowett is particularly happy. He never worries as to whether his car will get 'there.' When he gets 'there' he knows he has done so at a cheaper cost than any other means of transport.

A Jowett owner is a happy motorist.

AND IT'S ALL ABOUT A
# JOWETT
## THE LITTLE ENGINE WITH THE BIG PULL

We wish to contradict the rumours respecting the Jowett models at the Show for 1928.

1. There will not be a Jowett four-cylinder.
2. There will not be a Jowett six-cylinder.

What will there be?

Our only model will be the famous Jowett horizontally opposed two-cylinder engine.

"The Little Engine with the Big Pull."

Why?

Because during 22 years' manufacture of this engine we have proved to the hilt that it is—

A. Cheapest in running costs and upkeep.
B. The most efficient light-car power unit.
C. As free from trouble as it is possible for machinery to be.

Petrol 40/50 m.p.g.        Tax £7.

## Prices from £134

Tear this page out and post it to us with your card. You will receive some very readable booklets.

*Dunlop Balloons and Stewart Speedometer standard.*

# JOWETT CARS, LTD., IDLE, BRADFORD

*TO DISBELIEVERS* (shows a rear view of a short-2 parked overlooking a lake, with a couple taking in the view)......*When a man tells you his dog is champion of its class you smile and probably disbelieve. When hosts of people confirm his claim, you will begin to sit up and notice. We claim our car is the best in its class, but you possibly prefer opinions from disinterested people, and perhaps you are wise.*

*Very well then, 'Jowett Owners' Opinions' is a booklet of which we are justly proud. A comprehensive selection from our thousands of testimonials is printed, covering as wide a range of conditions as possible. We cannot do it justice here, yet a post card brings it to your door.*

*Learn more about the wonderful 7hp Jowett; it is good to know, and this knowledge will make you wonder – can I afford to walk?*

*EXTENDING OUR PRESTIGE* (shows side view of a coupe in a stately home garden)...... *Owners of our latest model are writing in to say that this is the most comfortable car they have ever ridden in, and that the springing is wonderful. We see to these points before we allow a new model to be offered.*

*As yet we have not received any letters praising the coupe's performance and economy, but these will follow as our new model worthily upholds the Jowett traditions in these respects.*

*An exceptionally wide door, single screen with patented adjustment, and an artistic two-colour scheme have made this model a popular success and the price is only £168.*

*BEHOLD, A GIANT AM I* (shows a drawing of a family in a long-4 with a windmill in the background)......*The poet put these words*

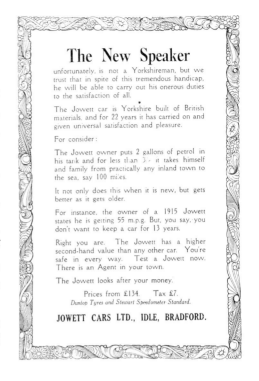

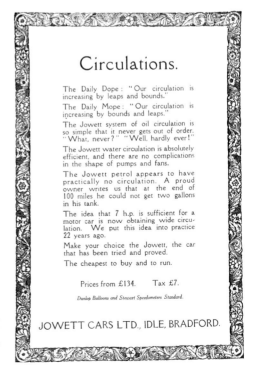

into the mouth of a windmill. The Jowett performs a giant's task throughout the year, and all you can hear from it is its contented purr. There is no fussiness. The little engine with the big pull is ready for any demand made upon it, and meets the demand cheerfully, willingly, efficiently. And the extraordinary economy!

Well might one of our friends say that his Jowett is as economical as a windmill. He's exaggerating of course, as petrol, oil, and tyres are hardly as free as the wind. Still the Jowett's appetite for these essentials is so small as to be incredible to the man who has never owned one.

Place your order now. You can't motor for less cost unless you are always a guest. Built to last a lifetime. Another friend states 'Jowett's never wear out, they are left to the next-of-kin.'

Advertising carried on in a similar vein through 1928. In October several advertisements were taken out to promote the Motor Show at Olympia, where the updated models for 1929 were on display. They all had the same picture of the new short-four; these are couple of them:

LOOK BEFORE YOU LEAP......Probably a quarter of a million people will visit Olympia
     But there are about 40,000,000 in the British Isles.
     This announcement is for the 39,000,000 odd people (odd refers to the number, not the people) who will not be at the show.
1. There is no car that can be run more cheaply than the Jowett.
2. There is no light car with better equipment or bodywork.
In support of the first we will send you our "Owners' Opinions" and "Running Costs," and in support of the second our Catalogue "The Big Pull," if you fill in and post us this page. Our prices are from 105 guineas.

JUST MISSED IT......This is our Short Four, 105 guineas "Why don't you cut a few things and give us the £100 car?" asked a friend.
We could have cut out the shock absorbers, speedometers, wiper, driving mirror, starter, two lamps, tool kit etc., fit cheaper tyres and upholstery that would look like nothing on earth after a few weeks use. We could have done this and it still would have been a car. We believe however, that the prospective motorist requires a full equipment, and as we can buy this cheaper than he can, we do so and let him have the benefit. Send for our catalogue 'The Big Pull.' All Jowetts are completely equipped.

Another all-text advertisement appeared in December, which I think, is fun, so typical of Jowett sales banter:

A BLUNDER!......Someone blundered and we had the Charge of the Light Brigade. A wonderful job, but costly.

We produced the Jowett Short Saloon. A wonderful job, but costly. Someone blundered, and our Charge was too Light......

In plain English, we are, from Dec. 10th, raising the price from £125 to £130. We are doing this because we believe the public would rather pay the extra £5 than that we should reduce quality. We regret the increase, but we can't help it.

The prices of our other models will remain as before, namely.

Short Four, 105 guineas. Long Four, £141. Long Saloon, £163.

THE LITTLE ENGINE WITH THE BIG PULL.

Moving on to 1929, this well-established style continued, as before. There was, however, a considerable amount of advertising devoted to the new Black Prince model. These all had the same three-quarters front view of the car, with a selection of texts. These ran from May right through to September. I will detail a few of these to give you the feel of them. The first two must have been before and after a general election!:

HOW WILL YOU VOTE?......The Jowett Black Prince (shown above) ran 210 miles last weekend, from Bradford to North of Newcastle and back.
Passengers carried, three adults and three children.
Luggage for the weekend.
Total weight 55 stones.
Petrol used 5 gallons.
Each passenger travelled 210 miles for 1s. 4d.
Whatever you're political convictions you can vote for a Jowett.
It is Conservative in its running costs.

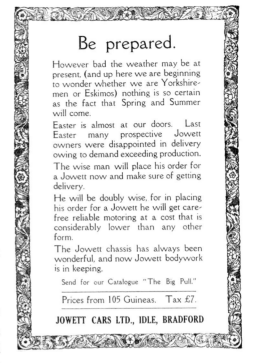

It is Liberal in the contentment it gives.
Its ideal is Labour. That is to say, the harder the work the happier it is.
Prices from 105 guineas.
VOTE FOR JOWETT.
Fill in the form below for (s)election literature.

RESULT OF THE POLL......The Jowett miles ahead and rightly so.
For we have been making light cars for 23 years, and experience does it.
In the Jowett, experience gives you the roomiest body ever put on a light chassis.
Experience gives you low running costs (lowest of any car), reliability (it takes you there and back), efficiency (any road with any load)....Finally.
The Jowett "Black Prince" is the handsomest light car on the road. It looks worth £300. It costs £175. Other models from 105 guineas.
The little engine with the 'Big Poll' (Sorry).

THE BLACK PRINCE......The owner of a Black Prince writes us to say that he considers his car stands out amongst light-cars of today as prominently as Edward the Black Prince stood out amongst his contemporaries.
    We blush modestly and leave it to you.
    We think that the Jowett Black Prince is the smartest light car on the road.
    We know that the Jowett is the cheapest car to run, and that for reliability and performance it is excelled by none.
    If pounds shillings and pence are a consideration with you, you should investigate our claims. The Jowett is definitely a money-saver. Prices from 105 guineas. Tax £7.

NULLI SECUNDUS!......Second to none is this Red and Black Jowett Saloon in appearance, and for economy of upkeep, performance and reliability it leads the field.
    To see it is to desire it, and to possess it is to be satisfied.
    It is beautiful outwardly, and when you sit inside the fittings and interior are just lovely. It is as comfortable and roomy as it is beautiful. Your luggage is accessible from inside and out, a great boon in bad weather.
    An alternative colour scheme is cream and black. Cream mouldings, cream stretchers and cream wheels.

ROUGE ET NOIR......The Jowett Red and Black Saloon.
    Everybody who sees one breaks a commandment. People come round one wherever it stops and have a look at the name on the radiator before they can believe it is a Jowett and not a car costing £400.
    The colour scheme is black with vivid red mouldings and red wire wheels.
    A one-piece opening, adjustable windscreen is provided.

The price is £175.

Production of this model will be limited, as we cannot allow it to interfere with production of standard models, therefore early application should be made.

Tear out this page and post it to us. Unsealed envelope, halfpenny stamp.

EE, BY GUM!......A correspondent, noting our use of Latin and French in recent adverts, writes to ask if we know any more languages.

Here's a bit o' Yorkshire for him.

It expresses delight and wonderment at seeing a Jowett Black Prince for the first time.

And it really is a lovely car.

Trimmed in red and black, with beadings and wire wheels in red or cream to choice, it is nice inside as outside.

Tasteful mahogany mouldings, silk rope pulls, parcel net, rear blind with door pockets and dashboard lockers; when you buy a Black Prince you only need to buy a licence and that's only £7 a year. Petrol consumption 40/50 mpg.

The handsomest light car on the road, and the cheapest to run.

Prices from 105 guineas

.

EIN, ZWEI, DREI......Latin, French, Yorkshire (claimed by Lancashire) and now German. What linguists we are!

There are three points about the Jowett which must appeal to the practical man:
1) Efficiency.
2) Economy.
3) Reliability.

There is a fourth point (we forget the German for four).

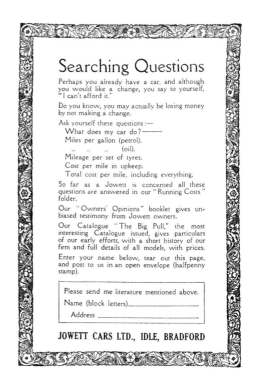
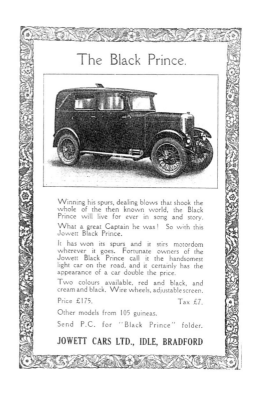

# A lying jade.

Dame Rumour has been busy again and the purpose of this notice is to contradict her and assure all and sundry that we are not bringing out a four-cylinder model this year.

Our programme for 1930 is laid out and it consists solely of our well-known two - cylinder engine. We can only as yet partially withdraw the curtain and say that our "Little Engine with the Big Pull" will, owing to certain improvements, have a bigger pull than ever.

It will actually be in your interest to send us your name and address so that we may, as soon as possible, advise you of these improvements, and also send you such details as will make you eager to become a Jowett owner as early as possible.

1930 will be a Jowett year.

**JOWETT CARS LTD., IDLE, BRADFORD**

The Jowett Black Prince (shown above) is the handsomest light car on the road. Its price is £175 and it looks a £300 car. Other models from 105 guineas. You won't be happy till you get one, so why miss happiness.

Our literature is yours for the asking, and whether or not you buy a Jowett you'll find it very interesting.

CAN YOU DO THIS?......After writing this, I shall start my holidays. My car is a Jowett long saloon.

I shall have 3 adults, three children (ages 14, 12 and 9). Luggage for all, and one large Alsatian dog.

We shall go up North among the hills. Our average petrol consumption will be about 45mpg. We shall climb all the hills we come across, and I do not expect to break down (touch wood).

Conditions will be rather crowded, but we shall have a jolly party, and the Jowett will be jolly too.

If your car won't do this, sell it and buy a Jowett, and you will start saving money. Verbum sapienta! (Languages again).

GNASHING OF TEETH......The heading sounds like we are going to speak of gear changing...... No, we are simply wondering if the petrol companies gnash (isn't gnash a funny looking word) their teeth when they read what wonderful mileage a Jowett gets on a gallon of petrol.

We've a letter from a Jowett owner, which states that he is getting 52 mpg on a long saloon. We claim 45 mpg, but we always err on the modest side. We can prove conclusively that the Jowett is the cheapest car to run, and is the car for you.

SWEEPS!......What uncertain things the Derby Sweeps are. You put down your money and hope for the best, entirely dependent on luck.

With the Jowett car, how different. You put down your money and find to your lasting delight that not only have you drawn a winner, but an actual money-saver.

For there are Sweeps and Sweeps.

The Jowett makes a clean sweep of high running costs, of inefficiency, and motoring troubles.

And further, for your satisfaction, it is the handsomest light car on the road.

A SURE THING!......This is not a tip for the Derby. We prefer to keep our feet on solid ground.

The Jowett Black Prince is a sure winner in the following classes:

ECONOMY! EFFICIENCY! RELIABILITY! ELIGANCE!

The Jowett has not hitherto been an entrant in the last class, but today the Black Prince is the smartest looking car on the road. Best quality highly glazed black fabric, with beadings,

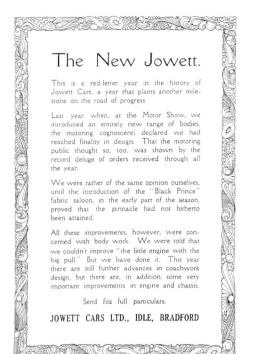

## The New Jowett.

This is a red-letter year in the history of Jowett Cars, a year that plants another milestone on the road of progress.

Last year when, at the Motor Show, we introduced an entirely new range of bodies, the motoring cognoscenti declared we had reached finality in design. That the motoring public thought so, too, was shown by the record deluge of orders received through all the year.

We were rather of the same opinion ourselves, until the introduction of the "Black Prince" fabric saloon, in the early part of the season, proved that the pinnacle had not hitherto been attained.

All these improvements, however, were concerned with body work. We were told that we couldn't improve "the little engine with the big pull." But we have done it. This year there are still further advances in coachwork design, but there are, in addition, some very important improvements in engine and chassis.

Send for full particulars.

**JOWETT CARS LTD., IDLE, BRADFORD**

## Back to the North

The Show closes next Saturday, and we're off back to Idle.

That's a comical name for a place where Jowetts are as busy as bees turning out cars for people who realise that in the light car world the Jowett offers the most comfortable and cheapest form of motoring.

We've got a lot of orders, but we would like yours, and the following points may help you to decide :—

A Jowett does 40/50 m.p.g.

Twenty shillings buys more horse power in a Jowett than in any other car.

Jowett tyre mileage is definitely longer than that of any other car.

These are facts, not fancies, and we can prove them to you.

Send now for our catalogue, "The Bigger Pull."

**JOWETT CARS LTD., IDLE, BRADFORD.**

stretchers and wire wheels in cream or red, according to choice, the Black Prince gives you plutocratic feeling at a democratic cost. The price is £175 complete.

*THIS GREEN AND PLEASANT LAND......* The long days are here, and this lovely land of ours (the finest in the world) is displaying her beauties for everyone to see. Make her acquaintance and do it in a Jowett. It does not matter whether it is the hills of the North or the valleys of the South, the lakes of the West, or the plains of the East, the Jowett is designed and built to take you there at a lower cost than any other means.

And when you take a snapshot of a beauty spot, with your family and the Jowett Black Prince in the foreground, this handsome car will hold its own.

'Gather ye rosebuds while ye may
Old Time is still a-flying.'

*two*

# The 1930s

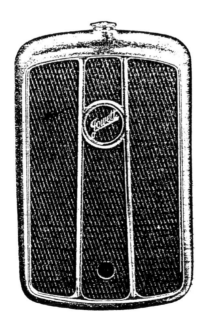

**JOWETT CARS LTD. IDLE, BRADFORD**

It is fair to say that there was no change at all in the advertising style, moving from the 1920s to the 1930s, it was just more of the same. The adverts for the Black Prince continued as previously, using the same picture as before. A typical example was from January 1930:

THE DAUNTLESS THREE
'The Black Prince.' A car for those to whom quiet refinement appeals. Black body, red or cream mouldings and steering wheel.
   'The Grey Knight.' The smartest car on the road. Wherever it stops the passers-by admire. Lovely shade of grey, with blue mouldings, steering wheel and wire wheels.
   'Silverdale.' A car for every occasion, business or pleasure. Fawn body, with mouldings, steering wheel and wire wheels to match.
   Each model upholds the Jowett traditions of economy, efficiency and reliability.
Price £177.10s. Tax £7.

Personal testimonials also continued in the same format as before. This is a typical example from March 1930, which was all-text in the traditional floral border:

LET OTHERS SPEAK......Dear Sirs, I have just taken over delivery of my 'Black Prince' and must tell you how delighted I am with the car.
   I have done 60,000 miles on one of your 1926 saloons, and although many people tried to persuade me to have something different this time, I felt it would be ungrateful to a car that had done such service.
   Now that the 'Black Prince' has arrived I am more than ever glad that I remained faithful to the Jowett – **I know** the engine to be good – just **because** it is a Jowett – and there is not a detail of comfort that could be added to the body.
   Many congratulations, Yours very truly Elsie Duniam Jones.
(Further letter in reply to ours asking for permission to use the above as a testimonial).
   Dear Sirs, By all means use my letter if you wish. You may add that I got a very good allowance on the old car.
   The new one is really lovely, and all my friends are as enthusiastic about it as I am.
   Yours very truly, Elsie Duniam Jones.

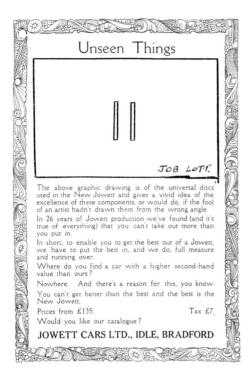

In October 1930 advertisements were placed in the motoring magazines, showing the new-style radiator grille for the 1931 models. The following selection of adverts are from October to December 1930, they all show the same picture of the Jowett saloon, sporting the new grille; the texts from these are as follows:

*STAND 11, OLYMPIA......The heading is for the benefit of visitors to the Motor Show, where we shall be able to show them seven of the best light cars ever produced.*

*To those who do not attend we have to say that our Catalogue, 'A Silver Wedding,' is now ready and will be sent on receipt of the form below.*

*The Jowetts we are now producing will lift Jowett prestige higher than ever, and orders should be placed early.*

*Prices from £142. Tax £7.*

*BACK HOME AGAIN......'The tumult and shouting dies. The Captains and the Kings depart.'*

*We don't think even our most fervid admirers would place us in the 'Captains and Kings' class but we are proud of the fact that to thousands the word Jowett is held in esteem; for this is the car that opened up to them the joys of efficient economical motoring.*

*We say to them, and intending motorists, that the 1931 Jowett is better than ever, and that they will do well to place their orders early.*

# The 1931 Jowett

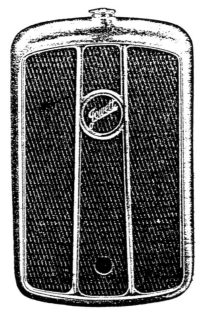

will carry this radiator, and it really is surprising how much more handsome our cars look. Improvements to the chassis have kept pace, and your new Jowett will afford you infinite delight.

Prices from £142. Tax £7.

Our 1931 Catalogue "A Silver Wedding" is now in the Printer's hands, and by filling in and posting the form below, your copy will reach you in due course.

Please send "A Silver Wedding" to—

Name...........................................................................

Address........................................................................

..................................................................................

Unsealed envelope, ½d. stamp.

## JOWETT CARS LTD., IDLE, BRADFORD.

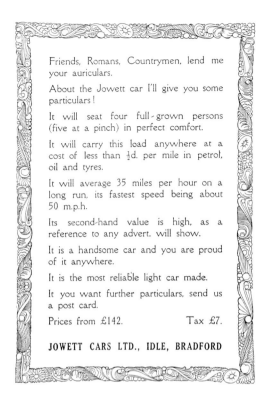

Friends, Romans, Countrymen, lend me your auriculars.

About the Jowett car I'll give you some particulars!

It will seat four full-grown persons (five at a pinch) in perfect comfort.

It will carry this load anywhere at a cost of less than ½d. per mile in petrol, oil and tyres.

It will average 35 miles per hour on a long run, its fastest speed being about 50 m.p.h.

Its second-hand value is high, as a reference to any advert. will show.

It is a handsome car and you are proud of it anywhere.

It is the most reliable light car made.

If you want further particulars, send us a post card.

Prices from £142.      Tax £7.

**JOWETT CARS LTD., IDLE, BRADFORD**

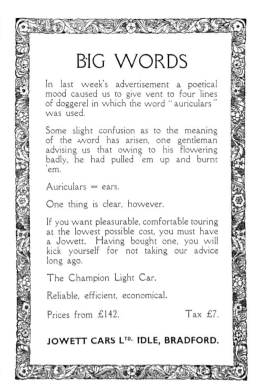

## BIG WORDS

In last week's advertisement a poetical mood caused us to give vent to four lines of doggerel in which the word "auriculars" was used.

Some slight confusion as to the meaning of the word has arisen, one gentleman advising us that owing to his flowering badly, he had pulled 'em up and burnt 'em.

Auriculars = ears.

One thing is clear, however.

If you want pleasurable, comfortable touring at the lowest possible cost, you must have a Jowett. Having bought one, you will kick yourself for not taking our advice long ago.

The Champion Light Car.

Reliable, efficient, economical.

Prices from £142.      Tax £7.

**JOWETT CARS L^{TD.} IDLE, BRADFORD.**

We are at home again, producing, but just now demand exceeds the supply. We will remedy this though
Prices from £142. Tax £7.

BACK TO METHUSELAH......We can't go so far back, but we have been making Jowett Cars now for, 25 years, and our wonderful record is due to our long experience in car manufacture.
Pedigree and experience must tell, and that is why the present-day Jowett holds the palm for cheap, economical, trouble-free motoring.
Our catalogue 'A Silver Wedding' tells you all about our cars.
Please send for it.

MONEY TALKS......and what it says about our cars is this:-
'I go further on a Jowett!'
There is no accident about this. It is the result of twenty-five years' unremitting toil towards this end. Lately (without resting on our oars) we have been able to devote some attention to the bodywork, and our bodies are now worthy of their chassis.
Investigate our claims, you'll never regret it; and sooner or later you'll join the happy band of Jowett enthusiasts.

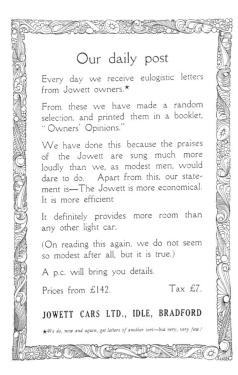

## Our daily post

Every day we receive eulogistic letters from Jowett owners.★

From these we have made a random selection, and printed them in a booklet, " Owners' Opinions."

We have done this because the praises of the Jowett are sung much more loudly than we, as modest men, would dare to do.    Apart from this, our statement is—The Jowett is more economical. It is more efficient

It definitely provides more room than any other light car.

(On reading this again, we do not seem so modest after all, but it is true.)

A p.c. will bring you details.

Prices from £142.              Tax £7.

### JOWETT CARS LTD., IDLE, BRADFORD

★ *We do, now and again, get letters of another sort—but very, very few !*

*LOOK AT IT!......It will take you, and your wife, and three children 80 miles for half-a-crown of petrol. It will take you there in comfort) and with speed, if necessary), for the Jowett is the roomiest light car ever built.*

*Its performance will astound and delight you as it has thousands of others.*

*Send for our literature now, as the first step towards making 1931 a Jowett year.*

*MERRY CHRISTMAS......to everybody, and may it be free from trouble, free from care.*

*The man who buys a Jowett is sure of this and also of a Happy New Year, for his motoring is trouble-free and economical.*

*Therefore, make your choice now, for better motoring, for "Jowetting," you'll never regret it.*

*'The little engine with the big pull.'*

*Prices from £142. Tax £7.*

*May we send you details?*

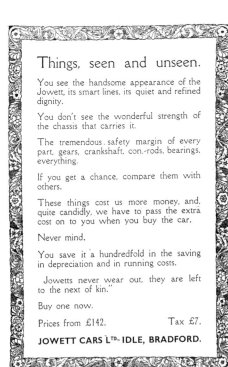

## Things, seen and unseen.

You see the handsome appearance of the Jowett, its smart lines, its quiet and refined dignity.

You don't see the wonderful strength of the chassis that carries it.

The tremendous safety margin of every part, gears, crankshaft, con.-rods, bearings, everything.

If you get a chance, compare them with others.

These things cost us more money, and, quite candidly, we have to pass the extra cost on to you when you buy the car.

Never mind.

You save it a hundredfold in the saving in depreciation and in running costs.

Jowetts never wear out. they are left to the next of kin."

Buy one now.

Prices from £142.              Tax £7.

### JOWETT CARS L^TD., IDLE, BRADFORD.

This same design of advertisement continued in 1931, using the same picture as the previous ones – they ran from January right through to June. Here are a few more examples, the first from January through to June. There were also more of the text-only testimonial-style advertisementsa – a couple of typical examples follow the pictorial ones mentioned above:

*BAG AND BAGGAGE......As you will see, there are no unsightly bulges on this body, yet concealed within its lines is a capacious compartment roomy enough for any amount of luggage, and **easily accessible**.*

*This is only one of the many features of this pioneer light car which make it the foremost of its class.*

*On the day you buy a Jowett you will commence an experience of motoring which*

will delightfully surprise you. Order one today.
Prices from £142. Tax £7.

THE BLACK PRINCE......Shall we send the address of the nearest agent? He will take you and your family up your biggest hill.

Then, if you are satisfied, ask for full details of running costs and our book of testimonials.

Bear in mind that our car is lower in tax than any other and our running costs lower.

When fully satisfied, place your order for a Jowett. You'll never regret it.
Prices from £142. Tax £7.

BREAKING UP......The Jowett, although it never breaks down (what never!), has certainly broken up a lot of misconceived notions on motoring.

It has proved that motoring may be enjoyed by the man with moderate means, and was the first to do so.

It has proved that it can be handled year in, year out by the man whose mechanical sense is nil.

It has proved capable of going wherever a big car could go; in fact it shows the way in this respect.

It has proved itself entirely and is the car you want.

HERRING OR SARDINES......Sometimes you are 'packed like herring' sometimes the phrase 'packed like sardines' is used, but if it is in this respect of a car and its passengers, the car will never be a Jowett.

The Jowett, in spite of being the lowest taxed car in these islands, is very much roomier than any other light car.

And – its wonderful engine carries on, day in, day out, "any road with any load."

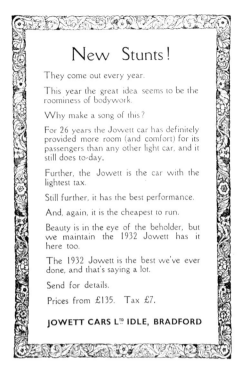

## New Stunts!

They come out every year.

This year the great idea seems to be the roominess of bodywork.

Why make a song of this?

For 26 years the Jowett car has definitely provided more room (and comfort) for its passengers than any other light car, and it still does to-day.

Further, the Jowett is the car with the lightest tax.

Still further, it has the best performance.

And, again, it is the cheapest to run.

Beauty is in the eye of the beholder, but we maintain the 1932 Jowett has it here too.

The 1932 Jowett is the best we've ever done, and that's saying a lot.

Send for details.

Prices from £135.   Tax £7.

**JOWETT CARS Lᵀᴰ IDLE, BRADFORD**

## Birds!

Our Blue de-luxe Saloon we have christened

### "Kingfisher."

Our Black de-luxe Saloon is

### "Blackbird."

These cars have rear petrol tanks, petrol gauge, 8-day clock, oil gauge, silentbloc oilless bushes, automatic ignition, warning light, sliding roof, etc., etc.

The bodies are of entirely new design which, however, still incorporate that unique Jowett feature, the concealed luggage compartment.

One word describes them—lovely!

Our chassis is of world renown, and the car is known as the most reliable made and the cheapest to run.

The range is from £135 and the tax £7.

Do it now.

**JOWETT CARS LTD., IDLE, BRADFORD.**

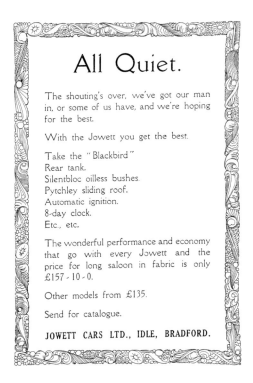

## All Quiet.

The shouting's over, we've got our man in, or some of us have, and we're hoping for the best.

With the Jowett you get the best.

Take the "Blackbird"
Rear tank.
Silentbloc oilless bushes.
Pytchley sliding roof.
Automatic ignition.
8-day clock.
Etc., etc.

The wonderful performance and economy that go with every Jowett and the price for long saloon in fabric is only £157 - 10 - 0.

Other models from £135.

Send for catalogue.

**JOWETT CARS LTD., IDLE, BRADFORD.**

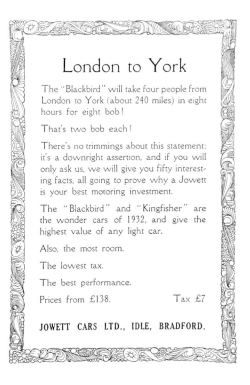

## London to York

The "Blackbird" will take four people from London to York (about 240 miles) in eight hours for eight bob!

That's two bob each!

There's no trimmings about this statement; it's a downright assertion, and if you will only ask us, we will give you fifty interesting facts, all going to prove why a Jowett is your best motoring investment.

The "Blackbird" and "Kingfisher" are the wonder cars of 1932, and give the highest value of any light car.

Also, the most room.

The lowest tax.

The best performance.

Prices from £138.                    Tax £7

**JOWETT CARS LTD., IDLE, BRADFORD.**

Economical, efficient, reliable.
'The little engine with the big pull.'
Prices from £142. Tax £7.

I AM BUYING A JOWETT......because –
Its appearance is handsome.
It is the roomiest light car.
It has been made for over 25 years.
It is reliable.
It is efficient.
It is economical.
Its all in running costs are less than 1/2d. per passenger mile.
Its equipment is complete in every particular.
Send for Catalogue 'A Silver Wedding,' which gives complete details of every model.

SPRING......Spring is here, and to enjoy it to the full you want a Jowett.
You don't want your motoring to be overshadowed by the thought of the expense – therefore you must have a Jowett, the economical car.
You don't want to be troubled by fear of breakdowns. The Jowett is the reliable car.

*Doubts as to performance. The Jowett is the efficient car.*
*The roomiest light car made.*
*The pioneer light car – The Jowett.*

*WE ARE PROUD to publish the following:*
*Gentlemen, In reply to your letter of the 8th instant, I beg to thank you for the literature received re Jowett Cars, also for your kind offer and valuable assistance in case of necessity. I have never driven a car before in my life, but have now proved what there really is in your claims for the Jowett and all my friends are amazed at its wonderful performance, its beauty and comfort.*

*Fortunately I have had as my instructor a friend who swears by and who lives for his Jowett car, and his advice has been my guide in buying one of your cars. There have been scores of people examining the car and one and all have been of the same opinion (it is the finest proposition they know of). I again sincerely thank you for your kind offer and will not hesitate to write if in doubt or unable to follow any part of the car's mechanism.*
*Wishing Jowett Cars Limited every success.*
*I remain yours truly J. H. Baines (Oldham)*
*Please send for a catalogue.*
*Prices from £146. Tax £7.*

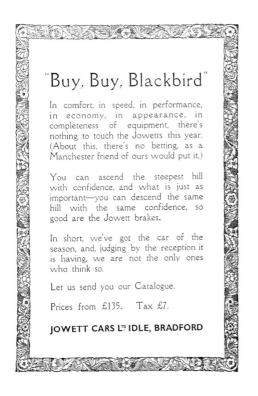

## "Buy, Buy, Blackbird"

In comfort, in speed, in performance, in economy, in appearance, in completeness of equipment, there's nothing to touch the Jowetts this year. (About this, there's no betting, as a Manchester friend of ours would put it.)

You can ascend the steepest hill with confidence, and what is just as important—you can descend the same hill with the same confidence, so good are the Jowett brakes.

In short, we've got the car of the season, and, judging by the reception it is having, we are not the only ones who think so.

Let us send you our Catalogue.

Prices from £135.    Tax £7.

**JOWETT CARS Lᵀᴰ IDLE, BRADFORD**

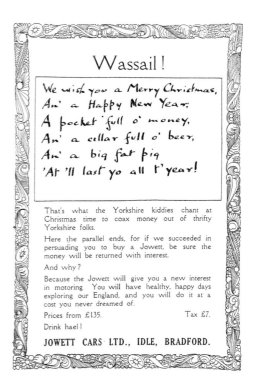

## Wassail!

We wish you a Merry Christmas,
An' a Happy New Year;
A pocket full o' money,
An' a cellar full o' beer,
An' a big fat pig
'At 'll last yo all t'year!

That's what the Yorkshire kiddies chant at Christmas time to coax money out of thrifty Yorkshire folks.

Here the parallel ends, for if we succeeded in persuading you to buy a Jowett, be sure the money will be returned with interest.

And why?

Because the Jowett will give you a new interest in motoring  You will have healthy, happy days exploring our England, and you will do it at a cost you never dreamed of.

Prices from £135.                                    Tax £7.

Drink hael!

**JOWETT CARS LTD., IDLE, BRADFORD.**

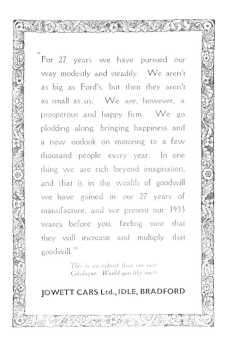

DEAR SIRS......Some six years ago I bought my first car, Susie Jowett, with which I was so pleased that I wrote you a little article of appreciation. She gave the greatest satisfaction always, if she didn't it was not her fault.

I have just invested in a Jowett saloon with a sunshine roof, and I want to congratulate you most heartily on the performance of Susie Jowett the 2nd, which is an extraordinary improvement on the old car, as good as she was.

You were good enough to get the new car finished for my holiday, and though she only came on the Saturday, and I was unused to the centre gear lever, after a few miles so good was her steering and gear action that I decided to go the following day for my trip of 800 miles, a real test which did not trouble her in the least. For 8 hours I drove in a deluge from South Wales to Shropshire, and not a spot of rain got into the car, neither did the wiper stick. Not once either was it necessary to go into bottom gear. In fact she has done 1,300 miles now and I have not used bottom gear yet, and will forget how to do it when it becomes necessary.

Her best performance was the stiff Warrington Hill outside Banbury on the Warwick road. With three aboard she climbed it well. With three up old Susie used to make a task of it, and always on low gear.

I could tell you so much more, but your splendid efforts must have elicited great praise from everywhere, but throughout our tour she gained the highest praise from all, especially from two Rolls Royce experts.

Yours Sincerely

F.R. Stanley (Herne Bay).

1932 would continue in the same way as before, with some adverts showing a picture of a certain model, some text-only and some testimonials from happy Jowett owners, extolling the virtues of the cars. I will detail some with pictures first:

*1 in 3.9 (shows rear view of a Jowett Kingfisher about to drive up a steep gradient)*
*It doesn't look it, but it is.*
    *And the Jowett Kingfisher stopped and restarted on this steep gradient with four full size passengers.*
    *Later, it took five men and two schoolboys up.*
    *This is what you get with a Jowett.*
    *Although it has a smaller tax than any other car, its climbing abilities are unsurpassed. It is reliable, it is economical, it is handsome, but why waste words: it is a JOWETT.*
*Prices from £135. Tax £7.*
*(The hill is Sutton Bank, near Thirsk, Yorkshire).*

*MOUNTAINS IN LABOUR (shows the front view of a Jowett Kestrel on a country lane).*
*All the big guns are labouring to produce engines efficiently to cope with the larger bodywork which motorists now insist upon.*
    *The Jowett set the fashion of roomy bodies and today we are still well in front.*
*But, then, we have the power unit, the only one of its kind, "the little engine with the big pull."*
*The new Jowett is as much ahead of its predecessors as it is of its competitors, and that is saying a lot.*
*If you haven't driven the New Jowett, you haven't experienced the full delights of 'light caring.' Try one now.*

*ONE in ONE (shows front view of a Kestrel in a country lane next to trees in blossom).*
*We are tr-r-r-rembling!*
*First, one manufacturer claims to be selling one car in three.*
*Then a second claims one in three.*
*We are waiting anxiously for a third claim, and then it will mean that all the Jowett cars we produce are like the Emperor's shirt (or was it clothes) – they don't exist.\**
*Until this fateful day we can claim that the Jowett satisfies a higher proportion of owners than any other car.*
*One in one, so to speak.*
*There is no better light car made, and we can prove it!*
*\* Where did we get this allusion? A small prize to the first to tell us.*

### Dry-as-dust details

1. Rear petrol tank.
2. Automatic ignition.
3. Finger-tip controls.
4. Sliding roof.
5. Oil-less spring bushes.
6. Concealed luggage compartment.
7. Streamline front.
8. Over-size tyres.
9. 8' 6" wheelbase.
10. Oceans of room.
11. Four doors.
12. Lowest tax.

Send a p.c. and try these for yourself, free of charge.

Prices from £135.                    Tax £7.

"The Englishman's Car"

**JOWETT CARS LTD., IDLE, BRADFORD.**

### More details.

13. Large efficient brakes.
14. Single plate clutch.
15. Dip and switch (finger tip).
16. Shock absorbers.
17. Clock, petrol gauge, etc.
18. Stainless steel radiator.
19. Rear blind.
20. Gloves and map lockers.
21. Magna wheels.
22. "Ripple-less" clearview windows.
23. Tool-box under bonnet.
24. Speed + comfort + reliability = Jowett.

You may try all these points for yourselves by using the coupon below. No obligation.

Prices from £135.                    Tax £7.

I want to test your claims.

Name _____

Address _____

Unsealed envelope, ½d. stamp.

**JOWETT CARS LTᴰ· IDLE, BRADFORD**

TRUTH IN ADVERTISING (shows a sideways view of a Kestrel).

There isn't a car made, no matter what make, even a Jowett, that doesn't at some time or other cause its owner to say, "Dash the thing!"

We do sincerely believe that an objurgation of this nature falls more rarely on the lips of the Jowett owner.

We are, all of us, striving after perfection and we at Idle believe that consistency is more likely to achieve this blessed state than chopping and changing.

For twenty-six years we have bent our energies toward one end, and it is now generally recognised that our engine is **the** engine for a light car.

It is vibrationless, reliable and economical.

It deals with, efficiently, the largest and most comfortable body in any light car.

You won't experience pride in motoring until you own the New Jowett. Try one now.

IN THE DOLDRUMS (shows three-quarters rear view of a Kestrel).

To our extreme disappointment we are compelled to announce that so far at the Show we have not signed any contracts running into millions of pounds.

Other firms seem able to do it, but we can't. Can it be that our Sales Manager is always off our Stand when these anxious buyers are floating round!

Never mind.

We're working night and day on our 'Kestrels' are winning golden opinions wherever they go, and 1933 is going to be a good one for Jowett owners and Jowett Cars Ltd.

Get our catalogue. You'll like it!

# Faint-hearts hon 'Onister

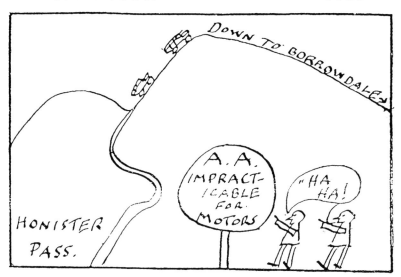

Sorry—Faint-'earts on Honister.   Faint-hearts hon —oh, dash it!

On Whit-Monday two of the New Jowetts climbed Honister Pass from Buttermere in spite of fore-bodings by the many car owners at the foot of the pass.   Further, the two cars were driven respectively by a youth of 21 and a lad of 17.

That's confidence.

The fact is we have the engine for a light car, and as we've almost 26 years start in this type of engine, we don't expect to be caught up.

THE NEW JOWETT.

Perfect in performance, excels in economy, reigns in reliability.

Our catalogue is almost as good as our advertising. Send for one.

Prices from £135.   Tax £7.

# JOWETT CARS LᵗᴰˑˑIDLE, BRADFORD

*P.S.—We shall make our next competition much harder. We were overwhelmed with replies for our last one.*

# Expensive Habits.

The Jowett hasn't any.

It watches its owner's pocket like America hoarding gold.

It gets the largest possible mileage out of its allowance for petrol, oil and tyres.

(An owner tells us he has got nearly 50,000 miles out of his front tyres and they're still running.)

It refuses to indulge in expensive repair bills.

Its yearly tax is the cheapest in the country.

It is, strange contradiction, generous also —

In the amount of room it provides its occupants, its comfort, the happiness it affords, the enjoyment.

There's nothing a light car will do that the Jowett won't do, a little better.

There's no part on a light car that isn't a little better on a Jowett.

We have the only engine for a light car.

Have a trial free of charge.

Prices from £135.    Tax £7.

**JOWETT   CARS   LTD.,   IDLE,   BRADFORD**

Now, a non-pictorial advertisement:

*THE WANDERER'S RETURN*

*'Here we are again!'*

*We've been so busy that we haven't had the pleasure of talking to you for a few weeks. How's things?*

*Have you joined the Jowett band?*

*'In delay there lies no plenty.'*

*We've got the finest light car in the world, bar none, and if 'you've a brain and cerebellum too', you eventually will get a Jowett, so why not get it over?*

*(This sounds like having a tooth out. Our hand is losing its cunning!)*

*Bradford to Newcastle on Good Friday, four up and luggage, 97 miles in 2 1/2 hours.*

*Pretty fair.*

*Comfort, who can touch us?\**

*Economy. The last word.*

*\*The last man who tried to touch us muttered something about 'getting blood out of a stone.'*

Now, a testimonial:

*YOU ARE NO GOOD TO ME!*

*Dear Sirs, A few lines to let you know my 1926 Jowett car has covered 100,000 miles.*

*I am a commercial traveller covering some 20,000 miles each year, and can truthfully state that the car (now in its sixth year) has never let me down.*

*The car is always ready – just a press on the starter and away; whether it is raining, snowing or fine, it makes no difference.*

*At a garage where the car is kept the proprietor says; 'I wish you could take that Jowett away. You are no good to me, never any repairs, you only buy petrol and oil and precious little of either of these.'*

Never Beaten!

72 hours continuous running, at an average speed of 38.5 m.p.h.

Further, the Jowett "Kestrel" was towing a trailer weighing 14 cwts. and throughout the whole of the 72 hours terrific pounding, not one moment's trouble was experienced. Now, what about the "little engine with the big pull"?

The Hon. Victor and Mrs. Bruce, who drove the car, send us their congratulations on making such a car.

We, in return, congratulate them.

You may have a Montlhery Jowett exactly as Mr. Bruce for his Jowett is absolutely standard.

Prices from £135.        Tax £7.

**JOWETT CARS LTD., IDLE, BRADFORD**
(Observed by Auto Club de France).

Do it yourself.

The Bruces' wonderful performance at Montlhery is no fluke.

It takes confidence in your products to create a world's record of this nature, but the Jowett's middle name is reliability

You, if you are a Jowett owner, have a car that is equal to feats of endurance that cannot be approached by any car in its class. If you are not a Jowett owner, we are turning out cars every day as good as the Bruces', and we advise you to investigate them as regards efficiency and economy.

You can try one for nothing.

Prices from £135.      Tax £7.

**JOWETT CARS LTD., IDLE, BRADFORD**

# The Fourth Test

If we don't win at Leeds we oughtn't to win at the Oval in the fifth match. Larwood ought to be in, but he can't, therefore we must have Bowes.

(Judging by the Old Trafford match we could do with a few fielders, too. The dropped catches, the missed chances!)

However, we shan't lose at Leeds. Five Yorkshiremen (we hope) wili be on their own "midden." A Yorkshire crowd, with additions, will provide that electric background, and the Australians will bite the dust.

Incidentally, our works are only seven miles from Headingley, and if anyone from the South would like to look around, we shall be very pleased to receive them, and to show them exactly how we make that very good car, the Jowett.

Prices from £150                    Tax £7

## JOWETT CARS, LTD., IDLE, BRADFORD

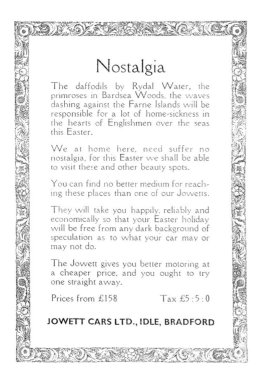

## Nostalgia

The daffodils by Rydal Water, the primroses in Bardsea Woods, the waves dashing against the Farne Islands will be responsible for a lot of home-sickness in the hearts of Englishmen over the seas this Easter.

We at home here, need suffer no nostalgia, for this Easter we shall be able to visit these and other beauty spots.

You can find no better medium for reaching these places than one of our Jowetts.

They will take you happily, reliably and economically so that your Easter holiday will be free from any dark background of speculation as to what your car may or may not do.

The Jowett gives you better motoring at a cheaper price, and you ought to try one straight away.

Prices from £158          Tax £5 : 5 : 0

**JOWETT CARS LTD., IDLE, BRADFORD**

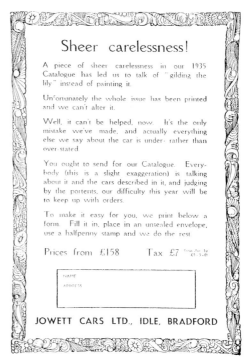

## Sheer carelessness!

A piece of sheer carelessness in our 1935 Catalogue has led us to talk of "gilding the lily" instead of painting it.

Unfortunately the whole issue has been printed and we can't alter it.

Well, it can't be helped, now. It's the only mistake we've made, and actually everything else we say about the car is under- rather than over-stated.

You ought to send for our Catalogue. Everybody (this is a slight exaggeration) is talking about it and the cars described in it, and judging by the portents, our difficulty this year will be to keep up with orders.

To make it easy for you, we print below a form. Fill it in, place in an unsealed envelope, use a halfpenny stamp and we do the rest.

Prices from £158          Tax £7

NAME
ADDRESS

**JOWETT CARS LTD., IDLE, BRADFORD**

*It may seem hard to believe, but it's a fact the engine has never been out of the frame; no one has ever seen the big end bearings since they were first fitted in the factory, and they are still quite tight. Only the usual decarbonising and a very few replacements have been required in all those thousands and thousands of miles.*

*I congratulate you and consider that only the engineering skill, the thought, the workmanship, and the many little refinements all go to prove that the Jowett is a car far ahead of anything yet produced.*

*Many glowing advertisements appear in the press tempting one to purchase a new car. Here I score again – my Jowett is good for a deal of hard work yet; thus at the present moment, I can claim the car is saving me the cost of a new one.*

*You may make what use you like of this letter, as it is the only way of showing my appreciation.*

*Yours faithfully, C. Rowland Maile (Bedford)*

From September right through to early 1933, there were a large number of adverts for the Kestrel. They featured a three-quarters view of the car pictured from the rear. Here are a few examples:

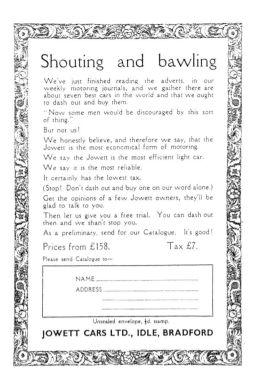

*INDIVIDUALITY!......The possession of a Jowett Kestrel invests you with an individuality hitherto only obtainable by a heavy expenditure on specialised coachwork.*

*There is nothing that you could suggest that isn't already on this car.*

*12-volt lighting and starting, bumpers, silent second, thermometer, safety glass, sliding roof, ashtray, rear tank, etc., etc. this car is so much ahead of present design that it ought to be modern for years.*

*The materials of which it is built ensure long life and it has the unexcelled Jowett attributes of efficiency, reliability and economy.*

*Price £175 (4-speed box £5 extra). Tax £7.*

*EXADUS!......North, South, East and West, the Kestrels are flying out to their new homes.*

*You'll see them in increasing as the days go by, because they're built so well and look so fine that every Kestrel we turn out will definitely sell others.*

*So much extra care and painstaking go into every Kestrel that we shall be obliged to limit the production. Don't think this is eyewash. We really mean it. You see we make other cars, also very fine lorries and vans, and we must keep the faith.*

*Shall we send you full details. Prices from £135. Tax £7.*

# Laodiceans!

May we not apply this word to describe a lot of the gearboxes of to-day?

That is, easy change in the top half, and the deuce to pay in the bottom half.

The Jowett, with its special clutch, gives an easy change through the whole of its range.

It also gives a multitude of other good things which are too many to set forth here, but which are mostly shown in our Catalogue.

It engenders more, we believe, than any other make of light car, a pride in ownership, a sense of comradeship, and a feeling of contented happiness.

For happy motoring, a Jowett every time.

Prices from £150.          Tax £7.

NOVEMBER ELEVENTH
PLEASE GIVE A LITTLE · MORE FOR YOUR POPPY
REMEMBRANCE DAY

**JOWETT CARS Ltd., IDLE, BRADFORD**

# Lowest tax, most room

There's no argument about the tax. The Jowett beats the lowest tax of any car in the country

As regards the roominess, the efficiency, the reliability, the economy of the Jowett, they have to be experienced to be believed.

We regularly get letters from Jowett owners saying things about their cars which we hesitate to publish.
(Don't take this the wrong way; we mean good things!)

Our cars ought to be good.

We are the only firm in the country who, for 28 years, have concentrated our efforts on the one chassis.

If you say that that's putting all our eggs in one basket, we prefer it so, but, my words, how we watch the basket!

That's why our cars are good.

Send for our Catalogue, "Music and the Speed of Jowetts."

A p.c. will do.

Prices from £158.          Tax £7.
                         (£5-5-0 from 1-1-35)

**JOWETT CARS LTD., IDLE, BRADFORD**

# "O Happy Easter"

as Mascagni sang, or if he didn't, somebody else did.

The first holiday of the year, and how it is anticipated and welcomed.

For ourselves, we propose (D.V.) spending it in Northumberland, around Bambrough way. Our Jowett "Curlew" will take five, all adults, with luggage (a bit of a squash) and we shall get there at a less expense than by any other light car made.

And more comfortably too!.

That's fact, not fiction.

There is time for you to get a Jowett before Easter and spend your holidays under similar circumstances. It will cost you less in worry, fatigue and money. And, more than any other car, it will become part of the family.

Try one for nothing.

Prices from £158.          Tax £5 : 5 : 0

Catalogue on request.

**JOWETT CARS LTD., IDLE, BRADFORD**

# "and Glory Shone Around."

We are frequently told (possibly there is a certain amount of leg-pulling about this) that our adverts. are the first things that are read.

We hope this is so, for following our usual practice at Christmas time we make an appeal to you to try and make someone thankful that you exist.

In plain words, try, this Christmas time, to bring sunshine into the heart of someone less blessed than yourself.

Especially the children.

We shall practise what we preach, and, unfortunately, there will be plenty of opportunities.

A Merry Christmas to you all.

(We hope this will give us a chance of catching up with orders, so that we are not absolutely altruistic.)

**JOWETT CARS LTD., IDLE, BRADFORD**

*IF DOUGHTY DEEDS......my lady, please, we'll give her these in plenty. Sutton Bank, Provoke, Red Bank - a host of hills flatten out their crests when a Kestrel approaches.*

*But we give her more than deeds. The loveliest body that ever went on a light car, luxurious trimming, a well-thought-out colour scheme. And on top, 12-volt lighting, silent second, bumpers, thermometer, automatic ignition etc., etc.*

*Tomorrow starts a new quarter. Start it in right fashion by buying a Jowett. You'll never regret it. Prices from £135. Tax £7.*

*SORTING IT OUT......In the multitude of counsel there is wisdom, or supposed to be. Would hesitate to apply when buying a car.*

*'Buy this' says one. 'Buy that,' says another. 'Buy Mine,' says a third.*

*We say 'Try one and see if you like it, buy one. If not, don't.'*

*GIVING MONEY AWAY!......At the Show, one of our friends suggested that we could not possibly produce our Kestrel at the price.*

*We replied that maybe we were so full of the milk of human kindness that we were giving money away. This caused him to laugh heartily.*

*The Kestrel certainly does look as if the price should be more, with its handsome lines, 12 volt set, bumpers, etc., etc., and wonderful performance, but the price is £175, and that is jolly cheap. So are its running costs.*

*THE HEAVENLY TWINS!......We are turning them out in ever-increasing numbers, and when you take delivery of our new Kestrel you'll have a heavenly feeling that you* are having first-class motoring at third-class fares.

There is no car anywhere near the tax and cost of a Jowett which gives you room we do. Or the equipment; or the service.

That is why our friends come to us year after year for their car. Not for them third-class motoring at first-class fares. Follow their example. You'll never regret it.

There were also large numbers of other pictorial adverts and text-only adverts during 1932 and into 1933, here are a few examples:

TIME AND ITS FORELOCK (Shows a sideways view of the 1906 Jowett)
Six months before Dec 31st. 1932, our Designs showed our Sales the 1933 model.
'Splendid' said Sales, 'they're sold before they are made.'
'Then it is no good making 'em,' said Designs. The same day, 18 months before the end of 1933, the 1934 model was trotted out.
'Lovely' cried Sales, 'you won't be able to make enough.'
'Then we shan't try,' said Designs.
30 months ahead of time, the 1935 was submitted. Sales turned it down, said it wasn't sufficiently modern.
The following day 42 months (except for a day) in advance, Designs submitted the above.
Sales fell on his neck, 'Build three more factories' he said, 'we shall need 'em. It's the last word.'
'Fool' cried Designs, 'it's our 1906 model,' saying which 'e 'it 'im 'ard on 'is 'ead with a crankshaft which bent badly but left Sales unmoved.

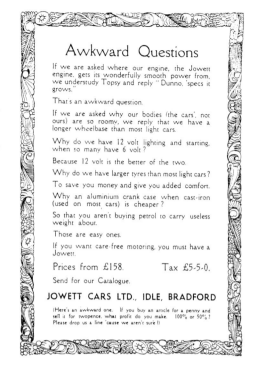

Awkward Questions

If we are asked where our engine, the Jowett engine, gets its wonderfully smooth power from, we understudy Topsy and reply " Dunno, 'specs it grows."

That's an awkward question.

If we are asked why our bodies (the cars', not ours) are so roomy, we reply that we have a longer wheelbase than most light cars.

Why do we have 12 volt lighting and starting, when so many have 6 volt?

Because 12 volt is the better of the two.

Why do we have larger tyres than most light cars?

To save you money and give you added comfort.

Why an aluminium crank case when cast-iron (used on most cars) is cheaper?

So that you aren't buying petrol to carry useless weight about.

Those are easy ones.

If you want care-free motoring, you must have a Jowett.

Prices from £158.            Tax £5-5-0.

Send for our Catalogue.

JOWETT CARS LTD., IDLE, BRADFORD

(Here's an awkward one.   If you buy an article for a penny and sell it for twopence, what profit do you make.   100% or 50%? Please drop us a line 'cause we aren't sure!)

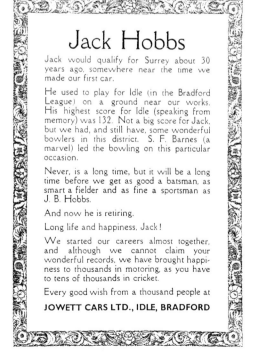

Jack Hobbs

Jack would qualify for Surrey about 30 years ago, somewhere near the time we made our first car.

He used to play for Idle (in the Bradford League) on a ground near our works. His highest score for Idle (speaking from memory) was 132. Not a big score for Jack, but we had, and still have, some wonderful bowlers in this district. S. F. Barnes (a marvel) led the bowling on this particular occasion.

Never, is a long time, but it will be a long time before we get as good a batsman, as smart a fielder and as fine a sportsman as J. B. Hobbs.

And now he is retiring.

Long life and happiness, Jack!

We started our careers almost together, and although we cannot claim your wonderful records, we have brought happiness to thousands in motoring, as you have to tens of thousands in cricket.

Every good wish from a thousand people at

JOWETT CARS LTD., IDLE, BRADFORD

# "Down South"

We've just returned from a business trip, through the West Country to Devon and Cornwall.

Church Stretton is a lovely place.

We got thoroughly lost in Bristol, and we imagine that most missing persons could be restored to their friends and their relations if Bristol were thoroughly combed. Providence was watching over us, however, and we escaped from the maze.

Devonshire was lovely; almost as nice as Yorkshire.

Most of the Cornish women seem to wear glasses.

We came across the ferry, Tor Point to Devonport, without payment. Is it free on Sundays, or can we send the fare on somewhere?

Out and home we put up nearly 1,100 miles with never a moment's trouble on a Jowett "Curlew" model. We climbed Porlock easily. Oil consumption was just over half a gallon. Petrol, just short of 40 m.p.g. Maximum speed, 59 m.p.h., but not on Porlock!

We're more than ever sure that the Jowett is the finest light car in the world.

Buy one. They're good.

Good buy! (Good heavens!)

Prices from £158.  Tax £5 . 5 . 0.

## JOWETT CARS LTD., IDLE, BRADFORD

The New Jowett is as much ahead to-day as was its great progenitor in 1906, and there were no vain regrets after buying.

Would you like our Catalogue? Prices from £135. Tax £7.

P.S. – Our crankshafts are made of finest alloy steel!

MAROONED! (Picture shows large numbers of children sledging down a snowy hillside). We were snow-bound at Idle for five days, and had just decided to eat our Sales Manager when relief broke through.

Busybodies! –

We have been much cheered, however, by the many letters we have received from Jowett owners saying they were able to carry on when practically every other car in the district was laid up.

When you buy a Jowett, you get a car that is always a little ahead of other makes.

In performance.

In appearance.

In room and comfort.

In economy.

In short, everything.

Would you like to know more about them?

Then send us a p.c. Prices from £135. Tax £7.

ALMOST HUMAN (Picture shows a Kestrel in a street from the rear, a lady with a small dog is talking to the driver, who is ready to set off).

The Jowett Kestrel is almost human in its responsiveness to your needs, but we must admit it cannot show you the correct road when faced with two of them.

It can show you how to save money in motoring.

It can lead the way to health, happiness and contentment. It will engender in your heart, more than any other car, a feeling of pride and affection because of its individuality and whole-hearted devotion to your needs. It is a car of cars for the owner-driver, and, to borrow a phrase.

'You won't be happy till you get one.'

The lowest tax and the roomiest body.

Prices from £135. Tax £7.

The plain-text adverts were very common through this period also, these are a few more examples, the first being from late December 1932, then leading into 1933:

WASTING SPACE!......This space is supposed to be used for selling cars, but dash it, 'Christmas comes but once a year.' –

Sincerest greetings then to all those thousands of Jowett owners who, since 1906, have loyally supported us. We **know** their Christmas motoring will be happy.

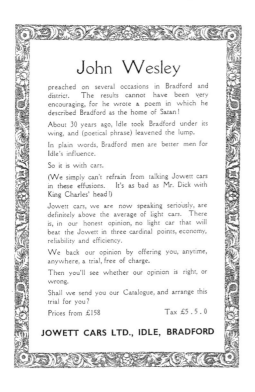

## John Wesley

preached on several occasions in Bradford and district. The results cannot have been very encouraging, for he wrote a poem in which he described Bradford as the home of Satan!

About 30 years ago, Idle took Bradford under its wing, and (poetical phrase) leavened the lump.

In plain words, Bradford men are better men for Idle's influence.

So it is with cars.

(We simply can't refrain from talking Jowett cars in these effusions. It's as bad as Mr. Dick with King Charles' head!)

Jowett cars, we are now speaking seriously, are definitely above the average of light cars. There is, in our honest opinion, no light car that will beat the Jowett in three cardinal points, economy, reliability and efficiency.

We back our opinion by offering you, anytime, anywhere, a trial, free of charge.

Then you'll see whether our opinion is right, or wrong.

Shall we send you our Catalogue, and arrange this trial for you?

Prices from £158          Tax £5 . 5 . 0

**JOWETT CARS LTD., IDLE, BRADFORD**

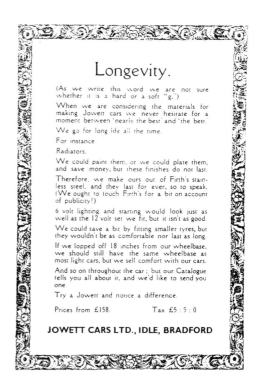

## Longevity.

(As we write this word we are not sure whether it is a hard or a soft "g.")

When we are considering the materials for making Jowett cars we never hesitate for a moment between 'nearly the best' and 'the best.'

We go for long life all the time.

For instance.

Radiators.

We could paint them, or we could plate them, and save money, but these finishes do not last.

Therefore, we make ours out of Firth's stainless steel, and they last for ever, so to speak. (We ought to touch Firth's for a bit on account of publicity!)

6 volt lighting and starting would look just as well as the 12 volt set we fit, but it isn't as good.

We could save a bit by fitting smaller tyres, but they wouldn't be as comfortable nor last as long.

If we lopped off 18 inches from our wheelbase, we should still have the same wheelbase as most light cars, but we sell comfort with our cars.

And so on throughout the car; but our Catalogue tells you all about it, and we'd like to send you one.

Try a Jowett and notice a difference.

Prices from £158.          Tax £5 : 5 : 0

**JOWETT CARS LTD., IDLE, BRADFORD**

Greetings, almost as hearty, to those many friends who, although running other makes of cars, have been good enough to write to us praising our cars and expressing their goodwill and interest.

We **hope** their Christmas motoring will be happy.

In short, 'love and joy' to everybody.

(Perhaps, after all, we had better try and sell something, but this concerns Jowett owners only. We have some neat imitation leather wallets, made to hold and protect the Jowett Instruction Book. The price is 7 1/2d. post free, and stamps to this amount should be sent with your application).

ESSENTIAL DETAILS......A car must be handsome in appearance.

It must give unfailing service.

It must be economical in operation.

The Jowett meets these three conditions, and on acquaintance you will find it meets a lot more.

You will never hear us claim our car is the best in the world. (You will have to go to Derby for this).

We do claim there is no better light car, and it is a fact that to get the Jowett comfort and performance you will have to go into the 12hp class.

Why throw money away?

Try one free of charge. If the test won't convince, no spoken words of ours will.

Send for our Catalogue. It's readable.

CAMARADERIE!......Why should one Jowett owner when meeting another on the road give a salutation by the wave of a hand?

Does it not suggest satisfaction, and that in full measure?

As the owner of a Jowett you are never lonely on the road. A friendly wave of the hand is yours a dozen times on the shortest journey.

Why not investigate the car that generates such **camaraderie** of the road?

Satisfaction and pride of ownership are the secrets.

DRY BONES......Two men witness an incident.

The first relates it later to his friends and all they hear is a rattling of dry bones.

The second relates it. He clothes the bones with living flesh, invests them with his personality, and hearers see the whole episode as a glowing, living picture.

At the works here, we take various materials, dull and lifeless in themselves, shape them, invest them with a living personality, and make them a car which is not merely a car, but a comrade and a companion.

How do we do it?

We can't tell you. Perhaps it is the 28 years' experience, perhaps it's the individual as against mass-production.

It's certainly there.

Try one today for nothing.

ASKING JOWETT OWNERS......Just in case you have not been able to follow out our

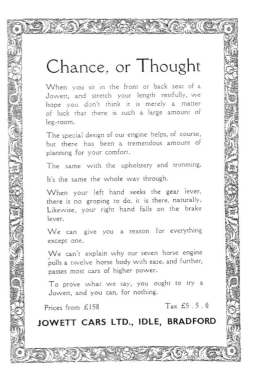

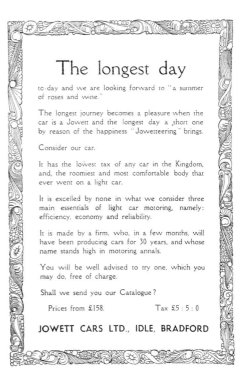

# The Rosetta Stone

Just as the Rosetta Stone provided a key to the ancient writings of the Egyptians, so does the Jowett car provide a key to motoring.

You are, perhaps, wondering whether you can afford to run a car, or maybe you already have a car (not a Jowett) and finding things a shade expensive.

The Jowett is very definitely the cheapest form of motoring, and when we say motoring, we mean motoring, and not being carried about like sardines in a box.

It has stood the test of time (nearly 30 years since we made the first), and despite fierce competition, we have maintained and enhanced our position as leaders of the light car class in economy and luxury.

Therefore, let all your doubts take wing and try a Jowett.

Prices from £158.                     Tax £5 : 5 : 0

## JOWETT CARS LTD., IDLE, BRADFORD

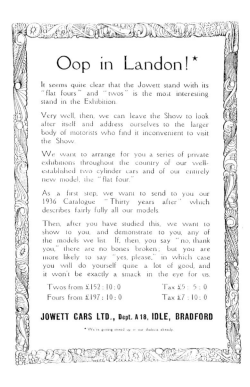

## Oop in Landon!*

It seems quite clear that the Jowett stand with its "flat fours" and "twos" is the most interesting stand in the Exhibition.

Very well, then, we can leave the Show to look after itself and address ourselves to the larger body of motorists who find it inconvenient to visit the Show.

We want to arrange for you a series of private exhibitions throughout the country of our well-established two cylinder cars and of our entirely new model, the "flat four."

As a first step, we want to send to you our 1936 Catalogue "Thirty years after" which describes fairly fully all our models.

Then, after you have studied this, we want to show to you, and demonstrate to you, any of the models we list. If, then, you say "no, thank you," there are no bones broken; but you are more likely to say "yes, please," in which case you will do yourself quite a lot of good, and it won't be exactly a smack in the eye for us.

Twos from £152 : 10 : 0        Tax £5 : 5 : 0
Fours from £197 : 10 : 0       Tax £7 : 10 : 0

**JOWETT CARS LTD., Dept. A 18, IDLE, BRADFORD**

* We're getting mixed up in our dialects already.

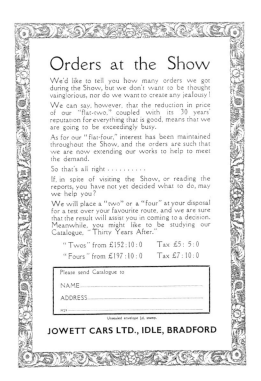

## Orders at the Show

We'd like to tell you how many orders we got during the Show, but we don't want to be thought vainglorious, nor do we want to create any jealousy!

We can say, however, that the reduction in price of our "flat-two," coupled with its 30 years' reputation for everything that is good, means that we are going to be exceedingly busy.

As for our "flat-four," interest has been maintained throughout the Show, and the orders are such that we are now extending our works to help to meet the demand.

So that's all right . . . . . . . . . .

If, in spite of visiting the Show, or reading the reports, you have not yet decided what to do, may we help you?

We will place a "two" or a "four" at your disposal for a test over your favourite route, and we are sure that the result will assist you in coming to a decision. Meanwhile, you might like to be studying our Catalogue, "Thirty Years After."

"Twos" from £152 : 10 : 0     Tax £5 : 5 : 0
"Fours" from £197 : 10 : 0     Tax £7 : 10 : 0

Please send Catalogue to

NAME

ADDRESS

Unsealed envelope ½d. stamp.

**JOWETT CARS LTD., IDLE, BRADFORD**

suggestion that you should take the opinions of Jowett owners anent the merits of our cars, please read this letter.

Sirs, I am the happy owner of a 1928 Jowett which I bought new in that year. I can most thoroughly endorse all your statements and advertisements regarding the reliability, performance and economy of your most efficient product.

During this period I have not spent £10 (ten pounds) on repairs. Two of the original tyres are still in use, and only today have I replaced the battery, which was still in good order. But, starting on a long tour thought it only fair to the car to fix a new one.

As a Somerset farmer said to me last summer, when wishing me goodbye from our holiday: - 'No need to wish you a safe journey, you are driving a Jowett.'

Gentlemen! When the time does come for me to make a change, my next car will most certainly be **Another Jowett.**

You can make whatever use of this letter, it is unsolicited.

I am, Yours faithfully,

'Thoroughly Satisfied' (London SE5)

BUTTONHOLING......The spoken, being more powerful than the written word, if only we could meet face to face, and tell you all the things that cause the Jowett 'to brightly shine'* amongst its competitors.

*We could describe the thought given to the choice of steels and other materials.*

*The willing engine, the four-speed easy-change gearbox. The 12 volt lighting and starting*

*The immense comfort and roominess of our specially built bodies.*

*Oversize tyres, strongly built and braced frame, stainless steel radiator, etc., etc.*

*We could then leave you to your slumbers, satisfied that the seed implanted would bear fruit and that you would become a Jowett owner.*

*Not being able to do this, can we send you our Catalogue? It is almost as good as the spoken word.*

*Prices from £150. Tax £7.*

*\* If W.S.Gilbert can split an infinitive, so can we. In which opera did he do so, and through which character? A small prize to the first correct answer.*

The same style of adverts continued on in 1934, and this is an all-text example from early January to start the year off:

*A RIGHT START......Start the New Year in a proper fashion.*

*Find out what it is about a Jowett that makes Jowett owners the most loyal and happily contented people in the whole of motordom.*

*Stop any Jowett owner and ask him to tell you all about his car. He'll be friendly and courteous and his praises will be very much louder than ours.*

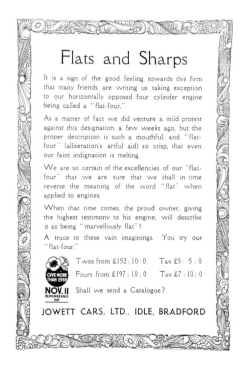

Flats and Sharps

It is a sign of the good feeling towards this firm that many friends are writing us taking exception to our horizontally opposed four cylinder engine being called a "flat-four."

As a matter of fact we did venture a mild protest against this designation a few weeks ago, but the proper description is such a mouthful, and "flat-four" (alliteration's artful aid) so crisp, that even our faint indignation is melting.

We are so certain of the excellencies of our "flat-four" that we are sure that we shall in time reverse the meaning of the word "flat" when applied to engines.

When that time comes, the proud owner, giving the highest testimony to his engine, will describe it as being "marvellously flat"!

A truce to these vain imaginings. You try our "flat-four."

Twos from £152 : 10 : 0     Tax £5 : 5 : 0

Fours from £197 : 10 : 0    Tax £7 : 10 : 0

Shall we send a Catalogue?

JOWETT CARS, LTD., IDLE, BRADFORD

# Primroses in Northumberland.

We stopped the Jowett on the roadside near Ford (Lord Joicey's place). Scattered in the grass verge were primroses, cool and pure. We crawled through the hedge, to the detriment of our flannel bags, and there in the wood were millions of primroses. We went no further, we didn't gather any, we daren't tread on them, we simply stood and worshipped, our bosoms filled with noble thoughts. (Later, when we found we had lost half-a-crown, our thoughts were less noble.)

If ever you are going North, spend a night at the Blue Bell, Belford, a fine hotel, and visit Etal and Ford, especially the latter's church, churchyard and schoolroom, and drop us a postcard from each, thanking us for telling you.*

All these things we did on a Jowett Four, beautiful, and you'll enjoy them a lot better if you do the same.

The finest light four in the world!

## JOWETT CARS LTD., IDLE, BRADFORD

*As regards the Churchyard, this is, perhaps, asking too much!

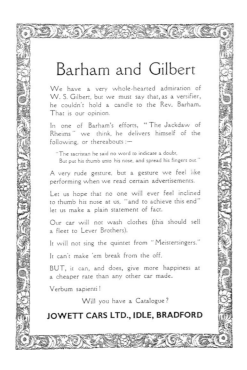

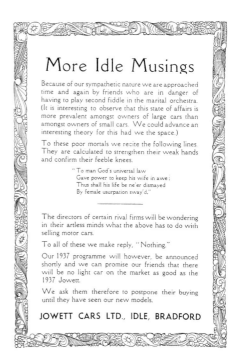

(*That's because of our modesty*).

*Then, place your order for one of our models, knowing full well that every claim made for our cars will be proved to the full.*

*Do your 1934 motoring on a Jowett.*

*Following years will look after themselves.*

*Prices from £150. Tax £7.*

Pictorial adverts for the Kestrel featuring a side-view of the car ran from October 1933 right through to July 1934. These are a selection of them, they are all from 1934 except for the first one, which was from October 1933:

*OOP FOR'T SHOW......We're trying, not very successfully, we are afraid, to disguise our Yorkshire accent during the Show. The people are very kind though and put up with our broad vowels, when they see the car we have to sell.*

*It's a good Show for us. The Kestrel, illustrated above, is going to be our best seller, followed very closely by the standard saloon. Next in popularity is our Flying Fox two-seater for which we are getting some very handsome compliments, and more important, some orders.*

*And now we long for Yorkshire, where, when you say **Coom 'ere** to a man, he comes, and doesn't wait until you say **Cam har**.*

*Have you had our Catalogue yet, the best we have ever produced?*

THE DIFFERENCE......We have never said our car was the cheapest to buy. (Probably by reason of the individual attention given to each car, it never will be).

What we do say is, that our car is the cheapest car to run, and probably the foregoing remarks in parenthesis accounts for it.

Our car is £1 per year less in tax than the next lowest, and if you are continually going to run a higher taxed car than ours, then you ought, as a level-headed individual, knock at least £25 of the price of our car, for in these days of low interest 4% is pretty good, and the payment of the higher tax means you are demobilising at least £25 of your capital.

Do you see what we mean? If you don't, drop us a line.


WHITE SUN TIDE......The sacrificial rites of the Druids were generally held in May at sunrise.

The victim was laid upon the slab at Stonehenge, and the strictest silence was observed by all (except possibly the victim) until the sun rose. If he rose white, that was to say bright, the victim was eulogised as being a worthy sacrifice and then, down came the knife.

Although this barbarous practice was discontinued after the suppression of the Druids* the name of the season remains as Whitsuntide.

Now, Whitsuntide is a happy break between Easter and summer holiday, and it will be all the happier if you do your motoring on a Jowett.

For, it is comfortable, the most reliable and the most economical light car.

*May we give you a run on one for nothing, to prove our words? Prices from £150.*
*\*By Henry VIII, we think, although we are not sure of our facts. Au contraire, every word we speak about a Jowett is a true word.*

*THEY LOOK WELL......They do look well, but there's other things about a Jowett besides its looks.*
    *It performs well, and it has an individuality about it that causes its owner to bang on about it for years, and years, and years.*
    *(We don't know whether to feel depressed or proud about this). Because of this individuality, we shall never make cars for the million, and, confidentially, we don't want to.*
    *We have a specialised market, and all the people who want a car with an endearing personality come to us sooner or later.*
*Would you like our Catalogue?*
*Prices from £150. Tax £7.*

*HAPPY DAYS......Happy days are knocking at the door.*
    *The beautiful early morning freshness and fragrance as you get the car out for a run.*
*The exquisite sadness of a summer evening (I believe George Eliot mentions this) and all the happy, happy time in between.*
    *And if you stay out just a little late for the children they can nod off on the back seat with no fear that they will be thrown off their temporary beds by road shocks.*
    *That is of course if your car is a Jowett.*
    *If it isn't, try a Jowett, and don't put off your happy days.*

*TAILOR MADE......We are neither fluttered nor flattered by receiving so many orders for our Kestrel model, but we are gratified.*
    *Even if we received twice the number of orders, we should still pursue our calm deliberate way and not attempt to increase our output by one single vehicle, if to do this would mean sacrificing in the meanest particular our name for tailor made as against the reach-me-down article.*
    *You can therefore place your order now for a Jowett, knowing that although you may not get it off the shelf, when you do get it, it will be worthy both of you and of us. Meanwhile, you may have our Catalogue per return.*

The text-only advertisements also continued through 1934. Here are five more examples:

*CHANCE OR THOUGHT?......When you sit in the front or back seat of a Jowett, and stretch your length restfully, we hope you don't think it is merely a matter of luck that there is such a large amount of leg-room.*
    *The special design of engine helps, of course, but there has been a tremendous amount of planning for your comfort.*

# 168,000 MILES ON A
# JOWETT SINCE 1931!

Branxholme,
Woodthorpe Drive,
Nottingham.

2.9.37.

Messrs. Jowett Cars, Ltd.,
Idle, Bradford.

Dear Sirs,

It seems only fair to you, as makers of the "Jowett" car purchased in 1931, to let you know of, what I consider, its wonderful performance. I have just completed One Hundred and sixty-eight thousand miles and not been "let down" once.

My wife and I have just finished a 1,400 miles tour of East and South East England and during the whole run had not the slightest trouble with it, and after the mileage it had previously done I think it only fair to give my testimony on the reliability of the Jowett.

The car has been rebored once and all adjustments have been made at once and not allowed to interfere with the running for want of expert attention, also the car has been greased regularly each Saturday morning which, to my lay mind, has helped materially to keep her going.

In conclusion, I can only say that for Reliability, Economical running and 'Getting you there' – the Jowett – every time !

Yours faithfully,

(Signed)  T. Holt.

# SEE THIS YEAR'S
# CAR WITH "BALANCED POWER"
# AT EARLS COURT STAND 80

JOWETT CARS LTD., IDLE, BRADFORD  *London Showrooms* : GODFREY'S LTD., 365-368, EUSTON ROAD, N.W.1  *Phone* : Euston 2644-7
J.40

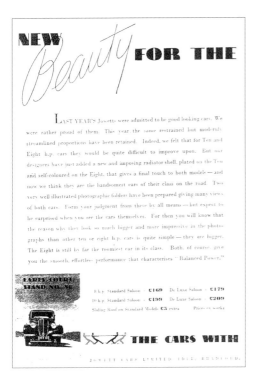

The same with the upholstery and trimming.

It's the same the whole way through. When your left hand seeks the gear lever, there is no groping to do, it is there, naturally. Likewise, your right hand falls on the brake lever. We can give you a reason for everything except one.

We can't explain why our seven horse engine pulls a twelve horse body with ease, and, further, passes most cars of higher power.

To prove what we say, you ought to try a Jowett, and you can for nothing.

Prices from £150. Tax £7.

214,000 MILES. REPAIRS £25......This mileage represents, to the average motorist 25 years of running.

You'd feel very happy, wouldn't you, if you thought that for the next 25 years your repair bill for motoring was only going to be £1 per year.

Yet this mileage for the cost stated was achieved by the owner of a Jowett – see his letter to the Light Car of May 11th.

Talk about dependability and safe investment; you only realise the meaning of these words when you are the owner of a Jowett.

Try one now. You can do, for nothing.

Prices from £150. Tax £7.

ORPHEUS AND MORPHEUS..At Jowetts, we have a works orchestra, 6 violins, 2 violas, Cello and bass, 2 clarinets, 3 trumpets, 2 trombones, piano, drums, and banjo in G. (Oh and a conductor).

Every Wednesday lunch the band gives a half-hour concert to the work-people in the canteen.

Now, this is the amazing thing. If the music is of the **maestoso** or **grave** type, for the remainder of the day, not one Jowett will do 70m.p.h.!

On the other hand, if we play a **tarantelle** – but why pursue the theme. Let us leave it to the student of psychology.

For the practical man, a few facts: –
The Jowett will do 35/40 m.p.g.
It will keep up 45m.p.h. for hours and hours, without fuss.
It costs less to run than any other car.
It is more efficient.
It lasts for ever, and we wish it didn't.
It is the best light car.
**Verbum sapienti!**

SUMMAT FOR NOWT......This is accredited as the aim of the Yorkshireman, but were it his only characteristic then every man would have the mind of a Yorkshireman, for 'Something for nothing' has an irresistible appeal to us all; else where is the thrill of a bargain?

When you buy a Jowett you buy maximum comfort, economy, beauty and absolute reliability, but there is something for nothing.

WE give you the benefit of our twenty-eight years' experience as manufacturers of economy cars plus individuality as distinct from mass produced.

You also get the camaraderie and goodwill of every other Jowett owner free.

Make up your mind that your next car will be a Jowett and let pride of ownership add two inches to your chest measurement.

FAILURES!......In twenty-eight years of manufacture we have not yet produced a car that will run without: –
A. Petrol.
B. Oil.
C. Repairs.

We have succeeded, however, in producing a car that is cheaper under these three heads than any other.

In producing a car that holds its own in looks, and excels in performance.

A car that will gladden your heart.

So after all of that we are only comparative failures.

If your thoughts are in the direction of a new car, you should certainly try a Jowett.
You can do, you know, for nothing.

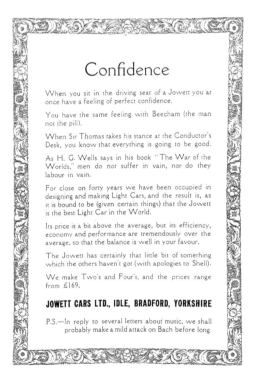

Then in 1935 there was a major departure for Jowett with the introduction of a flat-four engine fitted with twin Zenith carburettors with a 10HP rating. This was fitted in the new Jason and Jupiter saloons. These cars were identical in appearance, the Jason was the de-luxe version, and the Jupiter was the standard model. At this time, streamlined cars were very popular, and these two models were an attempt by Jowett to catch the mood of the day. The cars were displayed at Earls Court in October. They had a very steep raked radiator and steep sloped rear. Sadly, this model appeared too futuristic for most Jowett buyers, and sales were very poor. The brothers realised they had made a mistake with the styling, and within four months replacement models were introduced. The Plover replaced the Jupiter with a new radiator grille and bonnet, with the rear of a Kestrel. The Peregrine replaced the Jason; this had the same front end as the Plover, but retained the Jason rear. All four of these models were short-lived, each being produced for less than a year, with a total production of less than 300.

The new four-cylinder engine had been well received, so Jowett's chief designer, Reg Korner, was asked to design a new less-futuristic body style for the 1937 saloons. The 8HP model using the two-cylinder engine, and the 10HP model using the four-cylinder engine, were identical in appearance and proved much more acceptable to Jowett owners. Both these models were very popular and sold in large numbers up to the outbreak of the Second World War. The commercial range also used both engine sizes, but the 10HP only in relatively small numbers.

# Crescendo

The Loveliest thing in musical expression is a Crescendo, properly done.

The most perfect Crescendo in nature is the lowing of a cow.

In our opinion the most polished tenor of this Century, living or dead, was the late Gervase Elwes. If you want to hear a song well sung with a perfect example of a Crescendo, hear him in the song "So We'll Go No More A-roving." You can get this record from H.M.V.

The Jowett offers a perfect Crescendo in value, and is surpassed by no other Light Car. Unfortunately its price has crescendo'd, but there is good value for every penny.

Shall we send you a catalogue?

Prices from £169.

# Wiedersehen

## JOWETT CARS LTD., IDLE, BRADFORD
### YORKSHIRE.

P.S. Although we start with an Italian and finish with a German word, don't jump to conclusions.

During this period from 1935 up to the war, there was a marked change in some of the advertising. There were more pictorial adverts, which were more factual, and more like other car manufacturers' adverts. These did away with the floral border-style, and to me, are less memorable. I am pleased to say, however, that the text-only adverts in the floral border were retained right up to the outbreak of war. In my opinion, some of the ones published in 1939 were the best they ever produced. The following are a very small selection from this five-year period, as I am suffering from space constraints!

*Mrs. JOHN GILPIN......A friend informs us this is the name he has christened his car, and do we know why.*

*We turned up our Palgrave, and found Cowper's typically English ballad.*

*The following verse is, we think, the reason: -*

*'John Gilpin kissed his loving wife*
*O'erjoyed was he to find*
*That though on pleasure she was bent,*
*She had a frugal mind.'*

*(If you want to sing this, it will go to any common metre tune in your hymn book).*

*The Jowett certainly fills the bill as regards the last two lines, for it will give you more pleasure for less money than any other car.*

Try one for nothing. Prices from £158. Tax £5 5s

PS. – A little competition. How many words (English only) can you make from the letters Mrs. JOHN GILPIN? If there is a tie, the interest of the covering letter will be taken in to consideration when awarding the prize.

DEMONSTRATION at POONA......This sounds like more trouble in India, but we hasten to re-assure you.

A short time ago in one of our adverts we offered a free demonstration of the Jowett so that our car's undoubted merits could be tested prior to buying. Quite a number of our readers availed themselves of this opportunity with, we hope, benefits on both sides.

We have, however, received an application for a free demonstration from a gentleman in Poona. We find that our nearest agent is about 1,000 miles away.

How can we deal with this application?

We ask for your help in this matter and we shall be glad if you will forward your suggestions to the address below, and please mark your envelope with a capital 'P' in the top left-hand corner. To the senders of the most helpful suggestions we shall have much pleasure in presenting a set of Plugs for their car, irrespective of make.

(Carry on, Band Wagon).

Meanwhile we are still prepared to carry on with these free trials which are without obligation, and all you need do to obtain a trial is to scribble your name and address across this page, tear it out and post it to us in an unsealed envelope carrying a halfpenny stamp, but to make the matter clear, we had better point out that this refers only to England, Scotland, Ireland and Wales, oh, and, of course, Lancashire.

Prices – Two-cylinders from £159 10s, Four-cylinders from £179.

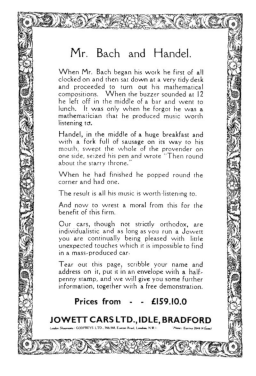

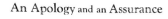

# SNOW, ICE, and FLOODS

◇◇◇◇

When you are dealing with things like this you must have a reliable car, and of course, we had a Jowett.

We have just completed an eleven hundred miles trip to Falmouth and back.

At Worcester we were told that we could not get through to Gloucester owing to floods. We got through.

At only one place were we daunted. That was at the ferry near Chepstow for crossing the Severn, and after waiting an hour and seeing the green faces of some of the passengers off the ferry we decided to go round by Gloucester to get to Bristol.

At Bristol we were warned that Barrow Hill was impassable because of the snow. We chanced it and got through.

At Taunton we were told the road to Exeter was blocked by 12 feet of snow. We chanced it and luck was with us as a single line channel had been cut through.

As often as not our car was garaged in the open but every morning the first touch of the starter brought the engine to life. We had not one involuntary stop during the whole tour.

If a car performs well under arduous conditions it will excel under easy conditions and that is what the Jowett does. Our car, incidentally, was a 1937 Four-cylinder Jowett.

You really must try a Jowett to realise what carefree, economical and reliable motoring is like.

## JOWETT CARS LTD., IDLE, BRADFORD, YORKS.

PS. We are snowed under with letters anent our advertisement "Demonstration in Poona." We crave the indulgence of the senders of these letters but assure them that, in due course, every one of them will receive an individual reply.

London Showrooms : GODFREY'S LTD., 366/368, Euston Road, N.W.I.

'Phone : EUSton 2644 (4 lines).

# VOLKES WAGEN

◎◎◎◎◎

We read with very great interest in a recent issue of the "Autocar" a letter from a correspondent who suggested that Jowett Cars Limited would be the best firm to make such a vehicle.

(We thought at first that the Volkes Wagen was a sort of Zummerset farm wagon.)

We appreciate very highly the compliment inferred in this letter, for we take it the man thought if anybody can produce an efficient and reliable car for the people it is Jowett Cars Limited.

We are sure of our powers in this direction but there is another point to be considered, and that is comfort. We provide the roomiest body of any light car with well-upholstered and delightfully sprung seats, and highly as we value our reputation for efficiency and economy we must also maintain our reputation for a well-designed, roomy and comfortable body.

Twenty years ago almost any sort of open body would do, and how we managed to endure the draughts and discomforts of these bodies goodness only knows.

To-day the first consideration in buying a car is, probably, appearance (we are pretty good here); secondly, comfort (we are second to none here) and lastly reliability, efficiency and economy, the very points on which we excel.

If you are going in for a change of car this Easter don't, for your own sake, leave the Jowett out of your deliberations. We will arrange a free demonstration for you and stand or fall by this.

Drop us a postcard and we will do the rest, or, if you prefer it, we will give you the names of a few Jowett owners in your district who will be very glad to tell you of the merits of our cars.

Two-cylinders from £159.10.0    Tax £6.0.0
Four-cylinders from £179. 0.0    Tax £7.10.0

## JOWETT CARS LTD., IDLE, BRADFORD, YORKS.

London Showrooms: GODFREY'S LTD., 366, Euston Road, London, N.W.1
Telephone: EUSton 2644 (4 lines).

KICKING AGAINST THE PRICKS......The choleric looking gentleman demanded to see our sales representative.

'Good morning' said our representative courteously.

Without replying to this greeting the visitor burst forth somewhat on the following lines.

'I want to test one of your eight horse power cars. I run a twelve horse now, but I am not going to pay 25s per horse power on that, and if the Government think they are going to get extra money out of me to run a car they are mistaken.'

We took him for a run during which his cholera abated very materially and in almost pleasant terms, he asked what the petrol consumption was. On being told he whistled delightedly and, perhaps a little incredulously, and for the first time he smiled. 'I shall be doing 'em both ways,' he chuckled.

He placed his order and took his leave a happier man than when he arrived.

We deliberately chose our headline for this advertisement for there is no getting away from the fact that things have got to be paid for, but the shrewd observer the fact sticks out a mile that if you want luxurious and at the same time, economical motoring you will have to include the Jowett in your calculations when considering your new car. It is the best light car on the market and withal, there is no other car that will cost you less to run.

If you want a demonstration to prove what we say send us a postcard.

Prices from £159 10s.

YORKSHIRE MODESTY......Headed by a brass band the united choirs assembled in the local cricket field.

We sang six hymns two choruses from 'The Messiah' and one from 'The Twelfth Mass.'

Where will you find better choral singing than we have in Yorkshire?

Where, for that matter, will you find a better ham than a York ham, a better cricket team than Yorkshire, and, rising in the scale, a finer Minster than at York, or a more beautiful monastic ruin than Fountains Abbey, near Ripon?

We will not mention our only lake – Semmerwater, as there is a scandalous legend attached to this sheet of water, we are almost sure, by a jealous Lancashireman.

And now as to cars.

There may be speedier cars than the Jowett, but we combine a fair turn of speed with reliability.

There may be cars with a better petrol consumption but we combine a petrol consumption of over forty miles to the gallon with the roomiest body of any light car.

Taking everything that goes towards good motoring – petrol and oil consumption, reliability, efficiency and good looks – we are excelled by none, and are ahead of most.

Would you like a demonstration of these points? If so, drop us a postcard.

Prices from £159 10s.

# A Nursing Home.

Where do individuals soonest lose their individuality?   Our answer to this would be, "In a Nursing Home."

"Drink this" says the nurse.   "Put out your tongue" says the sister.   "Swallow this" says the doctor. "Breathe deeply" says the surgeon.   You do all these things in spite of a wild impulse to snatch your clothes and dash into the street, and it is very well you do so.

You needn't do this, however, when you are buying a car.   Just because somebody shouts at you from an advertisement to buy such and such a car there is no need for you to dash out and buy one, and there is no need for you to dash out and buy one of our cars.

There is, however, a very strong need if you are desirous of the best type of light car motoring to try one of our cars before deciding which you will buy, and having tried one we are sure that in due course you will be a Jowett owner.

Therefore, drop us a postcard and we will give you a free trial wherever you want in this realm of ours.   There will be no badgering from our representative but your common sense will certainly do a bit of straight talking to you.   Why not send us that postcard?

Prices from £159.10.0.

## JOWETT CARS LTD., IDLE, BRADFORD, YORKS.

London Showrooms : GODFREY'S LTD., 366/368, Euston Road, N.W.1
Telephone : EUSton 2644/7

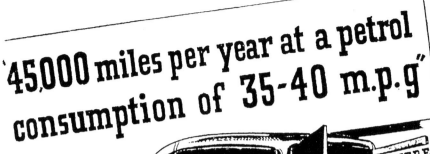

*Wonderful record of famous firm's fleet of*
**10 CWT. JOWETT VANS . . . . . .**
*easily the roomiest Van taxed at £10*

The *Commercial Motor* writes: "Hobday Brothers Ltd., the well-known cycle, motor, radio and electrical factors, which was founded in 1905 . . . . advertises free delivery in 42 counties, of which 15 are tackled from London, and the remainder from Manchester, Sheffield and Wolverhampton.

"Both light and heavy vehicles are used. After exhaustive trials, the company has decided to standardize the Jowett 10 cwt. van for light transport, and vehicles of this type now operate from London and the three provincial depots. Each Jowett van runs an average of 45,000 miles per

year. Despite arduous operating conditions, the vans give an average consumption return of 35-40 m.p.g.

"One of the features of the Jowett van which attracted the company was its large capacity of 107¼ cubic ft.— because, in a number of cases, it is not so much weight as bulk which has to be dealt with."

TRANSPORT MANAGERS and others interested in reducing running costs should send for folder giving comparative tables showing exactly what could be saved by running Jowetts (taxed at £10, with a capacity of 107¼ cu. ft.) in place of other vans in either the £10 or £15 tax class.

*There's nearly* TWICE *the* ROOM *in a*

# JOWETT 10 CWT. VAN

*compared with any other Van taxed at £10*

★  J O W E T T  C A R S  L I M I T E D  ·  I D L E  ·  B R A D F O R D  ★

# three

# The Post-War Years

*Easy with that throttle!*

**JOWETT CARS LTD. IDLE, BRADFORD**

Prior to starting this chapter off, I should point out that it will not be as long as the 1920s and 1930s chapters, for two main reasons. The first reason is that the post-war adverts were far less in number. The pre-war advertising was far more prolific, with new adverts appearing virtually every week in the motoring press. In some cases *The Motor* or *The Autocar* or *The Light Car* could carry different adverts in the same week! Most of the post-war adverts related to the Javelin, and later the Jupiter. These would appear in various publications for several weeks, or even months in some cases, at a time. Also, it was not until 1949 when most of the Javelin advertising took off, so there was only a maximum period of five years while these cars were actively marketed, as car production dropped off dramatically in 1953, prior to the company ceasing trading in 1954.

As regards the pre-war adverts, I really have been spoilt for choice, as there are literally hundreds to choose from, as virtually none have been published in recent publications, so all those featured in the text, or reproduced in this book should be 'new' to most readers. With the post-war models, there are far fewer examples to choose from, and of those available several have been reproduced in other recent publications. I am trying, therefore, to reproduce as many I can, which I do not think have been used before. There are a few that I have used in the text which I know have been seen before, but they were too good to not use again!

Jowett Car production ceased in 1940 and the factory was converted over to produce munitions for the war effort. Jowett owners were still able to have their cars serviced at the works and obtain spares, etc. Small advertisements were taken out from time to time to make these services known. This is an example:

*Although the War has brought the production of Jowett Cars and Commercial Vehicles to a halt, we can still give facilities in Service and Spares.*
*We invite JOWETT OWNERS to send us their problems.*
*Jowett Cars Limited, Idle, Bradford. 'phone Idle 341, 'grams Jowett 341 Idle.*

Jowett realised that a new model would need to be ready as soon as possible after the hostilities were over. To this end they appointed a young engineer in 1942 called Gerald Palmer, who at the time was working for MG. His brief was to build an all-new car suitable for use at home and abroad, at an overall cost of £500! The car he would produce would be the Javelin.

It's new right through

The engine is new; the body is new; the whole design is new. Under 14ft. overall, yet will take six and provides luxury seating for four. Capacious boot for luggage. Exceptional ground clearance. Light and softly sprung, but safe on corners. Powerful, speedy, yet economical to run. Deliveries start in the New Year. 1½-litre flat 4-cylinder engine. Price under £500 plus purchase tax.

THE **JAVELIN**

*a completely new car by* **JOWETT**

In May 1945 Jowetts took out a full-page advert in *The Motor* and *The Autocar* to advertise the new car. The advert had a picture of an empty shop floor at the works with this text:

*THIS SHOP HAS NEVER SEEN A JOWETT......For years this shop at the Jowett works has been tackling the tricky job of making breech mechanisms for anti-tank guns. Very soon now, we hope, it will be assembling the new Jowett car – a car that will have all the old Jowett sturdiness and reliability with verve, speed, comfort and style added.*

In September, another advert was published, this being a full page again; the page was basically white, with three bullet shapes on it with views of the shop floor within the bullet shapes. The advert read:

*A NEW SHOT IN THE LOCKER......During the war years Jowetts made hundreds of thousands of six-pounder armour-piercing shot – a job calling for considerable skill in heat treatment. But there is another shot in the locker now – the new post-war Jowett car which looks as if it's going to be something of a revelation to peacetime motorists.*

In November, another advert was published, and once again it was a full-page advert. It showed a view of the factory floor again, but this time it had the outline of a Javelin drawn on top of the picture. It has to be said that it was based on an early prototype mock-up and it bore little resemblance of the finished article! The advert read:

*FROM CARS TO CAPSTAN LATHES – and back again......In this new shop in the Jowett factory the highly skilled job of making capstan lathes was going on during the war. Now one*

*skilled job gives place to another – the making of the new Jowett car – a car that will astonish and delight the new motoring public.*

In 1946 Jowett produced a booklet called *War Production Record*, which listed in detail all the items produced for the war effort. It also had some nice photographs taken in locations in the factory where various munitions were produced. On the last page of the booklet there is a photograph of the new Javelin in a rural setting; this was in fact one of the first prototypes. There was also some wonderful text in the booklet regarding Jowett's involvement with the war effort:

*Then came the dark days of Munich and the start of the present war, when that fateful September of 1939 broke upon Europe, Jowett were peacefully turning out cars. We switched almost overnight to capstan lathes and aircraft components. When a man in the street saw the bombers roaring overhead and the guns go rumbling through the streets on their way to the ships, he could feel a certain glow of satisfaction and comfort in the knowledge that they kept him safe at home.*

*When Jowett workers looked up and saw the same aircraft, they could feel proud that they had helped put them in the sky. With their own hands they helped to make hundreds of guns and millions of ammunition for them. Day in, day out, nights as well, the Jowett workers stood at their benches and made the countless thousands of parts for planes, ground equipment, guns, ammunition, tanks, motor engines and machine tools.*

*But now we see the results in Europe, the results of all this labour and the work of the men who used the weapons made by Jowetts. During those six long years, did Jowett workers ever wonder how much the factory was turning out, and what the value of the output amounted to? Did they ever think that if those fittings they stood and made had been faulty, their own sons and husbands and sweethearts might so easily have been killed? Perhaps they did, for the standard of their work never slipped.*

In July 1946 a full-page text-only advert appeared, giving details of the new Javelin:

*THE 1½ LITRE JAVELIN a completely new car by JOWETT......Newly designed from bumper to bumper to include all the advances the post-war motorist expects. Light; under 14 feet overall. Very economical to run. Perfect control. Steering column gear change. Will accommodate four in luxurious comfort, and can take up to six. Soft sprung, yet firm on corners. Exceptional luggage space. Price under £500 plus purchase tax.*
*Deliveries start in the New Year.*
**Jowett Cars Ltd. 48 Albemarle Street, Piccadilly, London. W1**

Sadly the delivery dates stated in this advert proved to be on the very optimistic. Due to the chronic shortages of raw materials in early post-war Britain, the first cars were not available until early 1948. The price was also considerably more by the time the car

was road tested in April 1948, and had risen to £640 plus purchase tax of £178 10s 7d, making a grand total of £818 10s 7d.

The Javelin was designed as a car for the world, as Jowett had to be able to export the car to obtain raw materials. This was reflected in a series of adverts that appeared from November 1946. A typical example shows three artist's sketches of a Javelin in various exotic locations. The large sketch shows the car parked next to a massive cactus plant, with a Texan-type cowboy riding towards it. The two smaller sketches show the car in an Indian casaba-type setting in the first, and skiing in an Alpine-type setting in the second. This seems rather ironic to me, as sales in the USA were to prove very poor, with only just over thirty cars being sold there out of a total production run of over 22,000 cars. Sales would also prove to be very poor in Europe, with the exception of Sweden and Finland. They were a great success, however, in the Colonies, such as Australia, New Zealand and Canada. They also did well in some South American countries, particularly Uruguay. The text for this advert was as follows:

# Designed
## *for world markets*

## THE 1½ LITRE Jowett **JAVELIN**

Jowett post-war policy has been to concentrate all the features of design wanted in world markets into one model. Both policy and product have been enthusiastically received at home and overseas.

Now in production, the all-steel JAVELIN, built for motoring conditions all over the world, combines real roominess, comfort and restfulness for driver and passengers, with sports-car standards of acceleration, road holding, braking, steering and high cruising speed — but with soft yet bounce-free torsion-bar suspension. The overall length is only 14 feet. This is possible because of the compactness of the 1½ litre 50 b.h.p. flat-4-cylinder

engine which makes generous passenger space possible with an 8 ft. 6 ins. wheel base. Add such attractive qualities as high power-to-weight ratio, flat floor and outstanding visibility, good cooling and ground clearance, small turning circle and fuel consumption, ease of maintenance and durability — all of which have been given high priority in the "new right through" JAVELIN — and you appreciate why the specification of this British car appeals so strongly to critical motorists all over the world, and why nearly 100 overseas agents in over 65 countries look forward with confidence to its universal acceptance as one of the outstanding successes of our time.

## *it's new right through*

JOWETT CARS LTD. LONDON AND BRADFORD

## The 1½ LITRE JAVELIN
### a driver's car with passenger comfort

If ever a car was a "driver's car" it is the JAVELIN. Correctly placed controls (including column gear lever) great comfort, outstanding visibility — these welcome you to the driving seat. First-class steering, brakes, road-holding and suspension — these invite your confidence. Remarkable top gear performance, available almost everywhere regardless of gradient and road surface — these gratify and surprise you even if you are the most hardened driver. Because rapid acceleration and high cruising speed are remarkably free from fuss and noise, and because the JAVELIN'S road

behaviour is so good, you are fit and fresh at the end of a long day's motoring.

But equally, the JAVELIN is a "passenger's" car incorporating basic features which contribute to remarkable comfort and convenience. The back of the rear seat cushion is 15 inches in front of the rear axle; this, coupled with the all-round torsion bar suspension, provides a soft but bounce-free ride and allows the back-seat passengers to travel in real luxury. A flat floor, armrests, wide doors, rear parcel shelf and unexcelled visibility complete their satisfaction. Price £640 plus purchase tax £178 . 10 . 7.

### THE JOWETT
# JAVELIN
*it's new right through*

JOWETT CARS LIMITED · BRADFORD AND LONDON

DESIGNED TO SUCCEED ALL OVER THE WORLD

*A Javelin in the Austrian Tyrol*

### THE 1½ LITRE
# JOWETT JAVELIN

"We had a marvellous trip, and the car surpassed everything we had hoped. You cannot imagine the comfort, the roominess, and the docility of this marvel of British engineering. It takes a long test, such as the road section of the Rally, to bring home the value of a good suspension system — like that of the Jowett. One rides in the utmost comfort even cars of much larger capacity and costing very much more, had to give us best. Fine acceleration . . . a real joy to drive . . ."
SR. ELIAS LOBO, Portugal "O VOLANTE"

"The Javelin cruises at a quiet and smooth 60 m.p.h. and, indeed, does not feel stressed when taken along for mile after mile at 65 to 70. The all-out speed, it will be noticed, is above 75 m.p.h. It is the handiness of the car, its quick acceleration and the ease of fast cruising, which make it a lively and decidedly interesting means of travel. Traffic conditions

at the moment in England are specially favourable to the putting up of good average speeds, but it is none the less creditable to the Javelin that on a regularly employed main road route of slightly below 100 miles, which formed part of the testing, it covered 56 miles in one hour and a total of 91 miles in two successive hours, most of which was after dark. Two or three times on this run the speedometer was put on to the full 80 reading . . ."
"THE AUTOCAR"— 30th April 1948

**AUTOCAR ROAD TEST**
*April 30th. 1948*
Top speed 76 m.p.h.—0-50 m.p.h. in 17.0 secs.—up to 60 m.p.h. in third gear—and the inherent comfort of the Javelin with its torsion bar suspension all round is as outstanding as its performance.

"Clean hands" jacking system. No crawling in the mud or playing hide-and-seek after dark. Simply place the handle in a hole below the door sill, and wind. A child can raise the JAVELIN in one-and-a-half minutes.

### THE 1½ LITRE JOWETT JAVELIN
### . . . its new right through

PRICE £640.0.0 plus £178.10.7 Purchase Tax     JOWETT CARS LTD. BRADFORD & LONDON

---

*THE WORLD TURNS TOWARDS THE NEW BRITISH CAR – THE 1½ LITRE JAVELIN by JOWETT......The Javelin is a British car, and has the precision, finish and staunch workmanship associated with British engineering products at their best. But its appeal is universal, for it has generous lines, the high ground clearance, the unimpeded vision, the comfort and untiring power required for big-map motoring in all conditions and climates. Although under 14-feet overall, the Javelin provides generous comfort for four, and will carry six without cramping. Its boot has abundant capacity for long-journey luggage. Flat-4 1½ litre engine. Back seats well in front of rear axle. Torsion bar suspension all round. Steering column gear change. All these features, and many besides, mark out the new Javelin a worldwide reputation.*

This must have been a very frustrating time for Jowetts, as the public were wanting to buy the car, but were still waiting for it a year later! The next advert I am detailing was from October 1947, and it is still referring to, 'You're going to like the new Javelin by Jowett'. It shows a side view line drawing of a Javelin and a picture of the engine. The advert goes on to say:

*You'll be surprised to find the Javelin getting to 50m.p.h. from a standing start in well under 15 seconds, and then climbing to an effortless cruising speed of over 60m. p.h. This new 1 1/2 litre engine endows an exceptionally roomy, comfortable family saloon with sports car performance at instant command. Like everything else*

in the new Javelin, the engine is new right through. It develops 50 B.H.P. which, with the low overall weight of the car, ensures sparkling performance.

**You're going to like its flowing lines...** The smooth flow of the Javelin's lines helps performance and eliminates irritating wind roar, unexaggerated modernity that is a delight to the eye. Lamps and door handles are recessed into the panelling – there's an unbroken flow from trim nose to tapered tail.

**Its roominess...** The compactness and forward mounting of the engine, the flat floor and steering column gear lever give abundant legroom. The bench-type seats accommodate six people on occasion and ensure armchair comfort for four. The rear boot easily accommodates an unusually large amount of luggage.

**Its safely and economy...** For all its lively acceleration, the Javelin is untiring and safe to drive. Excellent road-holding, first class brakes and all-round vision add up to safety. And as for economy the Javelin by independent test has been proved to be 29 m.p.h. at a steady 60 m.p.h.

**Its smooth riding...** Here again the forward engine mounting scores. It means that rear passengers sit well in front of the rear axle and that, with torsion bar suspension all round (independent at the front) ensures a ride of exceptional comfort and smoothness for everyone in the car.

Another similar advert from November 1947 also featured a side view drawing of a Javelin, plus two smaller pictures from the front. One of these clearly shows a Perspex sunshine roof, which was to be offered as an optional extra. A prototype was produced, but it was never put into production. The advert reads:

THE 1½ LITRE JAVELIN – A DRIVER'S CAR WITH PASSENGER COMFORT
If ever a car was a 'driver's car' it is the Javelin. Correctly placed controls (including column gear lever) great comfort, outstanding visibility – these welcome you to the driving seat. First-class steering, brakes, road-holding and suspension – these invite your confidence. Remarkable top gear performance, available almost everywhere regardless of gradient and road surface – these gratify and surprise you even if you are a hardened driver. Because rapid acceleration and high cruising are remarkably free from fuss and noise, and because

The JAVELIN's road behaviour is so good, you are fit and fresh at the end of a long day's motoring.

But equally, the JAVELIN is a 'passengers' car incorporating basic features which contribute to remarkable comfort and convenience. The back of the rear seat cushion is 15 inches in front of the back axle; this, coupled with the all-round torsion bar suspension, provides a soft but bounce-free ride and allows the back seat passengers to travel in real luxury. A flat floor, armrests, wide doors, rear parcel shelf and unexcelled visibility complete their satisfaction

Price £640 plus purchase tax £178 10s 7d.

The Jowett JAVELIN it's new right through.

From April 1948, several Javelin adverts were produced, all with the same heading, 'Designed to succeed all over the world.' These featured a picture of a Javelin in a foreign location, together with some text and these are three typical examples.

The first shows a Belgian-owned Javelin on the docks at Ostend, and no less than three testimonials by motoring writers of the day, which read:

'With the requirements of buyers all over the world in mind, the designer has endowed the Javelin with features to appeal to all types of user... comfortable seating for four people, with adequate room for two more if necessary....and generous head and leg room. Close attention to the design of the steering and suspension have resulted

in outstanding qualities of easy control and comfortable riding in all conditions.'
Export Trader May-June 1947

'My test of over 200 miles covered many single-figure hills, rutty lanes, main roads and rough trackless common land intersected with deep gulleys and sharp rises and drops. Purposely I gave this car an exceedingly rough ride, and well did it respond.
Quite early in the test four features became noticeable:
1) Ample power for all requirements with a satisfactory reserve in hand.
2) Suspension.
3) Ground clearance.
4) Manoeuvrability due to light steering and turning circle of 32 feet.
These features, combined with stability, excellent visibility and easy control contribute to a very nice-mannered car.
Being unhampered by unnecessary weight, the power available is more than satisfactory. In consequence, the engine takes its load very easily at any speed up to its maximum of 75 miles per hour.
This car treats hills with contempt. In top gear tore up a 1 in 8 gradient at 35 miles per hour. The suspension is the best I have tested on any post-war car. It gives a soft, floating action over the rough spots, but is firm enough to prevent roll on corners. Another asset is a ground clearance of 7¾ inches.'
Ralph Feilden – well-known motoring correspondent, writing in Great Britain and the Far East, July 1947.

'The Javelin is one of the most interesting cars I have handled in this country. Driving with four passengers to the top of Effigenalp, one of the steepest roads in Switzerland, and with sharp hair-pins, the car did not overheat.
    Every enthusiastic motorist who has been in the car was surprised about the perfect road-holding and suspension. It was a great pleasure to drive the car round the circuit at Bremgarten, near Berne, and to appreciate the good braking and general comfort, which is far ahead of any other 1½ litre saloon at the present time.'
Hubert Patthey - Well-known Swiss competition driver.

THE 1½ LITRE JOWETT JAVELIN ...**It's new right through**
Price £640, plus £17 .10s 7d

The second advert shows a sideways view of a production Javelin descending the Jaun Pass in Switzerland, with large mountain ranges in the background. There is also a stylised drawing of the car's interior, which seems a lot more spacious than my Javelin is!
The advert reads:

**Easy with that throttle!**

Easy with that accelerator! This isn't a car where you put your foot down and *wait* for it to go faster. This is a car that you tell what to do. And it does it.

You thought you were getting into a comfortable family car. Well, so you are. But wait a minute.

Find a clear road. You want to go up into the seventies? All right—just put the needle where you want it. The stuff is in this car, just waiting to be used.

Now put it into a bend. Go on—give yourself a chance to be surprised.

There's much faster cornering than you'd expected—and no roll to notice. Safe as houses.

And what about the bumps that you remember on this road? Nobody's mended them yet—they just got kind of lost on their way through the torsion bar suspension of this car.

Yes  you can take your family. Up to six; with luggage. But you can still have driving fun.

This car is a waste of money if you don't care what a car *does.* There's such a lot built into it that doesn't really show until you have it in your hands. Once tried, you'll say I'd rather go by Javelin!

Top speed 78 m.p.h. Acceleration 0-50 in 13½ secs. Horizontally opposed flat-four 50 B.H.P. engine.

★ *Javelins came 1st and 3rd in the 1949 Monte Carlo Rally,* 1½ *litre class.*

1½ LITRE  **JOWETT JAVELIN**
*take a good look when it passes you*

**She's a Lady**

Sometimes you just don't want to use all the zip this car's got. Today you're feeling lazy.

Of course you could whip through the gears and jump to 60 in 22½ seconds and stream along the straight at well over 75, and you could . . .

But today it's different—you feel like crawling . . .

You light a cigarette and drift silently along. Yes, you notice things about this car—how the curved windscreen lets in so much more of the landscape—how practically the bonnet tapers away to give you a close-up view of the road. And the back seat passengers enjoy wide visibility and relax in complete comfort.

Your seat comfy? Want to be nearer the wheel? There's no need to stop. Just wind the handle and take the seat forward a bit. That's better. Forward a bit more. That's perfect. You relax and admire the way she takes the curves—the disdainful way she treats the hills.

This is the time to find out the gentle ways of this car. The slightest tiptoe for the clutch and brakes. And that 50 B.H.P. engine just waits for you to tell it what to do—and it does it.

Try and see from how slowly she'll pick up on top gear. That's a test for a 1½ litre car. She does it smoothly from a mere traffic crawl.

A big car flashes past. A whim seizes you. A touch on the throttle and—still in top—you could be . . .

But no. Today you are in the mood to enjoy the Javelin's other qualities—calm and quiet and instantly responsive. Yes—this car's a lady.

This car is a waste of money if you don't care what a car *does.* There's such a lot built into it that doesn't really show until you have it in your hands. Once tried, you'll say 'I'd rather go by Javelin!'

Top speed 78 m.p.h. Acceleration 0-60 in 22.2 secs. Horizontally opposed flat-four 50 B.H.P. engine.

*Javelin saloon:* £595 *plus P.T.* £166.0.7
*Javelin saloon de luxe:* £695 *plus P.T.* £193.16.1

1½ LITRE  **JOWETT JAVELIN**
*take a good look when it passes you*

---

*THE 1½ LITRE JOWETT JAVELIN*
'Developing power enough to give a six-seater car sensational performance, the flat-four Jowett Javelin engine is compact enough to be mounted ahead of the radiator, leaving the whole wheelbase available for passenger accommodation.'

**'Presenting British cars.' THE MOTOR**
'A short trial run with this car showed that for hill climbing, acceleration and useful range of speed it is far above the average 1½ litre family car. While the suspension is definitely comfortable the car has very good road-holding qualities. The driving capabilities of this completely new design earned altogether a very good report. The Javelin has a roomy interior, which is finished and fully equipped according to the English taste. In many respects the new Javelin comes very near to the ideal of a modern family car.'
**AUTOMOBILE REVIEW** *Switzerland 26th November 1947.*

**From THE MOTOR Road Test on a Javelin prototype 7/47.**
*Top speed 76.3 m.p.h. – 0-50 m.p.h. in 13.4 seconds.*
*33 m.p.g. at a constant of 50 m.p.h.*
*1 in 10 gradient climbed in top gear at 52 m.p.h.*
'And the inherent comfort of the Javelin with its torsion bar suspension all round is as outstanding as its performance.' THE 1½ LITRE JAVELIN...**it's new right through.**

The third advert has a picture of a very early production car, registered FAK 573, on the Middle Rhine Bridge, Basle. Charles Callcott-Reilly, the managing director of Jowett Cars Ltd, is standing with the car.

# Used to be a long journey

It's a big hill; steep, curving. No chance to take a run at it. Lorries block you to a crawl. Throttle. Brakes. Throttle. It takes the guts out of a car. And out of a driver, too.

But not this car; not this driver. A clear patch and you put your foot down in 3rd. In a flash the needle says 50 — you're away.

How long have you been travelling now? Two hours? Three hours? Travelling fast — 60, 65, 70, 75. But there's no strain. You're fresh; relaxed.

A corner comes and goes; and another and another. A surprising absence of roll. You work out your average. It's high. Somehow this car grips a bend and straightens it out: comes to a hill and flattens it down.

You sit enjoying it.

It's a good road now. But there have been bad patches; they got lost in the torsion bar suspension, and not a kick in the steering. Only your eyes noticed.

Two hours to go. The light fades.

You snap on the head lights; brightly reassuring in the dusk.

This used to be a long journey. But this car conquers distance.

And what about space? Plenty. You can take up to six with luggage — and still have driving fun.

This car is a waste of money if you don't care what a car *does*. There's such a lot built into it that doesn't really show until you have it in your hands. Once tried, you'll say 'I'd rather go by Javelin!'

Top speed 78 m.p.h. Acceleration 0-60 m.p.h. in 22.2 secs. Horizontally opposed flat-four 50 B.H.P. engine.

Javelin Saloon £595 plus Purchase Tax £166.0.7
Javelin Saloon de-luxe £695 plus Purchase Tax £193.16.1

*SEE THE NEW JAVELIN AT STAND No. 9 (and other stands) SCOTTISH MOTOR SHOW*

 1½ LITRE **JOWETT JAVELIN**

*take a good look when it passes you*

**I**t's new right through

Newly conceived to the last nut.  Light and economical, yet big in everything that
matters.  Powerful, with ample speed.  Exceptional ground clearance.  Real big-car
comfort.  Back seats well forward of rear axle.  Independent front torsion bar
suspension.  Spacious seating for all.  Deliveries start in the New Year.  1½-litre flat
4-cylinder engine.  Price under £500 plus purchase tax.

THE **JAVELIN**

*a completely new car by* **JOWETT**

*above the 60 mark*

**JAVELIN**

*take a good look when it passes you*

He had taken the car on an extensive test in Switzerland and this is a photograph taken on this trip.

This too had no less than three testimonials in it. The text reads:

*THE 1½ LITRE JOWETT JAVELIN*
*'We recently reported to our readers on the new Jowett Javelin, which embodies a large number of novel features.*

*A road test has confirmed that our information was by no means exaggerated. This 8CV (13.05h.p. – RAC rating) engine gives a speed of 80 k.p.h in third gear up a slope of some 1 in 12½ and will push the needle round to 135 k.p.h on the flat.*

*Alongside this performance, not often met with a car of this power, the latest Jowett has a luxurious interior equipment, very detailed finish, and new body shape, which makes a break with tradition. Added to these, a suspension system perfect at all speeds, powerful but silent acceleration and perfect road holding, especially on twisty stretches where the stability and steering of the car are shown to advantage. The Javelin is a case of bold design and excellent workmanship.'*
**ROBERT BRAUNSCHWEIG**......*Editor of the Swiss* **Automobil Revue**.

*'Acceleration in the saloon tested was up to sports car standards, and the maximum speed reached was a smooth 75 m.p.h. At this speed, thanks to the Javelin's torsion bar suspension and adequate shock absorbers, the car rode very comfortably and without bounce or swaying. The Javelin cornered very steadily.'*
**Extract from THE BRITISH AUSTRALIAN.**

*'This is undoubtedly an outstanding car...it satisfies the driver who knows fast cars...it evokes enthusiasm from back seat passengers, too, for they have plenty of room...foot wells are not used by virtue of a low level hypoid drive to the rear axle...the comfort of riding in the back seats is not inferior to that in the front seats.'*

*Top speed 76 m.p.h – 0 to 50 m.ph in 17 seconds – up to 60 m.p.h in third gear.*

*The inherent comfort of the Javelin with its torsion bar suspension all round is as outstanding as its performance.*

**THE AUTOCAR 30 April 1948**

With the Javelin receiving such excellent reviews, it was not long before rally drivers wanted to get their hands on the cars. Two well-known Yorkshire rally drivers, Tommy Wise and Cuth Harrison, contacted Jowett to see if they would provide them with a Javelin to take part in the January 1949 Monte Carlo Rally. Jowett agreed to this request, as it was felt it would keep public interest in the car, until it became more readily available. They made the stipulation, however, that the car's designer, Gerald Palmer, should also go on the car's International rally debut. Wise and Harrison agreed, provided that Palmer did not drive as they felt he would be too gentle with his baby! The car had a trouble-free run, and won the 1½-litre class and was placed 14th overall. There were also several other Javelins in the finishers.

In view of the Monte success, Jowett decided to enter a Javelin in the Spa 24-hour race in Belgium in June 1949. They felt a good result here would

enhance sales in Europe. Anthony Hume of *The Motor* and Tom Wisdom of *The Daily Herald* would drive the car this time. The car was driven to the event, along with another car carrying spares. It was then prepared and raced for twenty-four hours. The car was entered in the 2-litre class, which it won with ease; in fact it was lapping faster than the 4-litre touring cars.

Needless to say, these impressive results were detailed in adverts after the events, so must have enhanced the car's reputation. During the March–April period, the Monte Carlo Rally results were published. This had a publicity photograph of the Javelin registered FAK 573 at the top, with the following text:

*In the 1949 Monte Carlo Rally*
**JOWETT JAVELINS**
**came 1st and 3rd in the 1½ litre** *class*
*This outstanding success was due to a tested top speed of 78 m.p.h.*
*An acceleration that whisks you from 0–50 in 13½ seconds.*
*All-round torsion bar suspension.*
*Streamlined body.*
*Powerful brakes and power to weight ratio.*
**Jowett Cars Limited Bradford and London.**

The advert regarding the Spa 24-hour race appeared in July 1949 and featured a sideways view of the actual Javelin at speed in the race, sporting its race number 86. At the bottom of the advert there was a small drawing of the rear of a Javelin, and featured the slogan, 'Take a good look when it passes you.' The text read as follows:

## SPECTACULAR WIN BY
## 1½ LITRE JOWETT JAVELIN
### In the Belgian 24 hours Grand Prix (2 litre touring class)
Driven by Anthony Hume and Thomas Wisdom, a standard production Javelin: -
1) Won the 2-litre touring class at 65.5 m.p.h. covering 1,500 miles in 24 hours.
2) Covered a greater distance at a higher speed than any other 1½ car, sports or touring.
3) Covered a greater distance at a higher speed than any touring car irrespective of size.
**Take a look when it passes you.**

As mentioned before, production of the Javelin was frustratingly slow due to the shortages of raw materials, and it was not until mid-1948 that cars were available to the public. Even then most went for export, to qualify for more raw materials. By the end of 1948 only 1,558 Javelins had been built, but things improved in 1949 with 5,450, as raw materials became more widely available and as the car's reputation grew.

Due to the success of the Javelin in competition, the company felt there was a market for an all-out sportscar using the Javelin mechanicals. A tubular chassis was designed by ERA for the project and the body was designed at record speed by Reg Korner. The first two cars that were ready were shipped to the USA to catch the New York Motor Show. The third car was produced soon after and registered GKW 111. Jowett's then took the bold step of entering the untried and untested car in the 1950 Le Mans 24-hour race on 24-25 June. It was driven by Tommy Wise and Tom Wisdom. The car in fact won the 1-½ litre class at a record speed of an average of 75.8mph covering over 1,819 miles. The Jowett slogan for the Jupiter, 'the car that leaped to fame', was born!

Javelin sales in 1950 would also increase again to 5,551, and the Bradford would continue to quietly sell in large numbers with virtually no advertising. Ironically, this was a pre-war designed vehicle in every respect, and was the only post-war model to make a profit. The profits it generated were ploughed back into the Javelin and Jupiter projects, which never broke even financially.

Needless to say, Jowett cashed in on the Le Mans success straight away, with a small advert in *The Yorkshire Post* newspaper on 28 June. This had a drawing of a Jupiter travelling at speed, carrying the correct race number of 36. It should be pointed out that the first Jupiters were known as Javelin Jupiters, but they soon lost the Javelin prefix, as the car was an overnight success in its own right. The advert reads:

## SPECTACULAR WIN AT LE MANS!
JAVELIN JUPITER First in the 1½ Litre Class.
In the Le Mans International 24-hour Sports Car Race the only Javelin Jupiter entered gained 1st place in the 1½ Litre class, breaking the class record at an average speed for the whole 24-hour race of 77.1 m.p.h. This was the first time that a Jupiter has entered a race. The car was driven by Mr. T.H. Wisdom and Mr. T.C. Wise.

*(Subject to official confirmation)*
**JOWETT CARS LIMITED BRADFORD AND LONDON**

A very similar advert to that used in *The Yorkshire Post* on 28 June was carried in *The Autocar* on 30 June. It used the same stylised picture, the headline was altered, but the main body of the text remained the same. It was also enlarged in size to take up a full page; the new headline was:

**ANOTHER SUCCESS FOR JOWETT'S – this time at Le Mans with the new JAVELIN JUPITER**

It was hoped that the Jupiter would sell well in America, as at that time British sportscars were very popular. If the MG and Triumph were selling well, why not a Jupiter? The June 1950 issue of the American magazine *Road & Track* carried a full-page advert on the Javelin Jupiter. This was clearly produced prior to Le Mans, so there is no reference to the race in it, even though it refers to the 'race-bred 3-seater sports convertible', when Le Mans was its first race! The advert has a stylised drawing of the Jupiter at the top of the page and a drawing of the rolling chassis at the bottom. The text of the advert reads:

*Britain's latest car – The JAVELIN JUPITER – The race-bred 3-seater sports convertible.*
*The thrill of owning and driving a race-bred car is one of the world's supreme pleasures, and the Javelin Jupiter has been specially produced to give high speed motoring with supreme comfort in all weathers and under all conditions.*

*The Jupiter, a product of the craftsmanship of the famous firm of Jowett Cars Limited, England, is a development of the world-famous Jowett Javelin which gained 1st and 3rd place in the 1949 Monte Carlo Rally (1½ Litre Class) and 1st place in the 2 Litre class (65.5 m.p.h. for over 1,500 miles) in the Belgian 24-hour Grand Prix at Spa, in the same year.*

*On the basis of the Javelin the Jupiter evolved. The Javelin's horizontally-opposed, four cylinder engine has been increased from 50 to 60 B.H.P. and has been fitted with two special carburettors; a special type rack and pinion steering gives precision steering at high speed; an absolutely rigid tubular steel chassis gives lightness and tremendous strength; the shock absorbers have been strengthened; better brakes fitted and a special oil-cooling system installed. The Jupiter has an aero-dynamic lightweight aluminium body seating 3 abreast.*

*The Jupiter will accelerate to 60m.p.h. in approximately 15 seconds, and reach over 90 m.p.h. and cruise at 80 m.p.h as a matter of course.*

*The walnut dashboard you will, of course, find all the instruments essential to high-speed driving – revolution counter, thermometer and oil-pressure gauges. There is ample room for luggage, the upholstery is fine hide and the equipment is de luxe.*

SOLE DISTRIBUTOR EAST OF THE MISSISSIPPI : -

The Hoffman Motor Car Co., Inc. 487 Park Avenue, at 59 Street, New York 22

Branches; - 1877 Broadway at 62 Street.

65E South Water Street, Chicago.

## THE JAVELIN JUPITER – A PRODUCT OF JOWETT CARS LTD. IDLE, BRADFORD, ENGLAND

Several Javelin adverts appeared over the next few years. Many of these had a drawing of a Javelin with some nice text to go with it. A couple I will use in the text are entitled, 'To a man's woman' and 'The gay deceiver'. In this politically correct world we now live in, it is fun to think that a woman would have no interest in the capabilities of the car at all. Her main concern would be to know how comfy the back seat would be, as she was not expected to drive the car, and was more interested in knowing where the vanity mirror was! As regards the gay deceiver, how the meanings of some words have changed over the last fifty years. I would think it would be hard to sell a car now, aimed at gay deceivers. I have to say, I think these two adverts are great fun!

*TO A MAN'S WOMAN......As a woman you're probably not impressed with such triumphs...International trial and speed events. That's for the enthusiast. But you hope he won't buy a car that's built just for speed – you want comfort too.*

*Well here's the Javelin. Different from what you'd imagined – much more roomy. Not super sports but family design.*

The 1½ Litre Jowett *JUPITER*

Sit in the passenger's seat. Deep and plenty of room. Soft, lolling arm-rests. She's an intriguing car!

And in the back you can doze a journey away – so comfortable. Your eye flickers over the rich fittings...pleased...taking it all in.

And yet he said this was a high performance car. He talked about acceleration and speeds up to nearly 60 m.p.h. He mentioned the powerful brakes, and the torsion bar suspension that cushioned the roughest road, and gripped the corners.

This car is both. His for speed – yours for comfort. Seating up to six – a new form of travel – owning the road she rides.

This car is a waste of money if you don't care what a car does. There's such a lot built into it that doesn't really show until you have it in your hands. Once tried, you'll say "I'd rather travel by Javelin!" *

Top speed, electronically timed, 78 m.p.h. Acceleration 0-60 m.p.h. in 22.2 seconds (The Motor road test) Horizontally opposed flat-four 50 B.H.P. engine. Javelin saloon £595, plus purchase tax £166 0s 7d. Javelin saloon de luxe £695 plus purchase tax £193 16s 1d.

**\* There are over 200 fully qualified Service Agents in Great Britain.**
**1½ Litre JAVELIN take a good look when it passes you**


**GAY DECEIVER**...You've heard incredible stories about this car – stories of International race triumphs; unbelievably high average speeds. And frankly you're doubtful.

Now as you inspect her close up, you still think it can't be. She looks so comfortable even sedate...so harmless somehow. Can that neat, tapering bonnet house such formidable power?

Then you settle down in the deep driving seat and touch the controls...and after a while you know this Javelin's been smiling at you all the time because those cars ahead seem almost stationary; and as you glide silently up behind, you realise your travelling fast – very fast. And you brake...

Quickly the needle slips back to 40 – yes, you were up in the 70s and the whole car was smooth and steady. You didn't even notice. The torsion bar suspension holds you gently to the corners, the road seems velvet smooth, the short neat bonnet lets you see and relax at the same time and the precision steering is just that. It's all so easy in this Javelin. Now you know it. This car, so disarmingly innocent – so spacious – has all the speed of victory in its veins.

This car is a waste of money if you don't care what a car does. There's such a lot built into it that doesn't really show until you have it in your hands. Once tried, you'll say, 'I'd rather travel by Javelin!' *

Top speed, electronically timed, 78 m.p.h. Acceleration 0-60 m.p.h. in 22.2 seconds (The Motor road test). Horizontally opposed flat-four 50 B.H.P. engine. Javelin saloon £595, plus purchase tax £166 0s 7d Javelin saloon de luxe £695 plus purchase tax £193 16s 1d.

**\* There are over 200 fully qualified Service Agents in Great Britain.**
**1½ Litre JAVELIN take a good look when it passes you**

# purposeful

There are no frills on the Javelin—you're looking at the car and suddenly you realise . . . she's perfectly and pre-eminently efficient. We imagined, planned and perfected a tapering body that would seat the family in luxury and yet sneak through the air at speed with hardly a ruffle; making 70 seem like 50.

Like an aircraft, like a bullet, like a torpedo, that body was built for the job—space plus performance. It's the truest form of beauty.

And of course, designs like that are dateless—they are rare too.

The skill and brains of men can build a car, but you need that special something—that touch of genius—to get a Javelin, a family saloon with greyhound's grace.

This car is a waste of money if you don't care what a car does. There's such a lot built into it that doesn't really show until you have it in your hands.

Top speed, electrically timed, 80 m.p.h. Acceleration 0-60 m.p.h. in 22.4 seconds. ("The Autocar" Road Test, 1951). Horizontally opposed flat-four 50 B.H.P. Engine.

The man who wants even higher performance will like the Jupiter. It's Jowett's fast convertible with the famous flat-four engine giving extra B.H.P. It won its class at Le Mans in 1950 and won yet again in 1951. It came 1st and 2nd in the 1951 Monte Carlo Rally, 1½ litre class and won the Lisbon Rally outright.

## 1½ litre

## JOWETT JAVELIN

*take a good look when it passes you*

Jowett Cars Limited, Idle, Bradford, Yorkshire

## What car's he got?

He gave you a lift last week—now can you remember what kind of car that was?
Probably not.

*If that car had been a Javelin you'd have noticed.*

When you're in one you feel something happening—you know it's not an ordinary car.
There's that quick change gear all the experts praise ; flashlight acceleration (0 - 60 in
22.4 secs.) ; a genuine 80 m.p.h. and torsion bar suspension that does what only torsion
bars can do to bumps.

It only needs one short ride in a Javelin for you to start thinking, yes, one day this car's
going to be yours.

The Javelin is a waste of money if you don't care what a car does. There's such a lot
built into it that doesn't really show until you have one in your hands — real family
comfort — and performance.

Top speed, electrically timed, 80 m.p.h. Acceleration 0 - 60 m.p.h. in 22.4 secs. ("The
Autocar" 1951 Road Test). Horizontally opposed 1½ h.p. flat-four engine gives 30 m.p.g.

The 1½ litre
### JOWETT JAVELIN
*one day — it has to be YOURS!*

Made by Jowett Cars Limited, Idle, Bradford, Yorkshire, who make the Jowett Jupiter convertible — class winner
of 9 major trials and races in 1950/51 — and, of course, the famous range of 8 h.p. Bradford commercial vehicles.

---

## What about the poor chap in the back?

You can sit comfortably behind the wheel of a car and never
know what the chap in the back suffers.

That's one of the first points you notice about the Javelin — in
the back seats your knees are nowhere near your chin. Two men with
lanky legs can stretch and loll about. And there's a feeling of confidence
in the car — the way it helps out the driver and takes a grip of the road.

If you've not been in a Javelin before, just come for a short
drive ... effortless acceleration (0 to 50 in 15.4 secs.) — 80 m.p.h. from
a flat-four 1½ litre engine — cruising up in the 60's.

Perhaps this is the first time you've experienced what torsion
bar suspension can do to bumps — perhaps you've never cornered like
this before.

Perhaps you're already saying to yourself—what so many say
after just one ride in a Javelin — one day this car is going to be yours.

The Javelin is a waste of money if you don't care what a car does.
There's such a lot built into it that doesn't really show until you have
one in your hands — real family comfort — economy — and performance.

Top speed, electrically timed, 80 m.p.h. Acceleration 0-50
m.p.h. in 15.4 secs. ("The Motor" 1952 Road Test). Horizontally
opposed flat-four engine gives 30 m.p.g.

The 1½ litre
### JOWETT JAVELIN
*one day— it has to be YOURS*

Made by Jowett Cars Limited, Idle, Bradford, Yorkshire, who make the Jowett Jupiter convertible — class winner
of 9 major trials and races in 1950/51 —and, of course, the famous range of 8 h.p. Bradford commercial vehicles.

---

Here are a couple more Javelin adverts
from 1951. The first shows a country
cottage in the background, with a Javelin
picture superimposed on top, the second
shows a dark winter street scene with a
Javelin picture superimposed on top:

*TIME FOR A CLASSIC TO GROW...
Sometimes it seems as though the shape of
a car gets altered somehow. Each year it gets
harder to put names to the shapes you see.*

*And then there are the classics. Not many.
You can count them on the fingers and the
Javelin is one. They keep their character.*

*It takes time for a classic to grow –
concentrating all the time on improvements
that don't hit the eye. It's not spectacular
– nothing to make headlines – no gaping
crowds – no change just for the sake of it.*

*But quietly, unobtrusively the essential
qualities are made perfect. Brakes sound-
proofing, lighting, suspension, comfort – all this
and much more, is subtly changed. Racing
experience has a lot to do with improving things
you'd think couldn't be improved – and Jowetts
are internationally famous for their successes.*

*Just about now the Javelin is taking its
place among the classics – a car by which
others are judged.*

*This car is a waste of money if you don't
care what a car does. There's such a lot built
into it that doesn't really show until you have
it in your hands. Once tried, you'll say, 'I'd
rather travel by Javelin!' ***

*Top speed, electronically timed, 80 m.p.h.
Acceleration 0-60 m.p.h. in 22.2 seconds.
(The Autocar road test) Horizontally
opposed flat-four 50 B.H.P. Engine.*
**1½ Litre JAVELIN take a good look when
it passes you**

# Le Mans 24-hour race

*(1½ litre class)*

# JOWETT *JUPITER*

**WINS 3 YEARS RUNNING!**

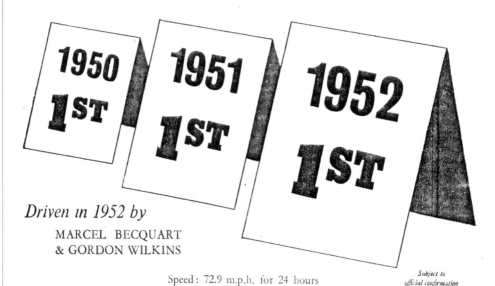

**1950 1ST**

**1951 1ST**

**1952 1ST**

*Driven in 1952 by*
MARCEL BECQUART
& GORDON WILKINS

Speed: 72.9 m.p.h. for 24 hours

*Subject to official confirmation*

**BASICALLY THE SAME ENGINE AS THE JOWETT JAVELIN**

## From the first gear change

So many cars are so alike today it's not always easy to know which one you're in — if you're a passenger. It's the inevitable result of mass production.

But the Javelin is not like that. If you have a noticing eye you can tell the difference instantly — sleek lines; very thorough finish; a functional look.

And from the first quick gear change, the car begins to tell you something — assuming you know about cars — as it settles down to its easy, eager stride.

Then you are getting those bumps converted into nothing, just nothing — only torsion bar suspension can do it that way. The Javelin's acceleration is not the old-fashioned sort; you do 60 effortlessly, in just over 20 seconds from standing — and cruise at that.

You look around and see all the leg room and largeness of the back seats and you don't believe that a 1½ litre engine will take 4 big people up to a genuine 80 — except that you've just done it.

The Javelin is a waste of money if you don't care what a car does. There's such a lot built into it that doesn't really show until you have one in your hands — real family comfort — economy — and performance. Incidentally, the Javelin won outright the Closed Car Section of the R.A.C. International Rally of Great Britain this year.

Best speed, electrically timed, 80 m.p.h. Acceleration 0–50 m.p.h. in 15.4 secs. ("The Motor" 1952 Road Test). Horizontally opposed flat-four engine gives 30 m.p.g.

The 1½ litre
**JOWETT JAVELIN**
one day — it has to be YOURS!

The Javelin's sister car, the JOWETT JUPITER
The 90 m.p.h., high performance Jowett JUPITER, winner of 9 major events in the 1950-51 season. Winner of Le Mans (1½ litre class) for the third year running in 1952. This amazingly successful 1½ litre sports convertible has basically the same engine as the Jowett Javelin.

MADE BY JOWETT CARS LIMITED, IDLE, BRADFORD, YORKSHIRE

## Ever actually driven a Javelin yourself?

There must be some very active reason why a person who has never been in a Javelin before looks on it as THE car after one short drive.

Perhaps you'd like to try her for yourself and find out. Hey, steady with that throttle! Maybe you're not used to driving a car that'll clock 50 in 15.4 secs. from standing.

Maybe you've never been in a 1½ litre saloon that will cruise all day in the 60's and touch 80. Maybe you never knew what torsion bar suspension could do to bumps or used a gear change that's so quick and positive.

And you'll notice another thing too—this car's got room behind for men with lanky legs. It's got room for all the family and all the luggage too. You don't feel cramped in a Javelin.

The Javelin is a waste of money if you don't care what a car does. There's such a lot built into it that doesn't really show until you have one in your hands—real family comfort—economy—and performance. Incidentally, the Javelin won outright the Closed Car Section of the R.A.C. International Rally of Great Britain this year.

Best speed, electrically timed, 80 m.p.h. Acceleration 0—50 m.p.h. in 15.4 secs. (" The Motor " 1952 Road Test). Horizontally opposed flat-four engine gives 30 m.p.g.

The 1½ litre
**JOWETT JAVELIN**
one day — it has to be YOURS!

The Javelin's sister car, the JOWETT JUPITER
The 90 m.p.h., high performance Jowett JUPITER, winner of 9 major events in the 1950-1951 season. Winner of Le Mans (1½ litre class) for the third year running in 1952. This amazingly successful 1½ litre sports convertible has basically the same engine as the Jowett Javelin.

MADE BY JOWETT CARS LIMITED, IDLE, BRADFORD, YORKSHIRE

WHEN ROADS ARE TREACHEROUS......
There's always that element of fear when wet roads turn to slippery greasiness...and fog threatens.

No driver can deny it – that extra tension of the muscles, that doubt...

But in this car you get greater confidence. The moment you take control you feel it – gratefully. That's just that extra precision and responsiveness. And in the fog the Javelin is always mistress of the situation – a short bonnet and a fine view of the road usually put you at the head of the line.

When the roads are bad and you've got to get there, the Javelin is the car to drive. And when the roads are good, and you want to keep her driving at high speeds – there's that high-geared steering again making it all fun driving far and fast, with the all round torsion bar suspension straightening out the corners, cushioning the bumps.

This car is a waste of money if you don't care what a car does. There's such a lot built into it that doesn't really show until you have it in your hands. Once tried, you'll say, 'I'd rather travel by Javelin!'

Both these adverts, and several others, had a box at the bottom left-hand side with a line drawing of a Jupiter, with some text:

The Jowett Jupiter is the new convertible version of the Javelin. Same engine geared for greater performance – all-weather equipment to make fast driving always fun. This car was first in the 1½ litre class at Le Mans in 1950 and yet again in 1951. It also came 1st and 2nd in the Monte Carlo Rally 1½ litre class, and won the Lisbon Rally outright. It came 1st and 2nd in the 1951 Tourist Trophy race 1½ litre class and easily won the 1½ litre race at Watkins Glen, USA.

CAR'S INSIDE STORY

# *Petrol — don't talk about it*

But haven't you noticed Javelin owners don't so much mind the subject of miles per gallon.

You see, an honest average of 30 m.p.g. is what they usually get on ordinary trips — and the Javelin's impressive performance thrown in.

Of course if you're always driving flat out at 80, which by the way the car will do, you'll use more petrol. But by and large, even making free use of the outstanding acceleration (0–50 in 15.4 secs.), you'll be round the 30 m.p.g. mark or perhaps a bit better.

The Javelin is a waste of money if you don't care what a car does. There's such a lot built into it that doesn't really show until you have one in your hands — real family comfort — economy — *and* performance. Incidentally, the Javelin won outright the closed car section of the R.A.C. International Rally of Great Britain this year.

Best speed, electrically timed, 80 m.p.h. Acceleration 0–50 m p.h. in 15.4 secs. ("The Motor" 1952 Road Test). Horizontally opposed flat-four engine gives 30 m.p.g.

### The 1½ litre
## JOWETT
## JAVELIN
*one day — it has to be*
*YOURS !*

★ ★ ★ ★ ★ ★ ★ ★ ★ ★ ★ ★ ★ ★ ★ ★ ★ ★ ★ ★ ★ ★ ★ ★ ★ ★ ★ ★ ★ ★ ★ ★ ★ ★ ★ ★ ★ ★ ★ ★ ★ ★

### The Javelin's sister car, the JOWETT JUPITER

The 90 m.p.h., high performance Jowett JUPITER, winner of 9 major events in the 1950-1951 season. Winner of Le Mans (1½ litre class) for the third year running in 1952. This amazingly successful 1½ litre sports convertible has basically the same engine as the Jowett Javelin.

★ ★ ★ ★ ★ ★ ★ ★ ★ ★ ★ ★ ★ ★ ★ ★ ★ ★ ★ ★ ★ ★ ★ ★ ★ ★ ★ ★ ★ ★ ★ ★ ★ ★ ★ ★ ★ ★ ★ ★ ★ ★

MADE BY JOWETT CARS LIMITED, IDLE, BRADFORD, YORKSHIRE

CAR'S INSIDE STORY

# *Woman at the wheel*

Women drive differently from men (oh — let's not start that argument again!)

Let's say a woman demands different things of a car. With the Javelin, the suspension that keeps a woman happy by taking the wickedes. bumps in its gliding stride is the same all round torsion bar system that cuts seconds at corners for a man in a hurry.

The quick, light steering and clear visibility are just what a woman wants for parking in the High Street . . . the same qualities that the rally experts praise.

The comfortable cleverly planned seating that lets a woman slip gracefully in and out of the car, sees a man through a 400-mile Continental run without fatigue. And there's plenty of room in the back for several children.

What more could a woman ask of a man's car that will do 80 m.p.h. and accelerate from 0 to 50 in 15.4 secs ?

There's a lot built into the Javelin that doesn't really show until you have one in your hands — real comfort — *30 m.p.g. economy* — and performance.

**The 1953 Javelin has the new Series III engine.**

**The Javelin Saloon with leather upholstery costs £1,082.12.3 (including purchase tax).**

1½ litre

# JOWETT   JAVELIN

*one day — it has to be YOURS!*

MADE BY JOWETT CARS LIMITED, IDLE, BRADFORD, YORKSHIRE

# The car so many have set their hearts on

Not for everyone this extra touch of class; not for everyone this extra comfort and safety and liveliness. The Javelin is for those who really appreciate a motor car with outstanding road qualities and fine appointments and who realise what a lot more they get for very little more money. The Javelin is for people who want the pleasure of driving an economical family car with a really fine performance.

You know of course that your local agent will always give you a trial run.

*JAVELIN SALOON*
**£886.10.10** *inc. P.T.*

*JAVELIN SALOON DE LUXE*
**£957.7.6** *inc. P.T.*

1½ litre
# JOWETT JAVELIN

JOWETT CARS LIMITED, IDLE, BRADFORD, YORKSHIRE.

The last advert I have seen was for the Javelin in May 1953. It had a small side view drawing of a Javelin at the top with the heading:

*THE CAR SO MANY HAVE SET THEIR HEARTS ON......Not for everyone this extra touch of class; not for everyone this extra comfort and safety and liveliness. The Javelin is for those who really appreciate a motor car with outstanding road qualities and fine appointments and who realise what a lot more they get for very little more money. The Javelin is for people who want the pleasure of driving an economical family car with a really fine performance.*
  *You know of course that your local agent will always give you a trial run.*
*JAVELIN SALOON* **£886 10s 10d** *inc P.T. JAVELIN SALOON DE LUXE* **£957 7s 6d** *inc P.T.*

Sadly, the Javelin would not be 'for everyone' as by now Jowett Cars were in serious trouble. Some 380 Javelin bodies were supplied to them from Briggs in early 1953, but they were the last they would receive. The company could not survive without the Javelin, so ceased trading. The factory was sold to International Harvester, the tractor manufacturers. The last Jupiters were finished off in 1954 in a corner of the factory. So one of the most original and illustrious of all British motor manufacturers was no more, after spanning a period from 1906 to 1954. At least they ceased trading as an independent car manufacturer, and were not absorbed into a larger conglomerate, where their survival would have been through badge-engineering, which was the fate of so many makes under the British Leyland group.

BRADFORD

JAVELIN

JUPITER

The Javelin now has the new Series III engine which retains the Javelin's well proved horizontally opposed principle but incorporates the modifications resulting from five years of successful international competition work and strenuous overseas use. The Jupiter also has the Series III engine tuned for specially high performance — and behind the driver is a roomy

The new Jupiter luggage boot

tonneau and luggage boot. The Bradford Commercial range — van, utility, and lorry, is known all over the world for its amazing economy and sturdy reliability. These three cars come from the same famous Yorkshire stable of Jowett Cars Limited who have been making cars for nearly half a century.

JOWETT of BRADFORD

JOWETT CARS LIMITED, IDLE, BRADFORD, AND 48 ALBEMARLE STREET, PICCADILLY, LONDON, W.I

# Other titles published by Tempus

## Jowett 1901–1954
NOEL STOKOE

When the Jowett brothers set about designing their first car, little did they
know that they would end up building thousands of Jowetts. A few cars were
built prior to and during the First World War, but it was the construction
at Idle, Bradford, of a new factory that saw Jowett expanded to become
Yorkshire's major car manufacturer. Always quirky, always fun, Jowett's were
the best engineered and designed of all the light cars. The post-war Javelin
and Jupiter models were successful too.

0 7524 1723 1

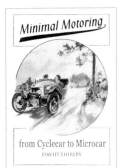

## Minimal Motoring From Cyclecar to Microcar
DAVID THIRLBY

From the dawn of motoring, light cars have played a major part in the growth
of the car. Many famous makers started with cycle cars including Lagonda,
Morgan and Fraser Nash. The cycle car boom period was in the 1910-1930
period and the start of the Second World War killed any car-ownership
aspirations overnight. During the 1950s, however, a series of manufacturers
from BMW to Bond, from Messerschmitt to Mochet and from Peel to
Powerdrive manufactured economy cars and the 'microcar' was born.

0 7524 2367 3

If you are interested in purchasing other books published by Tempus, or in case you have difficulty finding any Tempus
books in your local bookshop, you can also place orders directly through our website

www.tempus-publishing.com